We Got Soul,
We Can Heal

We Got Soul, We Can Heal

*Overcoming Racial Trauma
Through Leadership,
Community and Resilience*

PHYLLIS JEFFERS-COLY

Jefferson, North Carolina

LIBRARY OF CONGRESS CATALOGUING-IN-PUBLICATION DATA

Names: Jeffers-Coly, Phyllis, 1972– author.
Title: We got soul, we can heal : overcoming racial trauma through leadership, community and resilience / Phyllis Jeffers-Coly.
Description: Jefferson, North Carolina : Toplight, 2022 | Includes bibliographical references and index.
Identifiers: LCCN 2022007844 | ISBN 9781476684741 (paperback : acid free paper) ∞
ISBN 9781476644639 (ebook)
Subjects: LCSH: Resilience (Personality trait) | Psychic trauma. | Race discrimination—Psychological aspects. | Black people—Psychology. | BISAC: BODY, MIND & SPIRIT / Healing / General | SOCIAL SCIENCE / Ethnic Studies / American / African American & Black Studies
Classification: LCC BF698.35.R47 J44 2022 | DDC 155.2/408996—dc23/eng/20220302
LC record available at https://lccn.loc.gov/2022007844

BRITISH LIBRARY CATALOGUING DATA ARE AVAILABLE

ISBN (print) 978-1-4766-8474-1
ISBN (ebook) 978-1-4766-4463-9

Front cover artwork courtesy of Winifer Estevez

Printed in the United States of America

Toplight is an imprint of McFarland & Company, Inc., Publishers

Box 611, Jefferson, North Carolina 28640
www.toplightbooks.com

To my beloved husband
and business partner, Idrissa Eddy Coly,
my parents, Jackie and Ginny, and my extended family,
including my ancestors, my dear friends,
my elder-mentors as well as the many students
who have allowed me to support their capacity
to create change in the world over the years

Table of Contents

Table of Contents

Preface:
Here Is What We Know

We Got Soul, We Can Heal: Overcoming Racial Trauma Through Leadership, Community and Resilience reflects what we know about the capacity of Black people to extend ourselves for the well-being of ourselves and one another as well as our fundamental capacity to love ourselves and one another. *We Got Soul, We Can Heal* recognizes the urgency of investing our love as well as our time and energy into creating, sustaining, and restoring communities of care where we collectively and individually can consistently have a sense of hope and imagine the possibilities for a bright, abundant and prosperous future that meets the needs of more of us. This book reflects the importance of being deeply invested in healing justice, which means pursuing both our collective restoration, healing and well-being as well as transforming and dismantling the institutions and relationships that have been causing us harm, injury, trauma and misery.[1] It also reflects long-standing, radical Black traditions of resisting systemic racism and injustice and our collective capacity for resilience that makes experiencing "repeated assaults on [our] souls not as a reason to give up but as a source of power to keep on keeping on."[2]

We Got Soul, We Can Heal reflects the well-documented sobs and shouts, concerns and demands of Black people who have first-hand experience with the ways that anti–Black racism, systemic white supremacy and epistemic violence impact their minds, bodies, hearts, and spirits. Black people, the people we love, continue to face what often feels like "the constant threat of death and the flagrant violence of oppressive systems that obstruct justice and current systems that promise complex, compounded and nearly constant

1

trauma for [us] and ensure that we have little resources, space, time or energy to heal and little agency to protect ourselves and our loved ones from facing the same."[3] That is what we know as we continue to face, "even during a global pandemic, racism that is as pernicious as ever." And, that "not only has Covid-19 disproportionately affected the black community, but we can hardly take the time to sit with that horror as we are reminded, every single day, that there is no context in which black lives matter." And, we remember, we know, we sit with the fact that "no one is coming to save us," no matter who is in the White House or who has the majority of seats in Congress.[4]

We Got Soul, We Can Heal, therefore, reflects the fact that we have been and must continue to be willing "to fight for [our] liberation in the context of historical and ongoing dehumanization and oppression" through collective struggle that will ultimately allow us to alter our circumstances, and "to contain, escape, and possibly eviscerate the source of trauma; recover our bodies; reclaim and redeem our dead; heal ourselves and make ourselves whole."[5] In that vein, *We Got Soul, We Can Heal* reflects the fact that "it is absolutely necessary for us Black people to deal with the psychological, emotional and spiritual toll of racism. In lieu of adaptations for survival that are no longer helpful and are dysfunctional manifestations of historical trauma, we need to restore our connection to communal healing practices that foster resilience in our bodies and plasticity in our brains."[6] We need embodied practices, active and intentional interventions that will allow us to heal and to profoundly transform our lived experiences as Black people in our world.[7] *We Got Soul* recognizes that it is our SOUL that will allow for such personal and collective healing and transformation to take place.

SOUL is "a transformative healing resource that reflects long-standing cultural sensibilities of the African Diaspora."[8] As such, SOUL supports our capacity to be loving, courageous and connected to spirit so that we can practice self-care, experience well-being and be resilient and engage in resistance. SOUL as a healing resource reflects the important work of Malidoma Somé, who reminds us that "healing comes when the individual understands his/her identity—their purpose in the world of ancestral wisdom—and reconnects

2

with that world of spirit."[9] SOUL as a healing resource reflects the insights and wisdom of Alice Walker, the renowned poet and activist, who, in the essay titled "The Sound of Our Own Culture," explains that "culture is something in which one should thrive—the body and spirit simultaneously. But in the United States, [and globally] for many [Black] people that is not happening," in part because the dominant culture is typically injurious and disadvantages individuals who are not white males (53). Walker says, "healing means putting the heart, the courage and the energy back in our bodies with our own culture." SOUL *is* the culture that Walker speaks of. The heart that she speaks of is our capacity to love, to be in relationship with one another and extend ourselves for the well-being of others. The courage that she names is our capacity to tap into our personal and collective power in ways that allow us to be resilient and engage in ongoing resistance. And, when she speaks of energy, we recognize spirit, the life force, before all that which is living, that is divine. SOUL.

Thus, *We Got Soul, We Can Heal* explores how we integrate culture (SOUL) and contemplative practices so that we can experience healing and restoration that at the same time will allow us to deepen our capacity for resilience and resistance.

Yet, at the same time, because my husband Eddy and I are long-time educators, leaders and students of life, *We Got Soul, We Can Heal* reflects what we know about engaging in resistance and our awareness that choosing to lead might be intimidating for some. What we know is that in spite of the fact that our country is facing a racial reckoning that has been a long time coming, there are some who are just beginning to recognize their capacity to lead. There are others who are expanding their notions of leadership and beginning to recognize the importance of healing, restoration, self-care and their well-being as important to their leadership practice and priorities. What we also know from the healing and restoration experiences that we provide in Senegal is that some of us have not had the opportunity to develop the knowledge, skills and disposition to lead in ways that consider healing, restoration and the importance of our individual and collective well-being.[10] We know that healing and feeling whole, individually and collectively, are necessary if we want people to lead and create change. Thus, *We Got Soul, We Can Heal* is not just for those who have already decided to act; it is also for those who are not sure, who are struggling with fear, timidity or even their big egos. This book is also for those who seem to only be interested in leadership for personal gain and achievement rather than social justice or the well-being of the collective—those who perhaps believe that charisma, their social media persona and the positions that they hold are more important than their soul.

We Got Soul, We Can Heal reflects my extensive experience in higher education—experience that, at this point, has brought the jaded, cynical and disheartened part of myself to a place where it seems as if "universities will never be engines of social transformation." This reality deeply saddens me, and it represents an unfortunate truth that reflects my twenty plus years working at access institutions with stated missions to serve students from under-resourced communities, including a large community college, the access program at a large urban research institution, a small public HBCU and two college access organizations. What I know is that in spite of the ongoing demands of students across the country, universities are not changing in ways that many of us (after decades of service) still expect them to. Or hope that they might. Or wish that they will. What I know—what many of us in higher education know, when we are being honest, instead of being indifferent and complacent—is that universities continue to struggle, even in this climate, at this moment, even when the writing on the wall about racism and injustice is so clear and so cogent, to deliver on the promise to be "post-racial haven[s]" as they bobble about like litter in "a surrounding sea of white supremacy (Kelley)."

Yet, at the same time, *We Got Soul, We Can Heal* reflects the enthusiastic and hopeful part of me that loves students and believes in the power we have to create change. This part of me continues to hope and believe that some universities, or those within them, in spite of the looming threat and fear of the backlash blues, will commit themselves to and invest in the healing and restoration of their Black students, staff and faculty.

We Got Soul, We Can Heal gets us out of our heads and allows us to experience a healing that is embodied—an embodied healing that connects us to our bodies, our breath and our spirit. An embodied healing that reflects the fact that yoga, an ancient spiritual practice, heals. That "yoga offers us a vehicle for noticing and befriending the sensations in our bodies, which can produce profound changes ... that can lead to healing from trauma."[11] Embodied healing and restoration that I have experienced as a Black woman who has been practicing yoga since 2006 and who completed her 300-hour yoga teacher certification with a studio that accepted and supported her even when they did not always know how being a Black woman with working class roots impacted her experience on the mat, or how to manage their white privilege, fragility or guilt. My yoga experience in Cincinnati has recently been confirmed, validated and affirmed by a community of colleagues and fellow practitioners, which includes the Black Yoga Teachers Alliance (BYTA), Amplify and Activate, Sanctuary in the City and our wise elder-mentors, Dr. Gail Parker, Maya Bauer, Jana Long, Dianne Bondy and Shola Arewa as well as other important voices in the conversations about our well-being on and off the mat like Resmaa Menakem, Rolf Gates, Angel Acosta, the Rev. Angel Kyodo Williams, Anana H.-Perry, Michelle Johnson, and Octavia Raheem. *We Got Soul, We Can Heal* reflects what we know, what we have learned in community, in relationship to other Black practitioners such as these about the ways that restorative yoga, somatics and other complementary practices can contribute to the healing and well-being of those of us who have and continue to experience racial-based stress and trauma. What we know is what this community of practitioners has taught us as we continue to be invested in continuing to grow, learn and develop as co-creators and co-collaborators. *We Got Soul, We Can Heal* reflects a moment when Black healers, healing artists, yoga teachers, spiritualists and wellness practitioners have extended themselves for our individual and collective well-being by holding BIPOC−only spaces that are meant exclusively for our healing and restoration. In a moment when we refuse to leave any part of ourselves outside the studio or off the mat. In a moment when we bring all of our Black selves to the mat, all of our intersecting, overlapping and at times conflicting identities into each and every room we enter. When what we do on the mat is informed by our wounds and our pain as well as our struggle, our fight, our commitment to healing justice. When our mantras and affirmations echo the calls for justice of Black organizers and activists. When we are engaged in spiritual activism that relies heavily on self-study, connection to spirit and taking action when we know that we must.[12]

We Got Soul, We Can Heal reflects what spirit has shown us, even in the moments when we struggled to believe and trust that the universe was showing us the way and taking us to the exact places we were meant to be. *We Got Soul, We Can Heal* reflects what we know from the guidance and insights of our ancestors, our foremothers and forefathers who are always with us. The wisdom of those who are connected to centuries-old cosmologies that allow for multiple realities without steadfast demarcations or strict distinctions between everyday life and the realms in which spirit dwells. The wisdom of those who are simply at ease with existing with both the visible and the invisible. The realities that are layered and unfold in surprising and exciting (sometimes scary) ways that at times feel divine, magical, and incongruous all at the same time. The intuitive and divine knowledge of those who trust their guts, premonitions and promptings more than they would ever want or need to trust a Ph.D. The guidance offered in grains of sand, crashing waves, red bird sightings, cowrie shells, sacred decks, aura and dreams. Oh, and rainbows. Yeah, rainbows. *We Got Soul, We Can Heal* reflects what we know about the power of recognizing our own divinity, being open to spirit and allowing our SOUL to guide us.

We Got Soul, We Can Heal reflects what my husband Eddy knows. His wisdom, his expertise, his lived experience as a Diasporic Soul who hails from Senegal, West Africa, and who has lived as a Black man in both France and the United States. *We Got Soul, We Can Heal* reflects the ways that he loves—the way he radiates a deep, quiet, unwavering, stabilizing, grounding, anchoring and sometimes fiery stern care and compassion that makes me and the people who come to us feel safe, secure and like we belong in a place that we know, in our spirits, to be home. The way he continues to create and make space not only for us to heal ourselves but to hold space for others to do the same. And, not only the wisdom and lived experiences of Eddy, but those of his mom, Yaay and our extended family and community who lovingly contribute to the ways that we feed the souls of those who come to us to experience healing and restoration. This book reflects the way that they share their wisdom and knowledge, the way they offer insights and guidance that is refreshingly and reassuringly unpretentious, uncontrived, modest, humble and deeply loving. *We Got Soul, We Can Heal* reflects how Eddy and Ndey deeply value family and community in ways that exemplify how we might be more intentional about investing in, maintaining, creating and restoring communities of care so that we can without no longer having to compromise our innate dignity and worth.

We Got Soul, We Can Heal is what we know; it is a reminder of the ways that being at home with our SOUL, our culture(s) and in our own bodies is part of our capacity to be well and to lead in ways that are transformative. *We Got Soul, We Can Heal* is what we know about how SOUL, culture, and contemplative practices can offer us healing and restoration and to feel at home in our own Black bodies. This healing and restoration will allow us to deepen our capacity to be resilient and resistant so that we can practice and model a healing-centered leadership that transforms the very existence of Black people in this world.

CHAPTER I

We Got SOUL;
We Feel Good!

In 2015, my husband and I watched in horror from a pizza shop in Dakar as the news came in that nine Black people were murdered in their historic and storied church in South Carolina by a young white supremacist who I refuse to name. We were shocked, dismayed and heartbroken. We had, of course, been hurt by the murders of Tamir and Trayvon, Sandra Bland, Walter Scott, Alton Sterling, and many more. However, this particular attack felt deeply personal, in part because it happened in South Carolina, the state adjacent to my own home state of North Carolina. But the attack also felt personal because the racial terror took place in a such a very sacred space. Echoing the 1963 16th Street Baptist Church bombing in Birmingham, as well as the series of church burnings of the 1990s, this attack took place in a sanctuary that we have believed to safe and secure over generation after generation. Where we could find solace in one another and in God. Where we could feed our souls and find healing and restoration when the rest of the world insisted on marginalizing and wounding us. The 2015 Charleston Massacre was a game changer for me, and for my husband.

The Charleston Massacre, along with our month-long 2015 visit to Senegal, allowed us to see that moving to Senegal might just be in our best interest in the short term. However, we did not immediately decide that we would go after returning from vacation. Although, it is quite evident that God, the Divine, Source, Spirit guided us to the life-changing decision to move to Senegal. By that I mean that the space to go, to begin again in Senegal, was made for us when the fall of 2015 ended and 2016 began. In September 2015, I took a women's entrepreneurship class with Bad Girl Ventures—Cincinnati (which is now known as Aviatra Accelerators). At that point, I could not have told you that I would absolutely start a business, but for some reason I felt compelled to participate in the program. At the same time, I was working for a college access organization as a Post-Secondary Pathways Specialist in a public school after not working for a year upon leaving my last full-time job. While I loved the students who I served, most days I hated the job. I raged far too often. I brow beat everyone I thought I could, including the school's timid counselor. I was no different than I had been for much of my life. I was willing to challenge what I saw as the mistreatment of Black people and other folks struggling with poverty. I invested all I could in the students. I was creative and innovative in my approach. I mean, you should have seen my bulletin boards and where I scheduled college visits. I was vigilant as hell. And, frankly, my extensive previous higher education experience allowed me to do the job in ways that most access providers could not. I mean, most college access folks were naive and inexperienced, disproportionately white recent college grads who were completing a year of Americorps service, which added to my agitation. I mean, what did they know, really, about kicking down doors and taking names for the well-being of Black folks? So, yes, in spite of my heart-felt devotion, I would say that on most days I was miserable, combative and frustrated; I knew I would not last long. I was hoping I would find a way out—that I would find a new opportunity working in higher education. But, that would not be the case.

My soul, my spirit was not going back—just forward ever, backwards never. The divine one was not letting me do what I was comfortable doing; instead, she was preparing me for a new phase in my life. A new beginning. So, in addition to completing the Bad Girl Ventures program, where I first developed and fleshed out my initial plan for Diasporic Soul, I focused on centering and grounding myself in my home with Eddy, in yoga and the friendships that I did not nurture when I was working an hour and a half from home in a high-stress job. This included starting my 300-hour yoga teacher certification training with the studio where I had been practicing yoga off and on since 2006. It also meant that I began spending lots of time with my friend Carol, who I had met earlier when I worked at the University of Cincinnati. And, Eddy and I spent every Saturday morning after my walks with Carol at the local farmers market.

Carol and I walked two or three times a week, brunched and just hung out. It was marvelous; it was something I had never been able to do in Cincinnati after I moved there from D.C. I had put my work first, partly because I was good at it and it offered me a form of validation when I needed it. But, sadly, I did that at the expense of my marriage and overall well-being. I was, and still am, so very grateful for Carol and her willingness to make room for me in her life; her friendship and love mean the world to me. So, by the time the holidays rolled around in December 2015, Eddy was notified that his job was going to be eliminated, as the company was downsizing its training and development unit. He was told that he would be let go in March 2016. But, even when we got that news, we really did not consider living in Senegal as a real option for us.

Instead, we looked for jobs. At least I did, for both of us. We looked in places that we thought made the most sense for us based on where we had family and friends and where our SOUL might be fed consistently. So, of course, we looked in North Carolina where I grew up, attended college, and felt connected, and where my family lives. We looked in the DMV because of the time I spent there flourishing before Eddy and I met. We looked in Austin, Texas, because my former colleague and friend had just gotten a presidency there, and we thought living there might work for both of us. We even looked in Cincinnati, but we believed that moving would absolutely be a better option for us. But, nothing panned out. Both Eddy and I had a few interviews, but we received no job offers.

Then I got real clear. At some point, it hit me. Let's go! Let's move! Let's move to Senegal and live there! I had dreamt at some point early on in our relationship that Eddy and I would open a cafe in the desert. And, while we are not in the desert, the Sahel region where we live is not lush and green most of the year. If you sit in our cafe, beyond the flowers and foliage, you will see sand, which evokes the sense that you are in the desert, especially during the time of the year when the wind blows it around like snowflakes or dry fall leaves.

So, we decided that we would literally follow our dreams (at least that specific one) and open a cafe.

Also, as an educator, I have invested lots of emotional energy and labor into impacting the lives of Black students in a way that made sense to me after watching the shifts in higher education over the years. As I taught English as a community college professor and at the University of Cincinnati, and worked in Enrollment Management/Student Affairs at a public HBCU, I repeatedly reimagined how students, particularly Black ones (as well as others from underserved and under-resourced communities) might learn to lead and create change in the world. I engaged in this work in a variety of contexts, including by designing and facilitating leadership development trainings for much of my adult life. But, I never got the chance to do so full-time, and never in a way that fully resonated with my SOUL. There was no place where what I imagined (or what God would show me after I got to Senegal) that I could do healing-centered leadership development as it needs to be done. So, moving to Senegal also offered me the chance to hold space for young people to develop their capacity to lead and create change in the world. Therefore, Eddy and I understood that we would open Tangor Café and see if we could make something out of the business that I had conceptualized during my Bad Girl Ventures program—Diasporic Soul. It just felt right. And, when we decided to do it, it came so easy; all the doors to do it were so clearly open. We had a home there already, and we had the means to give it a try.

So, here we are five years later. Our café is flourishing; our love is stronger, and we are living a life that affords us the time and space to take much better care of ourselves, to rest, to have balance, to feel grounded, centered and rooted. And, we feel so deeply supported by the community we are in, one that includes our family and friends here and those who have come and had a Diasporic Soul experience with us. And, what feels so good, what is so rewarding is that through Diasporic Soul we are able to hold space where Black people can do the same, where they can experience healing and restoration. Where they can restore their connection to their SOUL, which is critical to our capacity to lead, create change and have the capacity for resilience and resistance. I am deeply, deeply grateful that my SOUL brought me here. And, that yours brought you here.

To be honest, as I write I am excited, energized and inspired. But, I am also anxious. I am anxious because the part of me that existed in the academy for over twenty years gets in the way of the me that wants to serve your SOUL. To meet you in a place where I impact you not just intellectually. I want to contribute to your well-being in part by getting you out of your head. My intention is to feed your soul. In a way that is embodied and that impacts you emotionally and spiritually. I want you to know more, but far more than that I want you to feel more. To be aware of more. To sense and intuit more. To be open and surrender to more. To experience more. To feel better and at home in your beautiful Black body. And, to feel better about all that is valuable, beautiful and magical about who you are in spite of the world being toxic because your skin is chocolate.

My hope is that you will expand and open up to the idea that you are a leader, one who is deeply deeply invested in our individual and collective healing, restoration, self-care and our well-being. My hope is that while you may not be able to come to Senegal at this point, you, in some way, have an experience that is similar to the ones our guests undergo. An experience that allows you to deal with yourself differently to see yourself far more clearly, to know yourself far more fully. I hope that reading this book, that hearing from me and members of our ever expanding, ever growing Diasporic Soul community, gives you with the opportunity to heal and to feel whole, "which is necessary if we want people to lead organizations effectively" and create the change we must see in the world.

We Got Soul is for you. It is a gift from me, a hip hop generation elder-mentor who has invested her career in young adults in particular. This book is an offering to support your ability to self-care and maintain your well-being as you continue to face white supremacy, epistemic violence and anti–Black racism. I intend for it to support you as you develop and sustain a self-care practice and do the healing and restoration work that will allow you to deepen your capacity for resilience and resistance. As your elder-mentor, I offer you SOUL, which is "a transformative healing resource that reflects longstanding cultural sensibilities of the African Diaspora" that can support our capacity to be loving, courageous and connected to Spirit.[1] I do so insisting that you pursue a version of social justice that respects and honors the fact that you have intersecting identities. Yet, I am putting Black at the center so that you can intentionally challenge, release and let go of ways that limit how you see and understand yourself and us. I center Black so that you can be well enough to resist and to create new ways of being, identify new solutions and build new institutions that serve far more of us.

We Got Soul takes a healing-centered approach to leadership practice. It about our healing and restoration as Black folks—work that includes a willingness to engage in resistance but to also practice self-care. The leadership of which I speak is NOT about a position you hold or your ambition. Instead, leadership is about having the courage and the agency to create and sustain healing communities where individuals can restore a sense of hope and envision the future possibilities for the collective. It is also about being self-aware. This type of leadership reflects Shawn Ginwright's thinking in "Radically Healing Black Lives: A Love Note to Justice" that healing justice "means pursuing both collective healing and well-being and transforming the institutions and relationships that are causing the harm in the first place."[2] A healing-centered approach recognizes that we have experienced various forms of stress and trauma, including race-based stress and trauma. A healing-centered approach recognizes that trauma is not simply an individual, isolated experience, but rather a collective one. Thus, trauma requires us to recognize that our healing is both individual and collective in nature. Our healing requires us to hold sacred communal space for Black people to address the psychological, emotional, spiritual and physical toll that systemic racism has taken.

A healing-centered approach to leadership practice requires that there be an intentional effort to prioritize well-being and self-care. Specifically, self-care in this context "carries on black radical traditions" by insisting that our health and well-being are not luxuries, but rather acts of resilience, survival and resistance.[3] A healing-centered approach to leadership practice recognizes the importance of Black leaders developing their individual and collective capacity to transcend obstacles and confront racism and white supremacy through their own personal and collective power. It offers relevant and compelling examples of Black cultural and political agency, as well as examples of Black leaders who recognize the need for healing, restoration and love as part of how we individually and collectively create change in the world.

Further, our healing-centered approach integrates culture and contemplative practices, including yoga, body-awareness practices, reconnecting with nature, healing rituals, and reflective journaling. I hope that in some way *We Got Soul* allows you the capacity to be a self-aware, loving, inter-culturally competent leader who practices self-care and recognizes our collective capacity for resilience and resistance so that we are able to collectively create change and pursue healing justice.

At this point, you might be wondering what I mean by SOUL. Well, of course, SOUL, at the most basic level, refers to Black folks or people of African descent, or using the term interchangeably. In fact, SOUL, as part of our name, serves as a 1990s-era hip hop style "yes, y'all," and a subversive wink and a nod to Black folks, particularly those from the United States as well as members of the broader African diaspora. Using the term also reflects the thinking of Dr. Sharon Harrell, as we define SOUL as a transformative healing resource that reflects longstanding cultural sensibilities of the African Diaspora.[4] Conceptually, SOUL, in this way, simultaneously names Black and African, and, of course, bumps up against much of the way that we understand these identities conceptually. And, in this case, using the term SOUL bumps up against conventional approaches to leadership, wellness and fundamentally how we define or perceive what it means to lead and be well.

In addition to the valuable and in-depth thinking of Sharon Harrell, the idea of SOUL as a healing resource for us is also informed by the groundbreaking work of Malidoma Somé, who offers that

"healing comes when the individual understands his/her identity—
their purpose in the world of ancestral wisdom—and reconnects
with that world of spirit."[5] The insights and wisdom of Alice Walker,
the renowned poet and activist, truly capture what we are doing, our
purpose, our raison d'être and how we see SOUL in relationship to
our healing and restoration work. In "The Sound of Our Own Culture," Walker explains that "culture is something in which one should
thrive—the body and spirit simultaneously. But in the United States,
[and globally] for many [Black] people that is not happening," in
part because the dominant culture is typically injurious and disadvantages individuals who are not white males (53). Thus, we integrate culture and contemplative practices that allow us to experience
healing and restoration, with the understanding that, as Walker says,
"healing means putting the heart, the courage and the energy back
in our bodies with our own culture." The heart that Walker speaks
of is our capacity to love, to be in relationship with one another and
extend ourselves for the well-being of others. The courage that she
names is our capacity to tap into our personal and agency in ways
that allow us to be resilient and engage in ongoing resistance. And,
when she speaks of energy, we recognize spirit, the life force, that
which is living, all that is divine. SOUL.

Thus, SOUL, as a transformative healing resource that is integral
to our healing-centered leadership development approach, consists
of various aspects and elements. We will explore them in a variety
of ways as we understand the ways in which culture and contemplative practices can offer us opportunities to deepen our capacity for
self-care, healing and restoration so that we may be resilient as we
collaborate with others in resistance.

On a spiritual level, when we use the term SOUL we mean the
energy that Walker names. We mean being fully open to and connected to the divine, to spirit and to that which is "an eternal, transcendent essence beyond" what we can see and touch.[6] It means
recognizing that energy is in all living things and that it is not
destroyed but takes on different forms. Thus, this most certainly
includes our ancestors, who are understood to be guiding and protecting us and who are constantly present in our lives which, for

some Black Americans, is a practice that has been overlooked or outright dismissed. Spiritually, soul also means recognizing energy and spirit in nature and in all living things and showing them reverence and respect. SOUL speaks to the "centrality of spirituality" in our lives. SOUL, too, is the unwavering faith that we express when we smile, as Seinabo Sey sings, when we truly believe in our future, knowing that we will move forward, not backward.[7] SOUL is faith in the notion that, indeed, as Sam Cooke soulfully sang, yes, sisters and brothers, change is most certainly gonna come.[8] SOUL is also Seinabo Sey imploring us to breathe so that we connect to the life force, spirit, to the divine. More so, when we speak of SOUL we mean that Black folks are in fact deeply connected to the sacred, that we embody spirit, energy, the life force. That we are divine and connected to all that is divine.

On a psychological or emotional level, SOUL is "the depths and dynamics of our inner world and our feelings."[9] SOUL is our capacity for emotional expressiveness that is deep, rich, complex and authentic. Emotional expressiveness means feeling what we feel when we feel it, unapologetically. And, out loud as need be, whether we are laughing or in deep, overwhelming, all-consuming lament. This includes being vulnerable and willing to surrender to the hurt, pain, sorrow and grief that we know inter-generationally, collectively and individually. It means recognizing these feelings, not apologizing for them, and finding ways to heal and grow so that we can flourish in spite of what hurts. SOUL on this level also refers to the mental and emotional fortitude and tenacity that allow us to be resilient and continue flourish in spite of adversity. It refers to our capacity to experience joy and pain, sunshine and rain.

And, love. Love is the heart that Walker names when she calls on us to find healing in our own culture. Love, then, is about opening our hearts to one another. Love is fundamentally about our willingness to extend ourselves for the well-being of others. Yet, at the same time, love, in a world that still seems to be confused about the fact that Black lives matter, includes loving ourselves individually and collectively, in spite of all the ways we have been encouraged to do otherwise. Love in this way means that we must be kind and

17

compassionate toward one another and ourselves. Love means that we must see our value both individually and collectively as Diasporic SOULS. It is love that will help us to feel grounded, centered and rooted.

Further, SOUL reflects the influences of diasporic African and African American cultural[10]—sensibilities that have historically and currently informed our way of life as Diasporic SOULS. A way of life that places high value on being interconnected and recognizes that we are responsible for one another, and that the collective and community are most important. That we belong to one another. That we must embody love, that allows us to extend ourselves for the well-being of others. Further, SOUL is our willingness to mend our individual and collective broken hearts, broken bodies and broken spirits. SOUL also includes a holistic orientation to human experience that allows us to truly value the wisdom and insights gleaned from our lived experiences, and which informs a deeply-held respect for our elders and the capacity to trust our many ways of knowing. Reflecting an African epistemology, these ways of knowing include "relational knowing (learning from reciprocal interactions), empathy, intuition reasoning (learning from heart-mind knowledge, which are linked not separate), divination (a learned discipline of decision-making based on integrated knowledge from the spiritual, scientific and unseen worlds) and symbolic imagery (use of proverbs, gestures, rhythms, metaphors and effect)."[11]

SOUL, too, is our authenticity, our depth, our vitality, and our joie de vivre. Our swagger, the way we move in the world, unapologetically, taking up space.

SOUL is the practice of being able to love nothing into something, which is a reflection of our creativity, ingenuity and capacity to improvise.

SOUL also consists of recognizing that our healing and well-being are not only tied to our capacity to be resilient and overcome adversity, but to our capacity for resistance. In this vein, SOUL is our insistent cry for freedom, equity and justice. SOUL is the declaration that "before I'll be a slave, I'll be dancing on my grave and go home to my soul and be free." It is the clarion call that Black Lives

Matter. SOUL is the "willingness to fight for liberation in the context of historical and ongoing dehumanization and oppression." SOUL is recognizing that through collective struggle, we, as leaders and change agents, "have the capacity to alter our circumstances; to contain, escape, or possibly eviscerate the source of trauma; recover our bodies; reclaim and redeem our dead; heal ourselves and make ourselves whole."[12] It is, in fact, the healing justice that Shawn Ginwright, Prentis Hemphill and other members of this generation of Black organizers and activists insist will allow us to heal, in part because we have successfully dismantled the systems that have fostered our pain and trauma and replaced them with institutions and systems that are rooted in love and life, and that affirm our innate dignity and worth.

I recently spoke to one of the young people who has spent time with Eddy and me and who I continue to mentor. She told me that she and a few of the others in her group had discussed my hugs. I was tickled to learn that they all felt so warm and welcome in my arms. I hope that what Eddy and I offer you here feels that way, even when you consider doing more for yourself and others. In their departing thank you note, these same students also mentioned that I yelled at them a lot, but that it was about love, about being held accountable and being pushed to show up and be present for all that we had to offer them, opportunities they ordinarily do not have as Black college students. So, if it feels like I'm fussing, I just might be. That's what I've done with other young people—fussed, pushed, nudged, hollered and shouted with deep, unbinding love. So, I hope you feel my warm whispers and my supportive shouts as you explore the ways you can deepen your connection to your SOUL. I hope you feel the love. I hope that you are curious and committed to this experience. I hope that you find yourself more in love with and more aware of your SOUL by the end of this book. I hope that you feel a sense of possibility and recognize your capacity to be both well and courageous and confident enough to consistently create change in the world. I hope you see your ability to live and lead with deep and abiding SOUL, unapologetically.

CHAPTER II

It Ain't Right

Race-Based Stress and Trauma

The world can be toxic (toxic)
Especially when your skin look like chocolate (chocolate)[1]
            —"Shine," Tobe Nwigwe
Something is holding me back
Is it because I'm black?[2]
       —"Is It Because I'm Black," Salaam Remi
            and Black on Purpose

Yes, as Tobe Nwigwe tells us, "the world can be toxic (toxic); especially when your skin look like chocolate (chocolate)." It often feels like "something is holding [us] back ... because [we are] [B]lack."

This was especially true in 2020. As *New York Times* contributor Roxane Gay stated just after the murder of George Floyd, "even during a global pandemic, racism is as pernicious as ever. Not only is Covid-19 disproportionately affecting the [B]lack community, but we can hardly take the time to sit with that horror as we are reminded, every single day, that there is no context in which Black lives matter." She goes on to state that "it seems to us [Black people] that when the doctors do find a coronavirus vaccine, [B]lack people will continue to wait, despite the futility of hope, for a cure for racism. We will live with the knowledge that there is not a vaccine for white supremacy."[3]

Or, as the Los Angeles Clippers coach Doc Rivers emotionally noted in late August 2020 when players decided to stop playing during the Disney-bubble-bound abbreviated NBA season after a 29-year-old Black man was shot seven times in the back by a police officer in Kenosha, Wisconsin, "It's amazing [that] we keep loving this country, and this country does not love us back." In 2020, even athletes who have historically not engaged in political action, including NBA, WNBA and MLB teams as well as tennis player Naomi Osaka, were speaking out against and kneeling silently to protest the fact that they had enough of the pernicious racism playing out in the streets of America.[4]

Indeed, as many of us have known for some time, "the world can be toxic (toxic); especially when your skin look like chocolate (chocolate)." Yet, it seems that 2020 was a year where this reality, the toxicity of and the wounding that comes with being Black in America became so crystal clear, as we spent the summer grappling with the murder of Ahmaud Arbery, Breonna Taylor and George Floyd. And, even as 2020 came to an end, Casey Christopher Goodson, Jr., a 23-year-old Columbus, Ohio, man, is shot dead by a deputy ostensibly searching for someone else.[5]

Yes, "the world can be toxic (toxic); especially when your skin look like chocolate" when we experience what Dr. Gail Parker refers to as race-based traumatic stress injury, which she explains is stress or trauma associated with racial wounding that has caused emotional pain.[6] According to Parker, it can be the result of racial hostility, racial avoidance, or aversive racial hostility. Our reactions to race-based traumatic stress injury may include recurring thoughts, avoidance, and irritability. The symptoms of it include anxiety, anger, rage, depression, low self-esteem, shame and guilt. And, she explains that "race-based traumatic stress injury is ongoing, recurrent and cumulative" (62).

Trauma of any form creates an imbalance in the body. In the body, trauma triggers a fight, flight, or freeze response in the limbic system that produces stress chemicals such as cortisol and adrenaline.[7] Trauma gets stuck in the body. Historical trauma, intergenerational trauma, institutional trauma, personal trauma, and vicarious or secondary trauma often interact.

In his seminal work *My Grandmother's Hands*, Resmaa Menakem explains that racialized trauma, like other forms of trauma, compound and new ones occur, our minds, bodies and spirits experiencing greater and ever-increasing damage.[8] He advises that "deep, persistent traumas live in many Black bodies. These compounded traumas contribute to a long list of common stress-related disorders in Black bodies such as post-traumatic stress disorder (PTSD), learning disabilities, depression, anxiety, diabetes, high blood pressure and other ailments."[9]

Reflected in the title of his text, Menakem ties racial trauma to his grandmother's hands; I tie it to my father's diabetes, the degenerative disks in his back and his depression.

My father was born in 1949 and he was raised in Jim Crow North Carolina in Guilford County well before it was incorporated into the current city of Greensboro. He most certainly carries trauma in his body. Like many of our ancestors and elders, he had his SOUL brutalized by white supremacy, anti–Black racism and epistemic violence. Trauma most certainly lives in his body. He has diabetes, fibromyalgia, acid reflux and often suffers from ongoing debilitating back pain. And, he has been taking anti-depressants for many, many years. He is a cogent example of the ways in which his own direct experiences with white supremacy and anti–Blackness manifest in disease. And, like many of us, my father exists in a way that is absolutely informed by what Dr. Joy DeGruy, author of *Post Traumatic Slave Syndrome: America's Legacy of Enduring Injury and Healing,* refers to as ancestral trauma.[10] He reflects the impact of the historical experiences of our enslaved ancestors and those subjected to racial violence and the extensive forms of anti–Black racism.

The racial trauma for my Daddy includes experiences that sometimes left him believing that he was nothing, or at least not "as good as." Not as good as certain other Black folks in his community of Guilford, which refers to his community prior to its inclusion in what is now Greensboro proper. Not as good as the light-skinned kids. Not as good as the kids whose parents had white-collar office jobs, ones who did not do manual labor or enter the homes of white folks through the back door. Or as good as the ones with bigger houses or nicer cars. He recently mentioned to me that after reconnecting with one of his high school friends, he recalled how their bond was due in part to the fact that she and he were not like the affluent kids who gave their teacher what was considered a lavish Christmas gift consisting of a set of cooking pots and pans. If you could have heard the sound in my father's voice. I could hear the mix of awe and hurt in his voice as he remembered the ways in which the social order played out in his childhood—an order tied not only to race and skin complexion but also to class.

Or as good as the ones with cache in the church communities that we know anchored the lives of most Black communities during that era. A church where everyone was Black, but their Lord and savior, Jesus Christ, was undoubtedly rendered as white.

The manifestations of white supremacy and anti–Black racism in my father's life and in his body are certainly exacerbated by the wounds he sustained from growing up in a house where his parents struggled with their own dreams deferred and drank heavily to numb that pain and hurt.[11] Self-destructive choices that deeply wounded them, my father and his ten siblings, as well as the generations who followed. Intergenerational trauma and hereditary alcoholism often intersect. It is important to recognize that my grandparents were simply trying to escape a world where dreams are deferred or crushed, where being Black felt so painfully toxic.

Yet, in spite of an omnipresent white Jesus, his parents' pain and the standing social order based on a white supremacist racial hierarchy, my father's spirit called him to break free, to get out, to resist, to run. So, he ran away. To New York, at first, to be an artist, a photographer. To make a way in a city that ostensibly would not subject him to the same strident racial, social and moral codes like those he faced down South. To express himself, creatively, out loud and unapologetically. To use his hands to capture and create beauty, to tell stories with photographs. To perhaps find healing behind the camera and to offer it, as artists do, through the photos he took.

However, when his own drinking got in the way, he left New York and returned home. Like his parents, my father used alcohol to numb his pain and to escape the feelings of anxiety, uncertainty and self-doubt that seemed to be his legacy at the time.

And, then he ran off again—this time with my mom. Not far off. Just two hours down highway I-70 to Raleigh, where he and my mom created a new life. A new life, thankfully, that after a few years, included sobriety, full and steady employment, home ownership and initially three children, which eventually became five. Not bad for a brother from Guilford.

But, in spite of his deep investment in his family, neighborhood, church and the Alcoholics Anonymous communities of Raleigh, North Carolina, my Daddy was not trauma-free. He was still haunted by the ghosts of his childhood. As a young father and husband in the 1970s, my dad was not fully afforded the opportunity to unpack and unravel his pain or heal his wounds. And, he, of course, continued to be wounded by anti–Black racism and white supremacy, because, as Parker advises us, racial stress and trauma are "ongoing, recurrent and cumulative."

My Daddy was a workhorse. He started working at around 10 years old. As a young man with a family to feed, he never stopped working. He pushed. He pushed hard. He had a work ethic that he got from his parents, one they had no matter how much drinking they did. There were times when he would work three jobs to make sure the mortgage was paid and we had enough to eat.

In fact, like many Black folks, my Daddy most certainly suffers from John Henryism. He could most definitely be the poster child for it. As Parker explains,

> John Henryism is a cultural adaptation of Black people faced with the daunting task of creating for themselves, an American identity in response to racism and white supremacy. Based on the legend of John Henry—the famous, Black steel driver of American folklore—it is an adaptation that can be understood that Black Americans must often attempt to control behavioral stressors through hard work and determination. It was to be authentic, that identity had to make possible a cogent expression of core American values such as hard work, self-reliance, and freedom. It is a condition identified by Durham-based researcher named Sherman James who found a disturbing correlation between high-effort coping or striving, i.e., African Americans who cultivate persistence, set goals and work diligently toward them, navigate setbacks, focus on the long term, and resist temptations that might knock them off course.[12]

A key component in the relationship between exposure to stress and the development of mental illness is coping. High-effort coping, defined as "sustained cognitive and emotional engagement," is described as a problem-focused coping strategy when Black individuals appraise stressful situations that are sometimes related to racial discrimination, such as job loss or being passed over for promotion, as situations that can be altered by hard work.

However, high-effort coping may be a "mental health cost" paid by African Americans who maintain greater levels of sustained effort and energy expenditures in order to cope with stress. Working class and poor black resilient strivers face a greater potential for illnesses that result from stress, such as diabetes and hypertension, from which my father suffers.[13]

Yet, in spite of all the ways that race-based stress and trauma has impacted him, my Daddy is most certainly also a perfect example of how SOUL serves a resource that has allowed him to be resilient and to be here in spite of the odds being so much against him.

Creativity, resourcefulness, inventiveness, ingenuity and improvisation, all aspects of SOUL, have all fed my Daddy's capacity to be resilient and to do more than just survive. When we were younger, he would supplement our income by making wood art and log reindeers during the Christmas season to make ends meet. Of course, there were other times when he would use his connections, his social capital, to get what we needed. Food. A car. Money to keep the lights on. Or to fix the furnace that broke in the middle of winter, leaving us all huddled in front of a single kerosene heater in our kitchen wondering what rabbit he would be able to pull out of his bag of tricks that would get the heat back on. And soon. Thankfully, he had sisters who adored him and folks at church and in his AA community who were willing to help. Certainly, American culture would have you focus on his tenacity and work ethic in ways that are rooted in individuality and personal responsibility. Yes, he did that. Held it down. He was always willing to grind. To push hard. To work harder. These characteristics that are deemed as admirable in our culture are actually part of what wounded him. In fact, his work ethic or compulsion to push and push harder or his high-effort coping are part of what is so deeply flawed about the ways that we exist in a society rooted in white supremacy and predatory capitalism.

Being a workhorse who started working as a kid took its toll on his body—a body that was already wounded and weary from beginning back-breaking work so early in life and being exposed to so much stress and trauma. A body that, as a healing arts practitioner, I would imagine was full of bound energy, tight and constricted spaces, unseen wounds and weight, knots of pain and grief. Fear. Anxiety. Shame. Humiliation and worry. Bound up, trapped in my Daddy's beautiful Black body. How on earth did he manage to breathe, to keep waking up, getting up, going out and getting something.[14] So, it was almost inevitable that, even though he worked with his body and for many years rode his bike to work, he developed chronic diseases—depression and diabetes. Diseases that disproportionately impact Black Americans. His diseases can undoubtedly be attributed to his experiences with white supremacy and anti–Black racism in the Jim Crow South. Diabetes is a disease Black folks have historically simply understood to be a foregone conclusion. "Having sugar," we used to call it. And, depression and addictions which, for us, have not typically been named, much less acknowledged, until very recently in our collective history.

And these chronic diseases have been compounded by the back injuries he suffered in his thirties, which compromised his ability to make a living and kept him off the bike he used to ride back and forth to work. All health challenges that are related to being from a Black family in the Jim Crow South directly impacted by white supremacy, anti–Black racism and epistemic violence. And predatory capitalism, for that matter.

Yet, my Daddy had SOUL and he sought and found healing. He started his healing journey by choosing to stop drinking and investing time and energy into his sobriety so he could be a husband and a father. He started his healing when he decided to approach fatherhood differently than his own father. He continued his healing in the hospital after multiple back surgeries when he began reading the works of spiritual teachers and after finding a guru of his own.

But, in spite of the heavy lifting he did to move forward spiritually and to grow and develop well beyond what might have been expected of him, his body, mind and spirit still held/holds trauma. He still struggles with the wounds of his childhood from growing up in the Jim Crow South, wounds that include working daily to manage his diabetes and depression. Wounds that include a deep and unabiding anxiety about his safety and the safety of his Black children, grandchildren and two great-granddaughters. For him, no matter how many white folks have helped him over the years, they still have the capacity to crush him, to crush us, systemically. Or in an interaction that goes completely wrong for a man living in a Black body. A man whose Black body carries the scars of all that makes America so deeply, deeply flawed. A man with a spirit that reflects the capacity of all the promise that America has had over the centuries.

These promises keep getting broken, over and over and over again. They are promises that, when broken, lead to wounds that keep getting reopened. Because my father, like all of us, experiences his own racial trauma compounded by the vicarious trauma of living in a society where the lynch mob, most recently at the United States Capitol seems to be back. Then there are the highly publicized murders of Trayvon Martin, the Charleston Nine, Sandra Bland, Nina Brown, Ahmaud Arbery, George Floyd and Breonna Taylor.

And I know when my Daddy's feelings are hurt—when he feels the sting of being slighted or dismissed because he is Black in our post–Obama era, when he puffs up and talks shit or tells jokes to move past the immediate hurt. Or when he goes off to find so(U)lace by painting with his music blasting. Soul music. John R. Carlos Nakai. Kitaro. James Brown.

Maybe it is easy to dismiss how my Daddy responds to or protects himself from racial wounding because of the trauma he has experienced. Maybe you can ignore his pain because he is the product of the Jim Crow South; he is a member of the civil rights generation; he is in his seventies. Perhaps, being young or younger makes it hard to realize or recognize the impact of white supremacy and racial injustice on our lives. Yet, the physical, emotional, mental and spiritual manifestations are not limited to our elders or the aging. In fact, we know that we are fundamentally experiencing what William Smith refers to as racial battle fatigue to label or name racial trauma or race-based injury, which "causes us to experience various forms of mental, physical, emotional, and physical stress that can lead to both psychological and physiological symptoms including headaches, elevated blood pressure, insomnia, mood swings, anxiety, and social withdrawal."[15]

In the same way that white supremacy and anti–Black racism forced my father to constantly try to prove himself and work so hard that he damaged his health and well-being, they also foster a degree of self-loathing that consists of having difficulty seeing our family members and cultural history as sources of spiritual strength and richness. Resmaa Menakem explains that "trauma decontextualized in a person looks like personality. Trauma decontextualized in a family looks like family traits. Trauma in a people looks like culture [bodies of culture]." This means that when we do not understand trauma and the systemic oppression tied to it, we judge our family and are disappointed with them for behaviors that are often outside of their control. So, while as an adult I have come to a place where I can sing my daddy's praises and write copious encomiums for him, I did not, for many years, understand how I contributed to his pain and suffering. How I and my siblings, impacted by judgments informed by white supremacy, anti–Black racism, and rampant materialism, hurt my daddy (and my mama, too). Our misinterpretations, our misreadings of ourselves, of others, and our wounds include the shame we carry. "A shame that has us act in ways driven by unconscious egotism that certainly hurt the ones we love."[16] Shame that even at times verges on disdain and self-loathing. We are disappointed in one another, in our parents, in our elders, in our loved ones, in members of our families and communities in this way because "there are huge gaps in our education from the larger culture that led us to focus on what we think are our shortcomings." Yet, how could my parents teach me when they didn't have the knowledge about our culture and about intentional and conscious ways to respond to and heal from racial wounding, stress and trauma? Beginning to understand that not all our families' "issues" are personal or "sourced in the recent past" allows us to release old judgments about our families, which, in so many ways, is healing in itself.[17] Learning to understand that my family (my father included) carries the wounds of racial trauma and ancestral trauma and intergenerational trauma (along with some recent EFT tapping) has allowed me to finally begin to release this shame I held about my beloved Daddy and my family. And to begin examining ways I might provide healing to my ancestors and elders that recognize the shame they carried over their lifetimes.[18]

Now, I can see my father more fully, with compassion, with respect and with grace. Now, I can absolutely see his SOUL. The parts of it that are still in pain, and the parts of it that radiate light and love. The parts of it that have allowed him to be my daddy and resilient in spite of all the obstacles he has faced and continues to face. I know now that my daddy has SOUL and had SOUL, "a healing resource rooted in the cultural sensibilities of the African diaspora." I know that he managed to put the energy, courage and heart back into his body repeatedly each time he got the breath knocked out of him by hardship, oppression and disappointment. I know that his SOUL, specifically his relationship with others, his creativity, resourcefulness, inventiveness, ingenuity and ability to constantly, like the dopest NYC dee jay, improvise, remix, make something new over and over and over again, has allowed him to experience healing and restoration.

Yet, as my sister told me a few weeks ago, 2020 showed us that the impact of white supremacy and anti–Black racism is not something of days gone by. As she said, the fear and apprehension around white terror and violence and its capacity to crush and destroy black lives is not a memory of my father's generation or your grandparents' generation. Your elders are not the only ones who have experienced race-based traumatic stress injury or racialized trauma. However, recognizing their trauma allows us to see concretely what long-term and recurring trauma look like in our individual and collective lives. And, it allows us to see that we all have experienced it. My generation, and yours. Yes, it is toxic and pernicious. And, as Dr. Gail Parker reminds us, racial trauma is "ongoing, recurrent and cumulative."

In the recently released book by Dr. Kyra Shahid, *Anti-Black Racism and Epistemic Violence,* five undergraduate students recall their respective experiences with racialized trauma.[19] They recount how they have

> exerted excessive amounts of psychological and emotional energy to manage stress in academic and social contexts, as well as systemic and

everyday racism, which can be overwhelming and taxing. In fact, the significant injustice of societal racism has taken a toll on our students who may to many appear to be tough, have grit and are successful. They have faced the constant threat of perceived intellectual inferiority rooted in notions of white supremacy, which has produced anxiety, trauma, and general unpleasantness for them and their peers.[20]

Constantly negotiating anti–Black in this way feeds and fuels our dis-ease—a dis-ease that disrupts our sense of safety, security and belonging, and erodes our sense of innate dignity and worth and self-esteem, at eighteen, at twenty-eight or at seventy-eight.

Sadly, what Shahid's students documented in 2018 still continues to be echoed by Black students In fact, just recently in a Fall 2020 series of articles titled "The Black Experience in Higher Education," *Inside Higher Ed* reported that "Black students continuously experience, fight against and bear emotional scars from racism, which can lead to increased anxiety and poor mental health outcomes." Yet, even after repeated protests across the country in response to cases of racial violence on and off campus, many "colleges are just starting to address these issues."

"Dealing with regular microaggressions and overt acts of racism on an individual level, while also living through the constant debates and discussions of systemic and institutional racism, can be sources of pain, trauma and stress," particularly for, but exclusively, students at PWIs. For some students, these experiences can also lead to more serious conditions such as anxiety and depression and leave them feeling hopeless that things will improve.

Additionally, "a 2020 survey report by the United Negro College Fund highlighted the emotional turmoil that students who attend historically Black colleges and universities [HBCUs] are experiencing due to the coronavirus pandemic and economic recession," which are disproportionately impacting Black folks.

Of course, many Black students have long been aware of systemic racism and have experienced examples of it firsthand prior to this year. Being racially profiled by campus police, receiving disparate treatment by staff members, witnessing a white professor using the N-word or being stereotyped by peers all contribute to heightened mental health concerns. Even if they attend colleges with large numbers of students of color where they are less likely to have racial problems and tensions on campus, students of color are still in greater need of mental health support for racism that occurs off campus. And while "[HBCU] students might experience some kind of an oasis in terms of cultural similarity and have a greater sense of belonging" on their campuses, "their experiences in the larger society are consistent with those of students of color who attend a predominantly white institution." Even for HBCU students, "[t]here's really no escaping these negative, racially-charged forces in our society, especially at this point."[21]

As a result, this generation of Black students are more likely to suffer from anxiety or depression than their white peers and are in need of culturally competent mental health support from colleges. Black students dedicating their time and energy to calling out or preventing racist incidents continue to hurt their mental health in myriad ways.

Also damaging are persistent notions of success mixed with classic John Henryism that ignore the communal good and the ways in which being in relationship with one another can allow us to flourish and be well far more often than being socially isolated and driven solely by individual gain.

In her essay in the *New York Times*, Jenna Wortham describes breaking out in a rash that "first appeared in the crease of [her] right elbow, ... that [she] ignored and [she] wrote it off as heat rash, or something similarly seasonal, until ... it started to spread. The topography of [her] body transformed into a foreign mess of hives and scaly patches."[22] I flashed back as I read the description of her spreading skin ailment in her August 2016 essay. I knew what she had immediately: psoriasis. Because, like her, I first got it during a summer when I was subjected to a level of stress that was quite high as I pursued "success" right out of college as a White House intern heading directly from undergrad at an HBCU to graduate school at a large research one PWI. And, like her, "my skin would heal for a [while], only to burst back into a weeping rash." Like Wortham, I also determined that my psoriasis outbreaks were stress-related. But in my case it was because I was success-seeking in ways that ignored my SOUL. She concluded that her rash was stress-induced after reflecting on the fact that her "first outbreak started in June, around the time that a man threatened to shoot up [her] local gay bar in Brooklyn, 'Orlando style.'" My psoriasis flared as outrage and grief over the killing of two black men, Philando Castile and Alton Sterling, by police officers began flooding my social media feeds, only to be followed by the murders of Sapphire Williams and Korryn Gaines in July.

The physical impact of race-based stress and trauma in Wortham's case was the result of state-sanctioned murders of Black people. Mine, pursuing "success" that may or may not have been in my best interest. Really I was doing what I had been told would be ideal. Ideals that one might think were based on achievement being tied to rejecting my SOUL in order to assimilate and advance. I certainly did not have the insight that my psoriasis was tied to my body keeping the score. That my body was telling me to slow my role and to look more deeply at my choices.

John Henryism and Sojourner Syndrome as explained by Parker is reflected by Barbara Holmes in her work *Joy Unspeakable: Contemplative Practices of the Black Church*.[23] She asserts forcefully that our effort to prove our worth and wipe out a history of oppression has taken its toll on us. She names the toll as a spiritual one, as do Malidoma Somé and Shola Arewa. We also know clearly too that the toll is also physical and more (114). In fact, Holmes suggests that the toll is intrinsically tied to consumerism, crime and a skewing of moral values combined with the prevailing social presumption of equal opportunity for all (113). This toll has come to include putting individual material success over communal well-being (122), holding fast to the notion that we might uplift the race as we rise in social and economic standing. Sadly, it seems, nothing could be further from the truth. Holmes insists that the capacity to reconcile personal gain and community well-being is not impossible but it is most challenging. And, one cannot certainly not be confused with the other. Our reliance on individual material gain as a marker of racial progress is one of the effects of white supremacy and consumerism that creates its own set of wounds in the long run. Some of us have robust shoe collections, name brand clothes and massive amounts of debt to prove it.

Additionally, our stories of our shared pain and trauma can be found in the music of some of our most popular artists, including Raphael Saadiq, David Banner, The Roots, Beyoncé and Jay Z, Maimouna Youssef, Michael Kiwanuka and so many others. And, the Black Lives Matter movement in its various iterations forces us to recognize this trauma, the wounds, the deleterious effect of white supremacy, anti–Black racism and epistemic violence on our minds, bodies and spirits.

For example, on his album *Damn*, on the track titled "D.N.A.," Kendrick Lamar reminds of the ancestral and inter-generational trauma in our bodies, both the pain and hurt in our DNA:

> *I got power, poison, pain and joy inside my DNA*
> *I got hustle though, ambition, flow, inside my DNA*
> *I was born like this, since one like this*

Yet, at the same time, Kendrick Lamar recognizes our individual and collective capacity for both resilience and resistance, which can both prove to be healing in their own right. My father, in spite of the trauma he carries deep inside his body and spirit, which he may never fully release in this lifetime, does reflect what Lamar celebrates in "D.N.A.": Lamar describes the complexity of how men like my father and women like Menakem's grandmother struggle to heal while fighting to survive. The in-your-face, I-will-not-be-broken bravado of Lamar's track is inspiring and reminds Black folks that we are strong and tenacious and resourceful against the odds. That we all have the capacity to be resilient and resistant, simply by being.

Lamar also, reflecting shifts in our culture, references yoga and meditation, two healing modalities that we can use to heal. My daddy, like many Black daddies (and mothers, for that matter), exemplifies how we negotiate the wounds we carry in part because we are so loathed in our society and the world. Yet, he also exemplifies our collective capacity for resilience and resistance. And restoration. And healing. And SOUL.

Reflective Journaling/Developing Self-Awareness

Consider your father, grandfathers, great grandfathers. Consider your mother, your grandmothers, great grandmothers. Aunts. Uncles. Your extended family. Consider your ancestors well beyond perhaps the elders in your family who you may have had the opportunity to meet, know and have relationships with. Consider what traumas do/did they co-exist with. Consider how racial trauma specifically exists/existed in their minds, spirits and bodies. What pain do you imagine is trapped deep inside their DNA?

Consider creating a genogram as a visual response to these prompts. A genogram is a graphic representation of a family tree that displays detailed data on relationships among individuals.[24] It goes beyond a traditional family tree by allowing the user to analyze hereditary patterns and psychological factors that punctuate relationships.

As you develop the element of the genogram that is you, take an honest look at your own experience with racial wounding and racial stress-injury. Take time to consider your firsthand experience with the ways that anti–Black racism, epistemic violence or the constant threat of perceived intellectual inferiority produced anxiety, trauma, and general unpleasantness for you. Consider how you may have expended psychological and emotional energy to manage stress in academic and social contexts, as well as systemic and everyday racism. Are there times in your life when you did not have the luxury to ignore the significant injustices of societal racism and the toll it took, even when you had to appear tough and continue to excel in your life—in school, at work, in community?[25] It may be best to respond to these questions before you integrate yourself into the genogram. You may even wish to interview or chat with family members as you work on your genogram, allowing them to tell you their stories, which can be healing, and allowing them to also give you feedback on how they see you moving in the world as you find ways to express your own SOUL in spite of the barriers and obstacles placed in your way.

Also, consider how you might be high-effort coping like Sojourner Truth or John Henry in your response to white supremacy and anti–Black racism. Do you see any overlap between yourself and your elders and your ancestors or other members of your family or extended relations?

Recognizing this aspect of yourself is a form of both self-awareness and self-care. Knowing what has hurt you and naming it is part of the healing process. We cannot heal without stopping to recognize what has hurt us. Sensing how those experiences impact you emotionally, mentally and physically is also part of knowing yourself more fully. However, it is also important to consider how you will release, restore and heal those wounds as you continue to live resiliently.

The following chapters will offer you a variety of resources for doing just that—experiencing healing and restoration, and practicing self-care as we continue to find ways to flourish and be resilient and engage in resistance as we create amazing lives for yourself and others in a world that can be "toxic (toxic); especially when your skin look like chocolate."

CHAPTER III

Getting to *Theibbu Jenn*
Surrendering to Love and Community

Theibbu Jenn is Senegal's national dish. To simply refer to it as fish and rice truly does it a major disservice. It is so much more than that—so much more. First of all, there is more than one variety. There is the red, the white and the *jagga*.[1] Each type is unique in the subtle ways it differs from the others. It is fundamentally soul food, food which Juliet JuJu Harris, founder and owner of Nana Juju Rocks Food, a culinary services and organic garden design business, characterizes as the food of love.[2] It is the food that our elders and fore-bearers have been preparing from the heart that radiates care and affection. Love and affection found in the hands that knead dough, shuck peas and chop tear-inducing onions. It is food where the sister or brother cooking it is clearly extending themselves for the well-being of those he, she or they are cooking for. And it is, as Juju suggests—food that is good for the SOUL.

While soul food is typically associated with Southern cuisine consumed by Black folks, Juju's description of it allows us to see soul food in a broader way—specifically, diasporically. It allows us to see *Theibbu Jenn*, a Senegalese staple, as soul food, particularly in the way in which it, as a dish, reflects so much about Senegalese culture, particularly the communal and collective nature of the society. And, the love. Like most meals here in Senegal, *Theibbu Jenn* is eaten for lunch from a large communal platter or bowl. Midday you will see young men on bikes with metal bowls wrapped in fabric darting about to get the bowl to its dining destination. Or you see young women with said bowls on their heads making a lunch delivery to a loved one or customers.

It is important to understand that *Theibbu Jenn* is soul food in part because it is slow food that takes hours to make. We make it for our café clients and our visitors. And I would say that it takes three or four hours to make in order to feed a large Senegalese family. One reason it takes so long is because there is typically not much of anything put in it that is processed, frozen or canned except the tomatoes for the red or *Theibbu Jenn jagga*. And, the subtle and deliberate way that each phase of the dish is prepared takes time. You can never rush a *Theibbu Jenn*—do not let those videos online fool you. You cannot rush *Theibbu Jenn*; it takes time to get to the *Theibbu Jenn*.

Understanding how we get to *Theibbu Jenn* offers us a way to see how SOUL informs our capacity for healing and restoration and for sustaining our well-being. Understanding how we get to *Theibbu Jenn* offers us a way to concretely understand how we put the energy, courage and heart back into our bodies with our own culture, one that is traditionally communal in nature.

In fact, sourcing your ingredients, like eating the dish, is a communal endeavor, one not done in solitude or isolation, or with any of that annoying rugged individualism we seem so fond of in the United States.

Speaking of annoying rugged individualism, let me back up for a minute, to an era gone by in my life. I did not know *Theibbu Jenn* before meeting my husband Eddy. Nor was I familiar with its close cousins in the *Jollof* rice wars that West Africans and other Diasporic Souls love to engage in. Even if I had, I know now that it would not be the same as eating it here at home in Senegal. And, as an American (albeit a Black one who came of age as a Catholic in the South, and who was raised to some degree to focus on "we" before "me"), I am not quite sure I would have fully understood *Thiebbu Jenn* or appreciated it when I first met my husband Eddy.

Eddy and I met in July 2003, and we lived apart for two years until I eventually moved to Cincinnati in 2005. During that period, we both committed ourselves to seeing one another in both cities. During that time, when he visited me in Washington and I visited him in Cincinnati, we got to see each other more fully. He saw me flourishing as a creative, intelligent Black female who was a proud

HBCU grad and who loved teaching at a large community college with a very diverse student population, living alone in a city that felt like home, a city with so much SOUL. And, in Cincinnati, on my visits, I saw him clearly as a leader who, in spite of living in a city that seemed to have little if any love for Black people, extended himself for members of the Senegalese immigrant community throughout the area, including the ones who lived in the same apartment complex and the same side of town—where Eddy lived.[3] And other folks, for that matter. He was a highly respected community leader who people trusted and relied on as they navigated being in the United States in racially and culturally contested spaces. But, as much as I thought I saw him back then during our long-distance courtship, and when I moved there, it is now, living in Senegal, that I have come to best appreciate and fully see who my husband truly is. Now I understand his roots; I see them clearly. They run deep like the roots of our beloved baobab tree.

In fact, to be honest about it, as an American who was conditioned to prefer privacy and individuality, I have often found myself bumping up against who he was as his mother's son and as a Senegalese man of a particular station. And, I can tell you that being with a man who grew up eating *Thiebbu Jenn* rather than hamburgers and french fries really challenged me, how I saw the world, and what I wanted to and needed to control.

I am self-aware enough to tell you that my need to be in control is an adaptation that I assume I learned from my mom and Aunt Rosanne. They are two women I truly love and adore, but who do not have a whole bunch of people in and out of their homes, or in their lives, for that matter. Ever. They have never eaten *Thiebbu Jenn*, either. Like them, the notion of my (yes, "my," as in mine) home, my private space, where I lived being open to a whole bunch of people was definitely out of the question. I'm not saying that my mom and my Aunt Rosanne are selfish; I am just saying that they have a fairly codified sense of what I think is a form of self-protection that they learned from their parents in some form or fashion. We (they, me) grew up in America and never ate *Theibbu Jenn*. And, yes, I lived in a residence hall for the majority of my time in college at an HBCU without complaint, and as the oldest of five children I shared a small bedroom with my sister. And, I was raised Catholic in a working-class community in the South, so in theory the notion of caring and sharing made sense to me.

But my sense of community, of being in relationship with others was not the same as it was for my husband and his mother. I most certainly wasn't trying to share my food. In our house (one where we, at times, grappled with food insecurity), as a teen, I was sure to write my name on my food to keep my siblings and parents from even thinking twice about touching or eating it. And, frankly, that is sad—the food insecurity and the way I responded to it. Ewww, Phyllis, just ewwww.

In any case, I grew up knowing each family adjacent to our home, and someone in my family had contact regularly with those families. Wayne and Joy were a couple with two large German Shepherds, Bread and Ginger. I never went to their house, but I knew them; I knew what kind of work they did. I knew when they were home and when they weren't. And, my father had a relationship with them. And, when my mother had a gallbladder attack and had to go to the hospital, it was Wayne who collected me after work as my father sat with my mother in the hospital. Yeah, we knew our neighbors and they took care of us and we them. To a degree. To the left of them were the Gartrells: George, Carroll, Brooke, Damian and Carlin. At least in my younger years. We rode to school with them up until the time we could no longer afford to attend the private Catholic school we attended. We rode bikes with them on the neighborhood greenway. We sat transfixed in front of their cable-connected television watching *Star Wars* and *Grease*. They played basketball in our huge backyard that included a jungle gym, a handmade club house and the beloved basketball hoop. So, yeah, we knew our neighbors, and in some cases we still know them decades later, even if only via social media. So, yes, we knew our neighbors and they knew us. Yes, we knew our neighbors. All the way to the end of the block and around the corner. The Black ones. The white ones. The Vietnamese ones who arrived later.

So, while we did not live communally as my husband and I do now in Senegal, we did belong to a community. One in our neighborhood. One via church, which we attended weekly up until the point that my father declared that our parish priest was racist and had his own spiritual awakening that took him on a liberating journey. So, in spite of the extensive critiques my Daddy and I have for the church, we were certainly able to make ends meet in part because of the fact that we were part of that particular community anchored by a particular faith and set of moral values. When my father was hospitalized or we needed help, we always got it—and then some. And, while I can certainly spend time unpacking the relationship of white folks and our Black family, I will not. I will extend grace to our fellow parishioners and assume they were well-intentioned rather than get into my feelings about possibly being a charity case for them.

I am grateful to have been raised in a church community, in a neighborhood and with extended family that allowed me to be a kid when I was a kid, that made my childhood less taxing and less difficult. I appreciate all the love and support that my aunties Joe, Hattie and Shirley gave my father. I appreciate the support he received from his AA community. I appreciate my Aunt Rosanne and my grandparents for supporting and loving us so well. And, while I felt deeply held, safe and secure and a very strong sense of belonging for most of my early childhood, I had never ever had *Theibbu Jenn*. Instead, as a child I ate the fish sticks my mom plated, and as a college student in Durham and young adult in D.C.—fried fish plates, which I still devour at homecoming. But they are just not quite the same as *Theibbu Jenn*.

And because I ate fish sticks sold in the frozen food section of Food Lion and Winn Dixie, the way that Eddy existed in Cincinnati at times felt in some ways foreign to me. Yet, thankfully, my childhood with a loving family and generous neighbors and my church community in some ways prepared me for our courtship, particularly during my visits to see him in Cincinnati.

When I spent long weekends with Eddy in Cincinnati, I was pretty adamant about not seeing or accommodating visitors or responding to calls for assistance on Sundays. With break-of-dawn Monday morning departing flights back to D.C. looming, I just wanted Eddy all to myself. I was not in any way, shape or form interested in sharing him or our time with others. We were courting. We were at the beginning of our relationship, and I insisted that I needed all the time I could have with him before going back to my life in D.C. We had "business" (wink, nod, wink, nod) to attend to. So, I was only amenable to going out or having a few folks stop by on Saturday afternoon and evening, but otherwise I wanted no part of nobody. We were absolutely not going to sit down with much of anyone to eat *Thiebbu Jenn*, that was for sure. In fact, I only recall us doing so once one Saturday afternoon on the one day a week that one of Cincinnati's three local Senegalese restaurants, Teranga, invested the time and energy to make the beloved fare.

There was certainly a gap. A disconnect. A tension. An issue. A challenge. In fact, for me the differences between Eddy and me were so significant that I wrote a short story about it in order to process my feelings and frustrations. I named it "The Culinary Culture Clash," which kinda says it all. In addition to my rhetorical affinity for assonance and alliteration, it captures my difficulty in adapting to being in a relationship in which community was so central to my lover's worldview and approach to life. And, if you read Dr. Gail Parker's book, you might advise my younger self that my emotional responses were certainly out of proportion (105).

In her bare feet, Celeste paced back and forth across the kitchen floor, stopping occasionally to lean dramatically on her oven for support, or to issue a menacing glare out the screen door at Ishmael. She was not quite sure how he could sit there on the patio for hours on end without eating. His nightly routine was way beyond her realm of comprehension. She was hungry, and she was starting to feel that she would pummel his ass, even though she had not really pummeled anyone before, except for that petite blonde Republican staffer on the opposing flag football team who was running downfield with the football tucked under her arm on an unseasonably balmy October afternoon along the majestic banks of the Potomac River basin. Celeste was struck by an unexplainable, vengeful, violent urge and just grabbed the girl by the neck and threw her ass down to the ground. At first, Celeste found it exhilarating. Perhaps as payback for the Republican takeover of the House and Senate the previous fall. Or perhaps it was some ancestral urging from those who had gone before me. But after being verbally castigated by the tackled hill staffer's teammates and realizing her flag football faux pas, Celeste responded with a quick "I'm sorry" and jogged off the field to soothe her frazzled nerves.

But, Celeste really had no just cause for wanting to pummel her beloved Ishmael. In fact, she was probably far more out of line than she might have imagined at the time. What Celeste did not quite fully understand was that she was married to a man from a different culture than her own. Although she had romantic and politically pan-Africanistic fantasies about dating and maybe even marrying someone non–American, she had not dated or dealt this closely with someone outside of her own culture before.

Celeste always suspected that she might marry a boy culturally different from her. In fact, she was ashamed to fully admit that run-of-the-mill African American men were no longer that appealing to her. And, well, no, she didn't want a white boy either, but she knew that the brother who she fell in love with or married had to be from somewhere in the diaspora or else she would not learn or be sufficiently stimulated.

Her fantasy man was born and bred in Brooklyn (what, what), but his parents were from Trinidad. He was a handsome, brown-skinned brother with a small gap between his two front teeth and donned a hip hop era afro. In her dreams, he reminded her of the dark-skinned, lanky union man who lead Black Workers for Justice after the tragic chicken plant fire in Hamlet, North Carolina, or the defiant, trash-talking, injustice-intolerant, Jamaican-born independent filmmaker she met one night at an informal, family-like dinner at the make-shift, organic C.L.R. James Institute located in a rent-controlled apartment in Manhattan just off Broadway. These men both closely resembled the bespectacled Eriq Ebouaney in the role of Patrice Lumumba, the formerly vilified and later redeemed leader of the independent Congo, which he played in Raoul Pecks' Lumumba *(2000).*

Of course, he, in his Malcolm X-ness, as her fantasy man, had to be well-versed in the discourse of the labor movement and liberation struggle. He had to be able to answer convincingly if political scientist and organizer Dr. Ron Walters asked him, "What, son, does what you are doing actually have to do with the liberation of Black people?" He was a community organizer or youth worker or maybe a spoken word artist. And he loved Black people, unapologetically and relentlessly.

The man of Celeste's dreams was willing to stand up and speak truth to power like St. Louis-born peace and environmental activist Damm Smith, who founded Black Voices for Peace after 9/11 and worked tirelessly as the executive director of the National Black Environmental Justice Network, or the head of Transport Workers Union Local 100, Roger Toussaint, a native of Trinidad, who demonstrated an unwavering commitment to fight for the livelihood of 38,000 New York Transit Workers who held the line against the city's Metropolitan Transportation Authority for better pay as well as full pensions and health insurance contributions. Or the Black Lives Matter Movement organizers responding to systemic white supremacy, anti–Black racism and ongoing state-sanctioned violence.

Oh, and he loved his mama dearly—actually more than life itself. He was just so sweet. And tender. And sensuous. And sensitive. And compassionate.

And passionate. And thoughtful. He was a man who would happily please Celeste and make her feel special, beautiful and appreciated.

And, her fantasy lover man, of course, as a member of the diaspora and global citizen, had to play soccer on the weekends with other beautiful sable-skinned brothers from all over the diaspora. He was so sexy in those shiny black, white-trimmed soccer shorts, matching jersey and Adidas sandals they all wore after removing their mud-caked cleats. In addition to soccer, he preferred live music, books (including the texts essential to Pan-Africanists, Black feminists and new age spiritual seekers), and swimming to watching mind-numbing amounts of television.

However, her reality had not quite caught up with her fantasy. Or, maybe it was the other way around: her fantasy had yet to be reconciled with her reality. In any case, Celeste as a novice newlywed, had not quite put two and two together. And while it was common in Senegal for dinner to be served at about 8 or 9 pm, her husband somehow managed to eat as late as midnight, given the opportunity, especially on nights like this when the sun hung in the sky until after nine. To Celeste, this was insane (another disproportional response, of course). Celeste, who, as a child and all the years following, had been taught that dinner was at six or not much later. In fact, her mom had consistently served dessert by seven. And, her aunt, who was also her godmother, never ate after eight. Ever.

But, what Celeste did not fully understand or recognize was that Ishmael simply did not care to eat alone. Eating for both of his cultures meant building community and connecting with loved ones. But, particularly as a West African, he was none too pleased to have to dine alone. West Africans typically did not. Even at work, they would congregate at a table, amidst their toubab (white) co-workers, to share a midday meal from the same platter, as they would have done anywhere back home or in their segregated enclaves throughout the city. In fact, it was not uncommon for members of Ishmael's community not to eat until someone else arrived to share the food.

For Ishmael, eating late as a bachelor may have been linked to an unarticulated hope that a friend or family member actually might arrive, unexpectedly and unannounced, to share his food with him. Celeste, in her rush to (over)react with violent impatience, did not realize that years of bachelorhood had grown increasingly empty and lonely for Ishmael, a man raised to share his meals and his evenings with family and friends. She did not even consider the fact that loneliness might have in some way contributed to his eating routine. Postponing dinner indefinitely while he sat outside on the porch, a place where he might socialize and interact with his neighbors, allowed him to avoid the silent, empty apartment he lived in. The fact was that if he ate late, he could eat and go straight to bed, avoiding the depressing time alone.

Celeste, had she slowed down just a bit and thought about it, might have understood this. She might have had the sense to recognize that her fantasy lover man was actually just a human being rather than the infallible heroic

figure she had created in her mind. But, nonetheless, none of that really
mattered on this summer evening a week or so after she arrived to live with
Ishmael.

Celeste was hungry. No, she actually believed that she was starving,
which placed her on the verge of pulling her hair out or jumping in the car
to head to the nearest burger joint drive thru.

And this was one reason why she had become so invested in cooking for
Ishmael. She figured that she had to alter the playing field and take con-
trol of the situation or she would end up killing him or herself in a fit of
starvation-induced rage. And murdering her magic lover, lover man would
simply just not do. Not at all.

Yes, of course—clearly, I am Celeste. And, Eddy is Ishmael. And, at some point, as the short story suggests, I have developed enough self-awareness and engaged in enough self-study to retrospectively see the error in my ways. I realized that my impatience and need to control and micromanage was not going to work if I wanted our relationship to last. I realized over time that I would, like Celeste, ultimately have to come to understand and accept a different way of life if I wanted to remain married and bound to my beloved. I was gonna have to eat and fully understand *Theibbu Jenn*. And, while Eddy never showed up in those Adidas sandals and shorts, he did manage to look quite dashing and debonair in his Levi's and tee shirts. And, he was patient with me, perhaps, because like Ishmael, he did not always see or hear or notice my rage and frustration and impatience. Or maybe he did and ignored it because he wanted our love to last.

In fact, although I had never had *Theibbu Jenn*, although I did not come from the same culture as Eddy, he always said one reason he loved me is because we shared a deep love and commitment to family. And, while that looked different for both of us, that was the case. He saw that, I imagine, when I took him home to meet my family and when my youngest brother drove to Cincinnati from Detroit to give him the once over, to see if he was worthy of his big sister Phyllis. Clearly, he passed the test. That shared value is just one reason we are still together in spite of a variety of "culinary" challenges along the way. And it is how, frankly, I am able to live in Senegal as a Black American, who, like Celeste, sometimes still struggles with letting go of my need to control everything to the point where doing so makes me sick and drives other folks, including Eddy, crazy.

However, over time and after eating *Theibbu Jenn* at least twice a week in our café and with members of our community, I have come to a place where I understand very clearly that what Eddy and Ishmael have—a communal connection to others, a deep sense of interdependency—is very powerful. And, I know quite clearly now that it is an aspect of SOUL that is critical to our capacity to heal, flourish and thrive. Existing without it, all balled up and contracted around the way we have been conditioned or raised like Celeste, is destroying many of us from the inside out. It is part of our individual and collective dis-ease. It is what Brene Brown describes as a spiritual crisis, one where we deny our life-threatening loneliness and need for social, life-affirming connection and communion.[4]

Of course, it is important to understand that the need that Celeste and I have to control our environments is deeply rooted in a number of factors. Some of it is simply because we come from our very, very, very individualistic American culture. Some of this need for control—staying all balled up, tight and constricted—is about our collective and intergenerational trauma that is tied to our intersecting identities as Black women. We are simply protecting ourselves. Our need for self-protection is due in part to identities as Black Americans who did not grow up around a communal plate or living in a family compound or intergenerational family dwelling. We are influenced by fear and the sense that if we fail to protect ourselves, to control our environment in order to surrender, to be open and vulnerable, we risk being victimized, and subjected to violence—both racially and sexually. So, we close up and take control even when we are falling in love (which requires us to open up) and hoping to find companionship. I see the inability to surrender in other sisters all the time.

And, to be clear, quite a few brothers are good with it to some degree because it means business gets handled, bills get paid and nothing is left undone. They are also good with it because it is familiar. Their mamas, aunties and elder females for generations have often operated in a similar manner—no nonsense, take charge, run the show from start to finish. We got this. That is how many of us have operated most of our lives in the same way that our elders and ancestors did. Simply as a matter of survival.

However, our need to control our environment, to decide who has access and who does not, is not only about self-protection that is tied to existing in tandem with white supremacy and other forms of what feel like looming violence and risk. Our need to be on guard, to control our environment (which means limiting who we interact with) is also tied to the nature of what it means to grow up informed by European values, assumptions and priorities. What it means to grow up and come of age and move away from the community of collective care that you grew up in. Yes, we get it in pockets, like I did growing up in the South, in our churches, on HBCU campuses and often with our families. But, we exist in a way inside of, beside and adjacent to a toxic and violent culture that runs counter to collaboration and being relational. One that ontologically is strongly oriented to individualism, competition and survival of the fittest.[5] We exist "in a culture that teaches us that safety is found in separation and disconnection."[6] As Parker Palmer laments, we are taught to live autonomously and not interdependently, to compete and win.[7] Our culture is one where the freedom to carry a gun or to not wear a mask is more important than the health and well-being of the community, of our neighbors, of others—even during a global pandemic.

So, honestly, in some ways, as intellectually invested as Celeste and I might be in the idea of existing in community and living with a strong sense of interdependence, we both have had a long way to go to get to a place where we shift away from focusing on ourselves as individuals and focus on "collaboration, social interaction, mutuality community mindedness and reciprocity."[8] Being in Senegal, in a culture that is still very much a communal society where the collective still matters, makes the individuality and isolation of life in the United States striking and glaring. Clearly, Celeste and I both had a long road to take in order to get to *Theibbu Jenn*.

Yet, it is when Celeste and I let go, surrender and decide to release our tight grip of control, when we open up to others, when we choose to be part of a community, to exist the way our ancestors did and the way Eddy and Ishmael do, that we experience peace, healing, restoration and well-being. And, healing and restoration. And, love. Which includes living and existing in a way that is communal, which means seeking and existing in collective communities of care. And, being able to happily and comfortably sit with others over the communal bowl of *Theibbu Jenn.*

Yet, as much as I was asked to open up and let go many of my conditioning as well as my assumptions and expectations about how life should look and flow, my experience in Cincinnati still did not prepare me fully for Senegal. Senegal is communal; it is a place where focusing on ourselves as individuals simply does not work—at least not in the way it works in the United States. It is a place where "collaboration, social interaction, mutuality, community mindedness and reciprocity" are very clearly the norm. Where everyone eats *Theibbu Jenn* pretty much daily.

CHAPTER IV

#CommunityHeals
Getting to Theibbu Jenn, *Part II*

It did not take Eddy and I long to see this emphasis on community play out after we moved to Senegal in 2016. When we first opened our cafe, we had to (or so it seemed) do everything for ourselves as we learned how supply chains worked (or didn't). But we also had the support of family and members of our extended community. For instance, Looky, who is not blood related, is our "son" now, as he so much of what makes our success possible. Of course, my nieces and nephews helped where they could. They helped make fatayas and marinate chickens. They helped move furniture and lay tiles. My brother-in-law made sure our guests were picked up from the airport and that we had transportation to Dakar and other places where we needed to go. My niece brought us our first bolts of wax fabric that our guests could choose from for the outfits all of our visitors have made. Our daughter and her husband helped us as we navigated opening the café and hosting guests simultaneously. They introduced us to their friends and helped us get a better lay of the land, particularly in Dakar. Our family contributed to our efforts without hesitation, negotiation, complaint or expecting compensation. They understood that, as family, they were responsible for us, that we belonged to them.

But, at the same time, we also had to make sure that we had all the supplies and furnishings we needed to grow our businesses, both the café and Diasporic Soul. That meant driving back and forth on the traffic-clogged road to Rufisque and Dakar during our first year here for so many things, ranging from wood to make beds to cooking oil and coffee. Yet, thankfully we (by "we" I mean Eddy, who speaks four languages fluently) eventually developed the relationships needed to stop running and find the resources we needed to run both businesses. These relationships included members of our extended family and our immediate community in Sebikotane.

This community is anchored most certainly by Eddy's mom *Yaay*, as we call her. She truly epitomizes what it means to exist in a collective community of care, to live in a way where we focus on "collaboration, social interaction, mutuality, community minded-ness and reciprocity." She is clearly where Eddy gets his generosity of spirit and commitment to community from. I cannot tell you how many people I have met over the years who explained to me that she fed them, cared for them, extended herself for their well-being either here in Senegal or in Marseille, where she immigrated and lived for years. I can only begin to imagine how many plates of *Thiebbu Jenn* she made to feed folks in Dakar and in Marseille over the years. There is Amir who calls her weekly for mentorship, guidance and advice from Marseille. There is Hassan, the son of Bilal, the fishmonger in Kayar, who *Yaay* cared for when he was a refugee in France in need of sanctuary. And, when she mentioned our cafe to him, he immedi-ately reminded her that his father, Bilal, the fishmonger, could help. It is this interconnectedness, this love, this generosity that ultimately allows us to sit down under the mango tree in the café, catch our breath and actually enjoy a plate of *Thiebbu Jenn* with one another as a couple and as hosts of our fellow Diasporic Souls.

And fishmongers like Bilal exemplify what community feels, sounds and even smells like in Senegal. They and the market women are the *poisson* purveyors to households and businesses all over the country who connect the nation to *Thiebbu Jenn*. They are critical to our capacity to sit together and connect over the communal bowl. To see them at work, to see the way they move and flow with one another is a sight to behold. What a sight it is to see Black folks out on hand-carved, beautifully painted *gaal*, which are wooden canoe-like boats, in the ocean. It is quite moving and awe-inspiring to see Black men bringing their boats to shore, collectively, collaboratively. It is quite a sight to see cool young men with swagger dressed in heavy rubber protective fishing overalls bringing in the boat as the elder men of a fishing village verbally guide them. To hear them, at times, singing or teasing one another as they bring in the brightly colored *gaals* as they are called, by rolling them over massive logs or large empty gas canisters. It is amazing to see others hoisting huge containers of fish onto their shoulders and bringing them to where it will be sold, often just a few feet from where their boat was just brought in, or sometimes in more formal fish markets like the one at Dakar's Soumbédioune beach.

This sense of connection, of community, is apparent in a heartfilling generosity of spirit. There is Demba, another fish monger, who helps us get to *Thiebbu Jenn*. His dilapidated coolers sit behind makeshift boutiques selling hardware. In them, he stores what comes in from Bilal's large fishing village, Kayar. It is here where you might come to get Kayar's catch without having to venture so far off the route. Demba is warm; his warmth makes me think of Cedric the Entertainer. He feels honest and trustworthy, energetically, as he shows you the fish (*jenn*) he has available. There is no hard sell. Just a matter-of-fact explanation of what there is and how much it costs. Not too much haggling, no hard hustle. Just an exchange.

Once we decide what fish to take, what will be used to make *Thiebbu Jenn* primarily and maybe *Yassa Jenn*, the fish is taken a few feet away to the women who will clean it. Some of these women are, in fact, our cousins—women from what Eddy calls the big house, the family compound of his maternal grandfather, where some of our cousins and nieces and nephews still live. These aging women, our cousins, squat on large logs and wooden benches underneath a tent made of logs and tarps to clean and cut our fish into steaks. They scrape off the scales, which pile up as the cats linger about hoping to eventually get something to eat. No one shoos the cats away; they know how close they can get. The women gut the fish, removing the parts that we cannot eat, piling those with the scales. And then with hand-carved mallets and machetes, they break the fish into large pieces. Once what we have bought is put in buckets or bags, we pay Demba and the ladies before heading back home.

But, this purchase is not simply transactional. We have a

50

relationship with Demba and the ladies who work there. We are, in fact, related to some of them. And, the way we engage with one another allows for us to connect beyond the exchange of money and fish. Demba has brought me a lotte and refused to take money for it, simply because we like one another. That is the kind of generosity here that I am deeply grateful for. I am grateful that he is willing to come all the way to Sebikotane to gift me my favorite fish. As an American, you might cynically see that as service, but it is not simply that. Instead, it is Demba's willingness to extend himself to gift me something he knows I adore. For me, it means so much, in part because I am still at times an outsider. For me, the fish he brings me is akin to him bringing me flowers or a box of chocolates. It means he sees me as special and valuable. He makes me feel the way singer Seinabo Sey and many others feel when they came to Senegal. Valuable. Magical. Beautiful.[1]

No matter where you are in Senegal, you are typically welcomed with open arms. It is a place where folks call out, *"Kai lekke an"*— "Come join us at the table and eat." Or, "Come join us for lunch." Where you are invited to sit and eat at the communal bowl of *Theibbu Jenn,* Senegal's national dish. Or come sit with us for *attaya.* Come sit with us and tell us where you are from. The call to eat is a welcome; it is hospitality. It is *teranga.* It is love. It is SOUL.

And, while Eddy and I don't eat communally every day simply because we run a cafe where we plate for individual customers, the energy remains, and eating communally resonates with me. So, I always appreciate it when I am given the chance to do so. Because eating communally means not only that we are eating, but we are connecting with one another. We are slowing down. We are paying attention to one another. And, they are paying attention to us. Taking time to sense and feel one another's spirits. There is such love, intimacy and affection when we eat this way, sitting knee to knee. There is SOUL. There is food created by someone who cares about the well-being of her loved ones. There is Soul Food. There is *Theibbu Jenn.*

One of my beloved former students and Diasporic Soul guest, Carmalita, who came to spend time with us for our 2019 Calm in the

Chaos Retreat for Black Women, describes how it feels to sit together and eat this way so well:

> Sharing meals elbow to elbow, thigh to thigh and spoon to spoon was somehow magical. I was able to laugh from my belly unabashedly. We got to let our hair down and comfortably share stories that lifted the weight of daily micro-aggressions that black women face in the workforce, grocery store and daily exchanges with folks who don't look a thing like us. This experience was a salve for wounds I didn't fully realize or know I had.

The connection that Carmalita describes is what our visitors experience during their time with us—a sense of belonging as a part of our extended family and community. She reminds us that community heals. #CommunityHEALS.

Carmalita's reaction to eating communally is reflected in how Andrick, an Olympic-qualifying semi-pro boxer and college student from California, describes his experience in Senegal:

> I will always feel like Africa, especially Senegal, is a special part of my heart. And, I definitely gotta come back and visit. You know for me, you know what it felt like? It felt like meeting new cousins at the family reunion. Like everything felt very welcoming. It felt like I belonged. It felt like I hadn't been there for the first time. It felt like I was going back to somewhere I had maybe forgotten as a kid. Overall, my Africa trip was a life-changer for me. It put a lot of things in place for me going forward.

The sense of belonging, the felt connection of communion that Carmalita and Andrick describe that happens here in Senegal feels automatic; it is the culture. Here, like Andrick and Carmalita and the other brothers and sisters we host, you will have *Theibbu Jenn* or another similar dish that is eaten communally. Here, you will eat in a way that allows you to sit and slow down long enough not only to enjoy what you are eating but to fully see and connect with the people you are sitting at the platter with. This is a healing and restorative experience that takes place in our home and cafe, but also in the homes of members of our extended community. It is an experience that will feed your SOUL.

For example, Lailya, our first Diasporic Soul-in-Residence, experienced this during her nine-month stay with us. She ate "soul food" with Eddy and me and others who spent time with us in our home before Covid-19 struck, including our dear friend Nana Lawson and my elder-mentors Ajamu and Rukiya Dillahunt and their eldest daughter Dara Monifa. For Lailya, being embraced by our community included breaking bread with our friends, such as Borso Tall, who is a former Obama Young African Leaders Initiative (YALI) fellow, founder of Young Advocates for Human Rights (YAHR), and a writer for the *Washington Post's* West Africa bureau.

Early on during Lailya's stay with us, Borso invited us over to her home in Dakar for lunch when she learned that the Dillahunts were arriving and that Lailya had just joined us for her residency. For them, along with a group of Black Americans visiting Senegal, Borso opened her home and her heart to virtual strangers. She spent hours in the kitchen with little assistance making huge platters of food. In this case, the dish was *Thiebbu Yapp*, which is a rice dish featuring mixed vegetables and beef, lamb or goat. She even extended herself to make meatless versions to accommodate those who no longer consume meat. Borso was so very generous with us, serving our drinks in family heirlooms that belonged to her mom, who had recently passed away. She was so gracious and generous with her home and her hospitality. Her *teranga*. She made it clear that we are welcome, that we are part of the same community and family. That we are connected and that we belong to one another. Borso showed us that cooking and serving food are most certainly expressions of love and a reflection of SOUL. And, food provides ways for us to create connection, foster community and say to one another, "You belong here, you are welcome, we see you." Being held this way in communion is healing and restorative. Being in community where we feel loved, inter-connected and a sense of belonging is an aspect of SOUL that makes healing possible.

Collectively enjoying food made with love while engaging with one another gave Lailya the feeling of a sense of connection and community and belonging. An experience that she says that she has only had twice in her life—here in Senegal, and on the campus of her beloved alma mater, an HBCU, Florida A&M State University (FAMU).

Later during Lailya's visit, we traveled to Casamace and the Sine

Saloum for the very first time—two places where she experienced the warmth, the *teranga* and the love that eating communally provides. Such was the case when we went to the village of my husband's father's family in Goudamp, at his cousin Fatou's house in Zinginchur, and at his cousin Omar's house, where we ate *C'est Bon* in the region where it comes from because Lailya asked for it.

And, when we vacationed in the Diofour (a small town in the Sine Saloum) Fatick region of Senegal with our friend Maimouna and her two children. There, after Maimouna met Lamine, a warm and generous merchant in the town where we stayed, we found ourselves sitting under a huge shade tree one early afternoon with his wife and children eating *Yassa Guinar* communally as we learned about the village we were in and about Lamine's life and family. And, of course, he expected nothing at all in return. He, like so many other Senegalese people, simply showed us what generosity and hospitality feel like. He not only had us over for lunch, he made sure we connected with other members of his community—his marabout, his nephew who works at a large eco-lodge in the area, the young man who took us across the massive lagune to one of the area's 200 islands, Mar Lodj, on his *gaal*.

Now back in the states, Lailya is very clear that she will always be a member of our community, of our family. And we are willing, always, to extend ourselves for her well-being. That is the collective nature of SOUL—one that has confirmed for Lailya in many ways who she truly is and who she intends to be moving forward.

It is interesting that like Celeste, folks are not always fully open to eating *Theibbu Jenn*. They are not always sure what it will be like, or if they will be able to coexist communally and closely. For example, some of our students and retreat guests come to the experience wondering how they will all get along when they have been so used to going it alone most of their lives. Yet, during what is a relatively short amount of time, typically between seven and fourteen days, most Diasporic Souls become connected with one another and support one another throughout the experience. As Carmalita noted, "There was a connectedness in Senegal that I didn't know I needed to feel until I felt it in Senegal. I felt at home there." As did Deshelya, who came to us as a part of Xavier University's 2019 cohort. She stated, "I felt at home in a place I had never been. On a continent I had never stepped foot on. I felt so connected to the people there even though I spoke English and they didn't. It just felt like home." Deshelya's sentiment was shared by her peers, who realized how much "they need(ed) each other" as they cried on each others' shoulders and contributed to the healing of one another. As one student stated, "being held while crying is so dope and needed." And, another indicated that he valued being there for those who needed the support. It is clear that the students who shared this communal space with us in Senegal felt as if they no longer had to keep themselves closed off or be guarded as they so often do at home. While in Senegal, one student, Ihsan, stated, "We were challenged to open up to [one another] and trust our peers with our truth, which was immense pressure … for [us as] a generation of young people who didn't have a lot of practice with this." Yet, it was in this moment that he realized the power he and his peers possessed to assist in healing each other. They had this power because they had the chance to engage in deep listening and to bear witness to each other's stories that "held answered prayers and truths for one another." To be in communion. To be in community. To feel safe, secure and a deep sense of belonging. To recognize their innate dignity and worth. To feel rooted, grounded, centered and supported. To feed their SOUL.

Our students' deeply felt sense of belonging was also due to the relationship they had with *Yaay*, who showed all of our visitors love and made them feel welcome each time she made her way into the cafe kitchen to oversee the plating of their meals to make sure they had more than enough to eat. Extending herself this way is significant because *Yaay* is an 80-year-old woman of great stature whose health has been impacted by years of hard work and aging, which makes every plate our visitors have truly a plate of soul food.

In fact, on occasion *Yaay* will even extend herself by making a meal for our visitors. For example, for the students from Xavier who came in 2019, she prepared Senegalese couscous made from millet that was served traditionally with lamb and chicken, veggies and tomato sauce. The meal was also special because it connected our students to our ancestors, as millet is a hearty, nutrient-dense grain that was traditionally consumed well before rice was imposed on the population by the French when the Senegambia was colonized. In addition to her *teranga,* they, like all our guests, experienced *Yaay's* love daily each time her face lit up as she greeted them with hugs and kisses when we prepared to depart and when we returned home.

Yaay's connection to our guests is also illustrated by the times she comes upstairs to see them, which is not easy to do at her age. For example, one morning during the Xavier University 2019 Diasporic Soul cohort's visit, *Yaay* shared her life story with the students, a story that exemplified the centrality of spirituality and the importance of family and community in her life. As she spoke to them lovingly and so openly, she implored them to open their hearts and be generous with their love and resources, reminding us that that is what God calls us to do. *Yaay* reminded them that they will be rewarded (as she has been) if they choose to love, if they choose to extend themselves for the well-being of others.

She recounted being a mother to seven children and living and working hard in two countries, France and Senegal, where she often fed and sheltered many people, including Hassan, Bilal the fishmonger's son in Marseille. In Marseille she invested her time and energy into supporting members of her community. *Yaay's* commitment to community was also apparent during her exchange with this group of young adults whom she extended love to by telling them that they are her grandchildren and they are now a part of her family. She showed them so much love and radiated so much SOUL and so much light. She was an integral part of their Diasporic Soul healing experience. And, she continues to ask about their well-being because they are now part of our community. And, she is part of their community. Now they belong to us.

But it is important to understand that this sense of community, the sense of belonging that is felt here in Senegal is not exclusive to Senegal. By that I mean, some of the sense of belonging that our visitors experience here is due in part to the connections they have with one another that can be deepened and nurtured in a space where community and family are the top priority in the culture. Being here allows them to see in very tangible and concrete ways what they value in terms of investing time and energy into the well-being of the collective. Being here allows us to see in stark contrast what we might be missing so deeply in our cloistered, isolated, fenced-in lives in places where we hardly know our neighbors or have time for our families, immediate or extended. Being here in Senegal allows us to consider that being in an intentional community may not be perfect, but our capacity for well-being and healing is intrinsically tied to being in community. Being here and going to villages and family compounds where the communal lives that people live is so apparent and so explicitly clear allows us to see that there is another way to exist. That our resistance to community and affinity for self-first and individuality is causing us great dis-ease.

We see it on trips to Eddy's maternal grandmother's compound, where three generations live together. On the way there, as we walk through the various sections of Sebikhotane, we are embraced and greeted warmly and enthusiastically by merchants, artisans and tradespeople along the way. We also met the village chief, the village's female elder, Fatou, who serves as the women's community health liaison as well as the mayor. And, in spite of their important status in the community, they all stop and talk to us as if they have nowhere else to be. As if spending time with us is all that matters. As if they have known us forever. As if what Dr. Gail Parker often reminds us, we do, in fact, have all the time in the world. To pay attention to one another. To fully see each other.[2] To feed one another's SOUL.

We experience this same generosity of spirit and warmth when we visit even more rural Serer-Sine communities to learn about traditional Senegalese spiritual practices that pre-date conquest, colonialism and the imposition of Islam and Christianity that are still practiced today.[3] As always, we experience from the *teranga* of our host—a well-regarded traditional Serere spiritual practitioner, referred to as a *marabout*. And when our guests can deepen their sense of interconnectedness, community and belonging as the day unfolds. For the students from Xavier, this means playing soccer and hand-clapping games and dancing with children of the village, including two particularly resourceful and creative girls who improvised and played drums made of large square ten-gallon water jugs. For the women who came to our 2019 Calm in the Chaos retreat, this means being invited to come out of the compound in which we were gathered to witness the celebratory parade of the village's young men returning home from their three-month long traditional initiation, as well as eating communally, even though they, like Celeste, were not quite sure they could go with the flow and do something that they had not quite planned to do. For the young men and their mentors from California, it means gradually softening their "hard" edges, letting down their guard, being open to others and co-mingling with a group of young people of the same age who are listening to music on the other side of the compound and dancing, laughing and having fun together, in spite of language and cultural barriers. And, of course, it means never being able to refuse the generous communal plates of food made by the healers' families for us to eat. These experiences where community and interconnectedness feel so good and foster feelings of being loved and belonging offer us a chance to imagine what it might be like to live in a way that allows us to feel far less disease than we feel now. And, that we have all the time in the world to pay attention to one another. To see each other. To make each other feel like we matter and that we belong. To feed one another's SOUL.

It is this communal energy that makes being in Senegal feel so good. Like home. Senegal offers us a cogent and important reminder that our well-being as well as our healing and restoration require that we must consider deepening our connection to one another, to community. Racial wounding often negatively impacts our sense of belonging and subsequently our capacity to feel safe, secure and loved. It hurts our root chakra, the chakra that helps us feel grounded, rooted and supported. A pain that can keep us from flourishing if we do not address the trauma or the wounds. However, as we consider the way SOUL is a healing resource, it is important to remember that community and our interconnectedness are key to our well-being, healing and restoration. Clearly, our capacity to feel safe, secure, loved and a sense of belonging requires us to live and be in communities of care and relationships rooted in love and the willingness to extend ourselves for one another. Where our innate worth

58

and dignity are seen, valued and respected. It is important to understand ourselves in relationship to others. It is important to know who
we belong to, who cares for and loves us in concrete and tangible
ways. It is important for us to find joy, courage and affirmation in
safe, brave, loving spaces where we will be able to sit together over a
huge heaping platter of *Thiebbu Jenn.*

Reflective Journal Prompt

So, what will you do to deepen your connection to community? How will you, like *Yaay*, Borso, Lamine, Looky and Maimouna extend yourself for the well-being of others? How will you
intentionally consider ways in which community can contribute to
your well-being? What choices will you make that center community in your life and that put others before yourself? How will you
choose to live day in and day out in a way that fosters connection in
lieu of isolation? How will you live day in and day out in a way that
allows you to be supported and held and seen, versus overlooked and
ignored? How will you choose to live day in and day out in a way
that fortifies your SOUL and your capacity to be resilient in a world
full of great challenges, including those directly tied to systemic
white supremacy, anti–Black racism and other pernicious forms of
oppression? How will you hold space for yourself and others to foster life-sustaining connection? How will we hold space for us collectively to feel safe, secure and an unwavering sense of belonging? How
will we foster community and seek connection for our individual and
collective healing? How will you intentionally create space and time
where you can slow down and sit with others over food that is made
with love and that feeds your SOUL?

How, my dear ones, will you get to *Theibbu Jenn*?

Chapter V

In Big and Small Ways
The Importance of Elder-Mentors

Recognizing the importance of our elders and ancestors is another aspect of SOUL. Our elders and our ancestors are integral aspects of SOUL who play a key role in our overall well-being. They offer us a sense of belonging and feed our sense of safety and security. This means that having SOUL, expressing SOUL and being connected to SOUL means deeply respecting our elders and all the wisdom that they possess from their experiences and of our traditions. It means asking them for guidance and advice. Respecting and recognizing the importance of our elders means caring for and attending to them with love. In a similar vein, SOUL speaks to revering and recognizing our ancestors. Throughout the diaspora, we understand that our ancestors are always with us. That they protect and guide us. As spirit, our ancestors, we understand, must be recognized as members of our community, as we recognize at the same time our elders. Our elders and ancestors can support our ongoing efforts to flourish and be well.

On the last Wednesday of April 2020, I had my weekly Covid-19 call with my elder-mentors, Ajamu and Rukiya Dillahunt, who had just recently visited Senegal for the second time for a week in February with their eldest daughter and my sister Dara. Since the lockdowns in both the US and Senegal, we had agreed to speak each week to check in. Their visit to Senegal bumped up so closely to what most of us never imagined might happen in our world—a global pandemic.

That afternoon after finishing up our lunch shift in our café, I received the text message that Ajamu had sent me earlier indicating that we might miss our call and lovingly noting how the day was special as it marked our connection to one another in more than one way:

> Here is how our day started. My FB feed popped up with 3 years ago today with us in St. Louis. The festival, restaurants, etc. And then you post about meat packing plants and then the Well-Being Wednesday post of which we watched even though not doing the yoga. Thanks. We are working on some trees being cut that threaten the house, waiting for Imani to pass by so we can wave and finally taking two mowers to be repaired. We may miss you if you call but we have connected in big ways today. Namaste.

I felt tears welling up as I read Ajamu's text. I was in my feelings to be sure. Ajamu is a stern, no nonsense New York native with energy like my maternal grandfather, so the sweet softness of his message was particularly moving for me. His message captured so much about who we are and how they have impacted my life as my elder-mentors. It reminded me that we belong to one another. That we are together, family, community. It also reflected how important our weekly calls have been during a period when our world seems to be unraveling and we have been challenged to channel our capacity to be resilient and resistant even when we are sometimes scared shitless.

Saint Louis was the capital of the French colonial empire that sits on the banks of the Senegal river, a stone's throw from Mauritania. It is a popular destination for tourists to Senegal, in part because of its colonial past and the associated architecture, which, in comparison to Senegal's other major colonial-era cities, has been fairly well-maintained. It is also home to an annual world-renowned international jazz festival held typically at the end of April. It is the Saint Louis International Jazz Festival that Ajamu refers to when he mentions Saint Louis. Ajamu loves jazz. That is the reason that we went to the festival during their visit to Senegal in 2017. In fact, on our call, I was excited to tell him about a recently released album by Christian McBride that the WNCU overnight syndicated radio host mentioned just that morning—*The Movement.*

In addition to being able to attend our first jazz festival on the continent of Africa, the Dillahunts' visit to Senegal in 2017 was special for many reasons. One, they finally got a chance to meet my husband and our family, including Eddy's mom, our family matriarch,

Yaay as well as our daughter Daba, her husband Malick and their first-born, Mohammed. Immediately, we were an expanded family of four generations connected and bound by love and respect for one another. Daba and Malick showed the Dillahunts so much respect. They also invested so much energy and love in hosting the Dillahunts, immediately, without hesitation. They were generous and attentive as we moved about the festival grounds and enjoyed our journey to Saint Louis and back, which included simply lingering and enjoying nature surrounding the home we stayed in that weekend. There was no language or culture barrier, even though the Dillahunts do not speak Wolof or French, and Malick and Daba only speak a little bit of English. However, the love and deep respect was palpable. And, even when the Dillahunts left Senegal, Daba and Malick were at the airport to see them off. And, to gift them a gigantic painting of Miles Davis done by Malick's close friend Laz, which was a loving and generous gesture that was an unexpected surprise.

And that same love and generosity was evident when the Dillahunts returned three years later in 2020. On their return visit, the Dillahunts not only came with gifts for Daba and Malick, but also for all of their four children, including the three daughters born after their first visit in 2017. And, again, Malick and Daba exemplified one of the aspects of our cultures across the diaspora—deep respect for their elders and family. They understand completely that Ajamu and Rukiya belong to them because I first belonged to them, and now they belong to me and Eddy. It was a joy to spend time with Malick and Daba one afternoon in Dakar and again here in our café with the whole family, which, at the time, also included our dear Lailya, who was just beginning her three-month residency with us that soon became nine thanks to our deep fondness for one another. Oh, and, yeah—Covid-19. The Dillahunts also embraced Lailya without missing a beat. And, she them. The connection between everyone was immediate and endearing in what has evolved into an ever-extending family.

The Dillahunts first visit in 2017 was significant not only for them, as it was their first time in West Africa, but also for Eddy and me, because they are my elder-mentors; they are like my parents.

Having Ajamu and Rukiya come was akin to having my mom and dad come to visit. And, actually, they were our first Diasporic Soul guests. They paid for the package without any hesitation, which meant the world to me. Doing so was them investing in me and the work Eddy and I are doing here. We felt so affirmed and validated by their decision to come and support our work.

Their visit also meant a lot because I can honestly say I would have never chosen to live in Africa without them. What I mean by that is my consciousness is the gift they gave me as my elder-mentors during my time in high school and college. My parents were busy and working to take care of my siblings and me, and, honestly, figuring out their own sense of what being Black meant to them. As noted in the earlier chapter, my father carried around some pretty deep racial wounds, including some shame and self-loathing that I don't think he had quite worked through when I was a teen. Plus, he was my dad, and what teenage girl wants to sit around with her dad and learn Black history and about Black cultures? Certainly not me, as an American teen, who at the time had yet to have *Theibbu Jenn* or to understand the profound importance of my parents and other elder family members. So, as a teen, I learned about Black history and political movements primarily from the Dillahunts. They ran Freedom Books, the Black bookstore in Raleigh, where I was raised. And, they were labor organizers active in Black Workers for Justice (BWFJ)—Ajamu as a postal worker and Rukiya as an educator. They taught me about the radical Black liberation struggle.

Thus, this explains Ajamu's reference to the meat packer controversy Facebook post. The infection of hundreds of meat packing workers during the spring Covid-19 outbreak has been deeply disturbing for me, in part because it brought back memories of the fire in a chicken processing plant in Hamlet, North Carolina, during my 20s that I will never forget. That fire revealed for me how nasty it is to put profits over people. Of the 81 employees working that day, 25 died and an additional 40 were injured at "the Imperial Food Products plant in Hamlet, North Carolina, when a fryer ignited and flames fed off grease and oils on the factory floor. As the fire raged, the building's sprinkler system failed, forcing workers to run through heavy smoke. Desperate to find exits, only to find locked doors, the victims collapsed into piles of bodies as the carbon monoxide overtook them."[1] Watching this horror unfold for me as a college student provided me with a disturbing and gruesome lesson that was so tangible, concrete and palpable for me at the time. My attention to it at a time when I was as a college student can only be attributed to what I had been learning about Black labor struggle and resistance from the Dillahunts since high school. In fact, the Hamlet Imperial Foods fire would inform how I understood the massive agricultural industrial complex, critiqued and condemned globally by environmental and labor organizers like the Dillahunts. Knowing that people were burned to death during the fire because the plant doors were locked to keep them from stealing chicken was and still is very disturbing to me. I was shocked and devastated. I remember that Jesse Jackson came, as he often did back then, as a voice for the voiceless during that era. But, I had, at that point, no real connection with or affinity for him outside of the image of him on the Lorraine Hotel balcony and as an 80s era Democratic presidential candidate. So, when the pushback began in response to the fire, it was the Dillahunts I saw and heard, specifically as active and engaged members of Black Workers for Justice willing to challenge the workplace conditions that resulted in the death of twenty-five innocent people.

In fact, it was the Dillahunts who took me to my first protest, in Washington, D.C., against the first war in Iraq. It was an experience that allowed me in 2000 and 2001 to show up and challenge the Bush presidency and the second war he launched in Iraq under the false pretense that we were ostensibly fighting global terrorism.

They also took me to my first grassroots organizing conference—the Malcolm X Conference at CUNY in New York City, which was actually when they introduced me to Assata Shakur and her autobiography, a book that eventually became the basis for my Master's thesis on the Black Power autobiographies written by women.

They also mentored my peers and me as we organized our first protest under the banner of what we so ambitiously and enthusiastically called the Black Youth Brigade. Then, we organized to challenge what could only be called racial profiling at our local mall. We were fully aware that Black youth were treated differently there than white youth. And, we called for a boycott. I can't say how impactful we were, but I can say that the courage and confidence we had to stand up and question authority and challenge an institution in our city can be attributed to the fact that we had guidance and support from our elder-mentors, the Dillahunts.

And, when I say I wouldn't be in Senegal without the influence of the Dillahunts, that includes Ms. Dillahunt serving as the advisor for the International Culture Club (ICC). Having her hold space for my peers and me at school and in the book store gave me the impression that my world was bigger than it might have seemed living in NC at the time. I had yet to meet anyone from the continent or the Caribbean. My sense or awareness of anything African or diasporic was limited to South Africa and the clear ways that the anti–Apartheid movement and Black liberation movements in the United States informed one another. Yes, by introducing my peers and me to the fact that there was a world well beyond North Carolina, Ms. Dillahunt planted a seed that allowed me to be open enough to marry a suave, debonair Diasporic Soul named Eddy Coly, who, when we began dating, had dreadlocks like my elder-mentor dad, Ajamu. She and Ajamu and my parents must be credited for giving me the ability to sit comfortably with an open heart and open mind at the communal plate of *Theibbu Jenn,* which, by the way tastes much better than the sushi Ms. Dillahunt had us try at one of the ICC events we had.

The Dillahunts were and remain part of my village, my community and my extended family. They are the elder-mentors who Malidoma Somé describes in his seminal work, *The Healing Wisdom of Africa.*[2] Somé explains that in traditional cultures, having mentors is aimed at helping the young person, the mentee, develop the genius within them, to help them tap into their true and authentic self so that they can share their gifts with the community (192). In this vein, mentors recognize and see the young person "as someone who already [possesses] the knowledge that he or she needs"; they are there to help the young person, the mentee, remember who they truly are, what they already know (191). The mentor is not simply a teacher, according to Somé—they are, in fact, mirrors, helping the mentee see what they can become even when they are struggling and how to embrace and accept the genius they possess (105). The mentor knows her mentee "from the inside out" and is willing to support and "serve her wholeheartedly" for the well-being of all of the collective (119). Put another way, our mentors are the "midwives of [our] spirit(s) as we experience the pain and discomfort of coming into [our] own genius and accept [our] true purpose" (106). We all have our growing pains, which are not easy and can be quite painful, particularly when that purpose seems to counter the ways we have been conditioned to conceive of what and who we should be and why. As elders, mentors offer us the assurances we need to take risks; they offer us stability, dependability and wisdom (123). They ground us as they serve as a frame of reference and resource that we can count on.

In *Journey to the Heart*, author Melody Beattie reminds us that

> sometimes we find ourselves with people and in places we can't adapt to. No matter how hard we try, no matter how much we want to, it just doesn't feel right. Doesn't fit. At these moments, in situations like this we revert to old ways of thinking, believing and feeling. There must be something wrong with me if I don't like this, if this isn't working. If I try harder, control my emotions, jam a little harder … [I can make this] fit. These are times we may begin to feel confused, weak, scatter, uncertain. We abandon ourselves. Our emotions, disappear. Our passion wanes. We may begin sleeping, escaping, drifting further and further away. Our soul begins squirming in reaction to what we're trying to force ourselves to do. We may become physically ill. It's as though we're allergic to our surroundings. Sometimes, we may spend years in the process—depending on what we're afraid to face or what we're afraid to lose (293–294).

Forcing what doesn't fit causes us pain and suffering, of our own making.[3]

Our elder-mentors can serve as guides, as mirrors, as resources who can help us during these painful and confusing moments that Beattie describes when we stray away from our authentic selves—when we falter and lose our way. They can help us restore our connection to our gifts, our talents, our knowledge. They can help us restore our connection to our genius. They can help us restore our connection to our SOUL.

As Black Americans, we don't necessarily grow up in a traditional village like Somé describes in his work. However, we do often belong to healthy and vibrant communities who love, affirm and value us. And, when we forget that, our value and our worth, our purpose, our true self, it is often our elder-mentors who remind us of our value and worth. When we flounder, falter and make huge mistakes—mistakes that feel like they will break us, it is the love and wisdom of our elder-mentors who can help us find our centers again. They are the ones that can remind us of our genius. Sometimes this happens without us seeking them or their wisdom out. Sometimes they appear at a divine time when we need them the most. Sometimes, years later, even, this happens when you never quite imagined you would reconnect with them again or restore your connection with their wisdom and insights.

I realize this, too, in my own role as an elder-mentor to the young people who I have supported and nurtured over the years. My capacity to be supportive and loving comes when one of my mentees asks me to read and give her feedback on a statement she intends to issue that takes her campus colleagues to task at a moment when most of them believe they are engaged in radically and significant anti-racist work, when in fact they are deluding themselves and merely doing what they have always done, maintaining the status quo and continuing with business as usual. Or when she needs feedback on a presentation for a new job she is being considered for because she has decided to practice self-care instead of doing the emotional labor for an institution that is still not sure of its commitment to Black students, staff and faculty.

I also stepped into my elder-mentor role when another mentee, a young man who also attended Central State University while I worked there, called on me to come do a training for his students and for the Black male student retention program that he was involved in at the University of Nebraska–Omaha. What became apparent pretty quickly as I lay tucked away in his guest bedroom nibbling on the pound cake he made especially for me (and Patti Labelle) was that I wasn't there for his students as much as I was there for him. I realized this fact as I listened to him, over lunch, on the drives to the campus, over dinner, and as we sat together tucked under blankets on the couch. I realized that what he actually needed was me, his Ma Dean, his elder-mentor to be there for him. To offer him solace and reassurance. To remind him of his value and worth. To advise and guide him as he figured out how not only to move professionally but how to navigate what felt like an unraveling domestic situation with his long-time partner and lover. And, since then, to talk about how he might continue to grow professionally even with the ever-looming pandemic disrupting all that seem to be in order, all while finding a new love to pursue. And, most recently, to congratulate him on the new love he has found and the new opportunity he has been tapped for that will allow him to impact some of the Black students on the campus.

I appreciate these connections, the relationships I have with the young people in my life, my former students who are now in their late twenties and early thirties. And, the students who they serve, including members of the Xavier Diasporic Soul and A2MEND cohorts who have had a chance to come to Senegal for their heritage and healing experiences. I owe them at minimum what my elder-mentors have given and continue to give me. They also remind me of my impact and contributions to their lives, as well as my value and purpose, why I am here, and what I am called to do. They belong to me. We belong to each other. We are connected in BIG (and sometimes small) ways.

Often, the teachers we find of this nature may be with us only for a season or for a specific time in our lives. However, there is great value in being intentional and committed to seeking them out and staying connected with them. As they are part of our communities of care, they are key to our well-being. As our elder-mentors, they can help us remember our roots, our true and authentic selves, and help us ground ourselves over the course of our lives.

I can't say I was always good at this. My early adulthood offered me new mentors, particularly in the context of my career. Yet, I do not take it for granted, nor do I believe it is an accident that my elder-mentors, the Dillahunts, came back into my life not long after Eddy and I moved to Senegal. I believe they came back because my SOUL needed them to. My SOUL needed them as a reminder and as an affirmation of my journey and where I had most recently arrived. I am deeply grateful that they came back into my life at this moment when I believe I have restored my connection to my SOUL, to my authentic self, to my purpose. They remind me now of what I believe in, what I value and what is important. As a teen and young adult, they taught me so much, but now they show me, and I can see, what love is. What it means to show up for others, over and over again. What it means to find joy in small, sweet things that earlier in my adulthood I know I most certainly ignored and took for granted. They are now teaching me how to be a better woman, a better elder-mentor, a better person overall. And, hopefully, in some way, what I am doing with my life, particularly for Black people, makes them proud of me. It feels rewarding to be able to offer them what Eddy and I have to give from the place we are now. To give back to them, to pour into them the way they poured into me. To show them appreciation for all they have given me.

And, interestingly enough, even as I write this book with my mentees in mind, I have not only been engaged with Ajamu and Rukiya—other mentors and elders who impacted me as a young adult have resurfaced and reminded me of my true and authentic self.

In one case, as I write, I have reconnected with the amazing woman who mentored me as a young woman who then and now is still so grounded and centered and very much about her business. And, more importantly, as my mentor, she, like the Dillahunts, consistently held space for me to learn and expand my horizons. She also opens her heart and home to me. Our time together went well beyond the years I worked with her at the White House Initiative on HBCUs. She served as a resource and a guide for me up until the time I left Washington to move to Cincinnati. In fact, she is the one who introduced me to the idea of knowing and honoring my authentic self, well before I ever knew anything about yoga. She introduced me to the book *Finding the Purpose of Your Life*. I remember her convening me and other young women she nurtured, including her eldest daughter, to discuss the book and do some of the activities in it so we could deepen our self-awareness and live far more purposefully than perhaps we might have been at the time or, frankly, even thought possible. She, like the Dillahunts, has and continues to do exactly what elder-mentors do best—she holds a mirror up so I can clearly see myself and reminds me still of how special I am. She, like the Dillahunts, reminds me that the choice I made to establish Diasporic Souls to hold space for Black people to find healing and restoration is so important. I am deeply humbled by her praise and grateful for her wisdom, love and support.

Similarly, as I wrote this book with my own mentees in mind, the week following the election and the confirmation of the Biden-Harris win, I sat on a conference panel for the International Leadership Association (ILA) with two former colleagues and two of the young people in my life who I admire and deeply respect. These two young people have me as their elder-mentor, their Ta Ta Phyllis, including Ajamu and Rukiya's grandson, who is now an activist in his own right. We were convened to discuss the ways that our work continued the work and legacy of Dr. Ronald Walters, who I worked for years ago when he came to the University of Maryland to establish what eventually became the African American Leadership Institute in the Academy of Leadership in the mid–1990s. Dr. Walters often asked an evaluative question in his work as a political scientist and advisor to elected officials and public servants: what does this have to do with the liberation of Black people? What, indeed, sir—what, indeed? Although my relationship with Walters was not as intimate and rich as the one I had with the Dillahunts or with my mentor Catherine, I realized in our exchange on the ILA conference panel that who I am today is due in part to his influence. That I am, in fact, contributing in some way to what he wanted to see in terms of holding space for young Black people to be supported, to be the kind of leaders who have the capacity to create change and pursue justice in order for Black folks to feel free, to experience liberation.

What I realized from our exchange on the panel was that Walters, the Dillahunts and Catherine have been and still are my teachers. They and others, like Drs. Stewart and Gravenberg, have and continue to provide me with a moral compass. My elder-mentors have offered me the assurances I needed to take risks. They have offered me stability, dependability and wisdom. They remind me of what matters, what has the most value in the world. They also have shown me what love and resistance mean. They have exemplified for me what it means to extend yourself for the well-being of others, especially Black folks and other marginalized people. For the Dillahunts, I see this love in the care they have provided their children, grandchildren and now great-grands. And, the loving care they have shown Eddy and me and our extended family. And, for the community. I see loving care in the more recent work they have done in Raleigh to bring the Fertile Ground Food Co-op to their community. Or, in Catherine's case, I see loving care in her ongoing work with the Black MBA association and her passion for supporting Black entrepreneurship. Their ongoing devotion to Black folks, even during this pandemic when they are forced to stay in and keep their distance; that, too, is the love and care they practice, in big and small ways.

Reflective Journaling Prompt

So, as a Diasporic Soul operating in a world filled with challenges yet with still so much promise, who is mentoring you? Who is offering you the assurances you need to take risks and asking you tough questions so you might avoid pitfalls or experiences that break your heart and bruise your SOUL? Who, in your life, is dependable and has the wisdom and fortitude to hold space for you to feel supported and stable, and who encourages you to try new things and pursue new dreams? Who sees your light? Who holds the mirror up so you can see your light and your genius? Who are your elder-mentors? Who is guiding you? Offering you support and encouragement while simultaneously challenging you to live with purpose and to pursue your heart's desire in ways that feed your SOUL and ideally the collective and the greater good? Similarly, who is calling you to task and holding you accountable? Who loves you and is willing to extend

CHAPTER VI

Waiting on Red Birds

Honoring Our Ancestors

I never really cared much for birds until my grandmother died in 2018, two years after I moved to Senegal. I got followed by one, an angry one, in high school when I was out walking once. After that, I was like ewwwwww. The bird might have not been too pleased with me being out and about the neighborhood in curlers and a head scarf. Or maybe the curlers scared her. In retrospect, I probably was looking rough. That, of course, was before I went natural. But now, each morning I am so tickled and warmed by the sounds of birds as the day begins. Except for pigeons—I have yet to get over my aversion to them, because they seemed to take over spaces in downtown Raleigh during my childhood. Oh, and geese. Ewwwwww.

Anyway, yes—the morning for me means being able to sit and listen to bird song. And, when I am near the balcony windows or sitting on the balcony amidst the plants and next to the mango tree, I watch them. Many are so small, like the size of hummingbirds. And, they seem so happy with one another when they are flitting about and seemingly talking to one another as they kinda fly dance above mostly fuchsia that straddle our terrace. And, there are the huge ones that soar and dip and bob in the sky. Lately, I hear them more; I think they are the black kite birds that we just learned about on our last visit to Goree Island. There is one that sits majestically in a trimmed down baobab tree in the lot next to our house.

My evolving (yeah, evolving) opening up to birds is because they remind me of my grandmother. I imagine that she is with me and enjoying their music and their flurry of activity each morning just as I am. They are now part of my connection to my grandmother.

73

Yet, connecting to nature as a way to connect with my ancestors, particularly my grandmothers, is not unique to my experience in Senegal or to me specifically. For example, my friend Carol and my sister have both spoken to me about cardinals when they see them. Carol, in recent months, before shifting to working from home, described to me her experience seeing a cardinal at her office window—a window that is located on an urban university campus that absolutely cannot in any way be described as verdant and particularly nature-friendly. To be clear, energetically, the campus feels stark and unwelcoming—it evokes feelings of unease in me that I associate with places like Bensonhurst, Brooklyn. There is a racial energy, a charge there, for me, that is palpable, especially on that side of campus (which is somehow reflected, in so many ways, in the lack of nature there). The energy there is hot and heavy and makes me feel constricted and ill at ease, which is totally not usually how I feel on college campuses. Perhaps, the fact that the campus police murdered two Black men there is what I feel energetically. But I don't think it is the energy of these deceased brothers. Honestly, my sense is that what I feel is actually the energy that fed the campus police's capacity to murder them in cold blood. The energy of racism and hate and white terror that killed Yossef Hawkins in Bensonhurst, and many others since then.[1] The same energy that many staff, faculty and students experience but perhaps brush past with their heads down as they high-effort cope and do what they have come to understand must be done to "succeed." I know from my time there and my relationships with folks who work there that when folks are honest, this campus is a place where being Black does not feel good at all most days. Where folks get racially wounded on a regular basis, reminding us, as Parker tells us, that racial wounding is "ongoing, recurrent and cumulative." Even when they are completely oblivious and unaware of it each day, the students trudge to class striving and hoping that a college degree will free them from what some might feel is the weight and burden of their Blackness.

But, in spite of this hostile environment and a campus where the climate for Black folks can only be described as cold—no, frigid, other energy exists there. In spite of Black men being murdered there, our ancestors show up. They show up there even though it is a dark place—a place, like far too many, where our trauma is in the soil, underneath the unyielding concrete towers and walkways. They show up to remind us that they are there and that they got us, that they are guiding and protecting us always.

So to be clear, in a place like this, the likelihood of my friend having a bird of any kind popping up in her office window is slim to none. Like, there ain't nothing there for a bird to want. Nothing at all. There are barely any trees, and the ones that are there are small and paltry because they were planted by someone focused on some non-life-affirming design concept that is supposed to evoke a sense of modernity and sophistication. The so not verdant campus is not at all the place where I would expect my friend to see a bird, much less a vibrant, burgundy-hued red cardinal (and, in this case, a cardinal that seemed adamant about getting her attention by banging on the window). My friend was clear as soon as this cardinal appeared that it was her grandmother Lizzie G. She knew this immediately. Her capacity to know is because she is open to spirit. She is a Diasporic Soul, one raised in both the Caribbean and the United States, who understands that our "ancestors continue to show an interest in the daily lives of the relatives [who] are still alive" (Mokgobi).

What my dear friend and I know about red birds and their capacity to connect us with our ancestors is reflected in my friend Angela's series of textile pieces where she processes the grief she experienced over her sister's death. In the series titled *My Soul to Keep*, there is one piece titled *When Feeling Blue, She Reaches for the Redbird.* This particular piece reflects Angela's understanding that red birds are a form of contact from the deceased, an understanding that my friend and I obviously share. A form of contact with the deceased that is what Dr. Daniel Foor, author of *Ancestral Medicine*, refers to as spontaneous or unsolicited communication.[2] The idea that red birds are ways that our ancestors show up for us is something I have been aware of for some time. Here, in Senegal, they are tiny red birds the size of hummingbirds. In fact, I saw a pair recently just beyond the balcony around the time I recognized my own grief for my grandmother, whose birthday had passed the week before. I saw my first one here in Senegal (also on the balcony), only for it to fly off when I tried to get a closer look.

Our ancestors are speaking to us, spontaneously, even when we do not seek them out, and our capacity to connect with them offers us another powerful way that we can heal our SOUL. Connecting with our ancestors, practicing the ancestor reverence that is common across many indigenous cultures, offers us another way that we can "restore the energy, heart and courage into our bodies with our own culture." It is another way we can feed our capacity to be well, to be loving and to stand in our personal power. And, to be resilient and resistant. Relating to and recognizing our ancestors, understanding the continuity of their spirits is part of our spiritual legacy which can absolutely contribute to our collective and individual restoration and healing. It is part of recognizing the value of our SOUL, specifically in terms of our connection to spirit, to energy, to the divine.

However, doing so may be challenging at first because we have been deeply conditioned in our culture, in our society, and in our education to privilege our minds over both our bodies and spirits. "In Western cultures, we tend to give the thinking mind priority, but ... the thinking mind does not necessarily come first," if we intend to experience healing, restoration and well-being (Parker 159). Of course, "the thinking mind is a storehouse of information and in our attempts to problem-solve and to increase our knowledge, our tendency is to gather more information. Gathering information has its place, but its focus is external and therefore limited" (Parker 159). However, if we want to experience healing and long-term well-being, we will, instead, have to let down our guard and be willing to embrace "a deeper, interior, intuitive level of knowing.... We must open to grace and surrender to the realm of the unseen, the unknown, and allow it to reveal itself to us" (Parker 159). In fact, we must "let go of our attachment to the mind as our sole authority and open to spirit as our guide."[3]

Or, put another way, we must begin to "let go of our 'socially-constructed world' and relinquish our need to be in control, like me and Celeste, if we are going to be open to spirit so that we can heal" (Holmes 6). If we are going to experience the effects of unspeakable joy unfolding, we must be willing to involve our bodies and our spirits and be open to that which defies what the thinking mind can comprehend and the limits of language (Holmes 6, 7). We will need to let go of being enslaved to the rigidities of the cognitive in order to make room for mystery and magic, as well as for a reunion with spirit, with the divine, with God (Holmes 3).

Doing so means considering the ways in which our traditional and ancient spiritual practices might support our capacity for healing, restoration, resilience and resistance. Yes, of course, this might be a bit of a challenge, perhaps in part because of what Parker and Holmes describe as our conditioned attachment to and privileging of the thinking mind over our bodies and spirits. And, our need to be in "control." And, it might also be a challenge, because most of us "have been taught and have come to believe that there is something wrong with any spiritual practices outside of Christianity" (Burton). Yet, what we fail to realize is that our ancestors often, throughout the diaspora, did not supplant one belief system or cosmology for another. Religions were layered upon one another, and indigenous beliefs coexisted with Christianity and Islam, "despite rigid prohibitions" imposed on our enslaved ancestors (Holmes 15; Burton). "We see this creolization or layering of spirituality in spiritual practices such as Hoodoo, Santeria and Voodoo. And, in the ways in which we practiced Christianity. Our layered or creolized spiritual practices offered us one of few areas of totally autonomous activity for our beloved ancestors that offered them a dynamic and unwavering source of psychological liberation because it enabled them to express and reaffirm that self-existence they objectively recognized through their own labor.... They allowed us to break away psychologically from the very real and concrete chains of slavery and to see [ourselves] as independent beings; in short [they] gave [us] a sense of human dignity and enabled [us] to survive."[4] And, to be resilient and resistant.

Layering, integrating, mixing and creolizing our indigenous practices with the imposed religions of the colonizers, Muslim and

Christian, allowed us "not only to see [ourselves] as independent beings and survive, but allowed us to experience deep joy and fulfillment. Our history is one where we have been blessed to be in communion with family members who have experienced the mystical nature of faith and spiritual practice, where everyday communal practices that began on the African continent nurture us, mind, body and spirit." Thus, sustaining us, feeding our SOUL, "generation after generation as they simultaneously undergird and bolster our fight for justice, freedom, and liberation" (Holmes xxxii, xxxv).

Of course, you may have not yet had the chance to travel to Senegal or other parts of the Diaspora. However, we do, in fact, have the capacity to embrace our African spiritual legacy and to tap into what Somé refers to as the healing wisdom of Africa.[5] We owe it to ourselves to have the backing of spirit (Somé 26, 34) as we seek to heal the wounds inflicted on us by a "world that is toxic (toxic) when your skin looks like chocolate."

Opening to spirit or being open to having the backing of spirit requires us to distance ourselves from "traditionally Westernized versions of [spirituality], which generally stress individualism and independence" and cosmologies that privilege the thinking mind over the body and spirit. Instead, we might consider spiritual practices that "are reliant upon collectivism, strong communities, and healthy interdependence" (Burton). According to Shola Arewa, spiritual leader and author of the groundbreaking book *Opening to Spirit: Contacting the Healing Power of the Chakras and Honoring African Spirituality*, these are practices steeped in traditions that "focus attention on the spirit realm, daily communal flourishing and an (*embodied*) spirituality rooted in culture."[6] This happens in an accepted reality where we "recognize the fact that [we] are sharing an animate life world that is fully imbued with energy" (Arewa 25). Reflecting our SOUL, "this is a spirituality that connects us with the unseen, community, nature and engages in ritual" (Burton).

As theology professor Barbara Holmes explains in her book, *Joy Unspeakable: Contemplative Practices of the Black Church*, "while, we cannot overly generalize an ethnically and religiously diverse continent, the cultural orientations of West Africa specifically consist of cosmologies that embrace multiple realities without steadfast and strict demarcations or distinctions between an everyday life and the spirit realm. From conception to death, spirit and flesh breathe as one; silences and ecstatic performance erupt during both ritual and daily routines, always pointing beyond the visible to the invisible" (24). I can tell you that after being with Eddy for over almost twenty years and in Senegal for five, here, in Senegal, in West Africa, reality is layered in ways that at times feels divine, magical, and "incongruous" all at the same time.[7]

In fact, if we simultaneously embrace feeling divine, magical, and "incongruous," we will be able to surrender, to release control and get out of our heads. We will, in fact, be able to put the "energy, heart and courage back in our bodies." However, to do so we must understand exactly what we mean by "energy," particularly in a way that considers culture or SOUL. Energy, as Shola Arewa advises us, has been established as the unifying principle the world over (10). Donna Eden, well-regarded healer and energy work expert, reminds us in her texts *Energy Medicine* and *Energy Medicine for Women* that Einstein told us that energy is everything, a fact that modern physics has confirmed.[8] In fact, Eden and Arewa, although operating out of two seemingly distinct cultural perspectives, both advise us that our bodies are not just made up of physical matter. In fact, the body is actually an energy system. Further, Donna Eden reminds us that "energy is all there is" (17). "Matter follows energy; therefore, when your energies are vibrant, then so are you" (23). Our bodies, Eden offers, "are vibrating, every atom, every molecule, every cell, every tissue, and every organ." In other words, we are bundles of energy, a fact that Arewa outlines by reminding us that "diverse cultures throughout the ages have understood that people exist not as solid matter but as vibrational beings in direct contact with the greater source of energy surrounding us, [which] is an understanding reflected in spiritual practices, rituals, mythology, astrology, physiology, [cosmology] and magic in cultures throughout time" (9). Non-Western societies have a different understanding on how energy is supplied and transferred. "Though different cultures around the world have their own defining terms for this concept of energy, they all encompass the same meaning, which is to elucidate the substance that creates and animates one's life, the power to take action, and prove that we are all one, connected to each other and our earth." For example,

> in the yoga tradition of India, this energy is prana; it is chi or qi in China, Baraka by the Sufis, Ka by the Egyptians, Wong by Africans on the Gold Coast of modern Ghana, Elima in the Congo, Ntoro by the Ashanti, Ntu by the Bantu, Mungo in Central Africa, and Ori by the Yoruba. For the Mande people of West Africa, Nyama is energy; it inhabits and animates all living things.... It is the energy that flows through all beings and allows us to connect with the earth and our spiritual nature. It is the spark of spirit that infuses the body with life and the brain with consciousness.[9]

Further, Arewa explains, "energy flows from a greater source, the Divine, or Spirit, the Creator, through the Soul to our physical bodies, where it exists as both subtle energy" (44). That greater source that Arewa references might be understood or referred to as Spirit, which is often, Eden notes, understood "as the all-pervasive, intelligent energy of creation, which manifests as the Soul at the personal level" (25). According to Eden, "our soul is the manifestation of spirit at the personal level" (25). "Subtle energy is the bridge between spirit and matter. The Soul is the source of our subtle energies, which gives form to and animates everything about us" (Eden 25–26). In fact, Arewa offers us that the Self, which evolves, develops and shifts over the course of our lifetime, is fundamentally "the constant changing of energy" (10). We are energy, seen and unseen, through and through.

Arewa writes, "In fact, we are surrounded as well by energies. In fact, those external energies impact our own. We are, the people in our lives, all living things are vibrating. Energy takes various forms in us and the environment around us. In fact, we are energetically connected to the earth, the cosmos, to the universe, to that which is divine, to the source, to God" (Arewa 44). This connection includes the ongoing existence of our ancestors as well as the important energies of nature that influence and impact us. Both Arewa and Holmes remind us that "ancient Africans, although nowhere near a monolith, held a unified belief in an eternal spirit and respect nature and the belief in the continuation of spirit." In fact, "several different cultures in West Africa share an underlying belief that all energy comes from our earth and there are special ways to harness this energy and use it to our own advantage" (White). Thus, spirituality that reflects our SOUL will connect us with the unseen, including our ancestors, community, nature, and will have us engaging in ritual (Burton). Understanding energy in this way allows us to "surrender to the realm of the unseen, the unknown, and allow it to reveal itself to us" (Parker 159). In fact, when we "let go of our attachment to the mind as our sole authority and open to spirit as our guide," we experience healing that engages our bodies and our spirits (Parker 158).

So, let's consider the continuity of spirit and the unseen, specifically the energies or spirits of our forebearers, our ancestors. Particularly in terms of how connecting with them can be healing and restorative, and foster our sense of overall well-being.

In the fall of 2017 and early 2018, my family experienced some consternation regarding my maternal grandmother's living arrangements. Specifically, as her health continued to deteriorate, we faced the question of whether or not to put her in an assisted living community where she could have more frequent access to immediate medical care and support. At that time, she had been alone for ten years since my grandfather died in January 2008. My aunt was having someone visit three days a week to help around the apartment with cleaning and running errands.

During my first trip back home in Fall 2017 just prior to this decision having to be made by her adult children, my grandmother told me that she was tired. I knew what she meant. I knew that she was ready to move on. To die. To join her sweet beloved Jamie, which is what she called my grandfather James, in heaven. She wasn't dramatic about it. She was just quietly clear with me about what her heart and soul desired.

When my aunts, uncle and mom began exploring their options for how to best care for her, my prayer was that she get her wish—that she get to go home and join the ancestors. I knew losing her would be hard, particularly on my godmother and aunt, who had been her primary caretaker. But, I also knew what my grandmother wanted. I knew she did not want to live in an assisted living facility away from the apartment she had lived in with my grandfather before he passed and where she had a community of friends in the apartment units around her. Each morning back in Senegal as I put the put the chairs and tables out in our café, I would talk to my grandfather about my grandmother's desires. I would say to him that he should come get her, now. I told my grandfather what I am sure he already knew: that my grandmother was ready. That it was time for her to go. And, I knew very clearly that he heard me, because I had heard from him during my time in Senegal.

Specifically, I found his eulogy on my desk in January 2017 around the same date that he passed away. I knew he placed it there because I had never seen or touched it since I had arrived. In fact, at that point, any printed documents I brought over remained in file folders in drawers and trays, untouched and unused. Further, if you had asked me, I would have told you that I did not even think I had a hard copy in my possession at all, although I knew exactly which thumb drive the eulogy was on. Finding my grandfather's eulogy that morning was a clear message to me that he was with me, and I believe that he supported my decision to move to Senegal. For me, my grandfather's affirmative gesture simply reflected the fact that he had always approved and respected my marriage to Eddy.

In the meantime, it was not that long before my aunt reported that my grandmother was certainly not thrilled about the idea of moving from the place where she had lived well before she lost her beloved Jamie. He was there—his things, their lives, their memories. Moving meant not only leaving a place—it met leaving him in some way. His spirit. She did not want to go, even though the place my aunt found would allow her to bring her cat Jakey and was affiliated with the Catholic diocese, which was important to my grandparents who were active, true believing Catholics.

However, just before my grandmother was scheduled to move, she got sick and went into the hospital. This was not a surprise to me. Not at all. I knew what my grandmother wanted, what her soul wanted. And, I knew that my grandfather had heard both me and her, and that she would go soon. And, in that same week, on that Saturday, I got a call from my parents informing me that they and my sister and brother were on the way to Maryland to see Grandma. We knew this visit would be goodbye. It was time. My sister wanted her to meet Madelaine, her most recent great-grandchild, before she left. It was not long after my sister and brother arrived with Madelaine that my grandmother passed away and left to be with her dear, sweet, beloved Jamie.

When I got the call, I began the first iteration of my shrine or altar for my grandmother. I had to do something concrete in my own life to connect to her as she left us. Initially, I used the piano that already had the two small framed pictures I had of her in our living room. Along with the pictures, I lit candles, added more photos and the angels that she had made for me over the years. Within hours of learning that she was gone, I "found" two of the heart-decorated bookmarks she had made for me as well, although I was not looking for them at all (just like I "found" my grandfather's eulogy sitting on my desk). I wept, knowing that she was speaking to me, saying that she was still with me. And, that she always would be. So, I added the bookmarks to the altar I had begun on our piano.

In the months that followed, I expanded my altar to be one for her and my grandfather James, as well as my other ancestors, including my paternal grandparents. Interestingly enough, I was able to have an expanded altar when my husband and I came across a corner church pew as we walked from our section of town to our family homestead across town to give our condolences to our extended family. I was so excited to come across it. Honestly, I just couldn't believe it was a coincidence that it was so close to our home and available for us to purchase. My ancestors were, like many Black Americans, so very invested in their faith, their belief in going to church to worship their savior Jesus Christ. For me, it only made sense that a church pew would serve as our altar to them. And, it would serve as a testament to the importance of spirit, of the divine of all forms in our life. So, after a bit of price haggling (which is part of the culture here), we had it delivered to our house and placed it in the back left corner of our living room. It is what I call my Amen Corner. And, it is fundamentally my ancestral altar—where I visit my grandparents and other ancestors on a regular basis. Of course, I have pictures of both sets of my grandparents. The silver bowl that my husband and I were given by my maternal grandparents as a wedding gift and my grandmother's cake box are the central components of my ancestral altar. In the bowl, I have symbols that reflect how I know my grandparents. I have feathers for the number of grandchildren that they have. I have a bird's nest and two ceramic cardinals, because my grandmother loved birds, especially cardinals. Red birds.

I have a daily morning ritual for honoring and acknowledging my ancestors. Each morning as I make my own coffee, I serve them water in the glasses that are family heirlooms, delicate glasses that my mother managed to get to me here in Africa without them breaking. And, I also place two red cups on the altar daily, one with coffee and one with tea. I also put fresh flowers on the altar each week. My grandmother always had mints in her house in this candy bowl that sat by the door of the apartment where my grandparents last lived. It either had those red and white plastic wrapped mints or peppermint lifesavers. Always. So, I give her the mints I have found here in Senegal that are light blue and refreshing. And, my grandfather liked shortbread cookies and sherbet ice cream. So, I give him shortbread cookies, and when I can't find those, I give him a pack of wafer cookies. And, I sometimes give him a bag of nuts that are so common here, especially in the late fall after the harvest season. And, on the cake box, which sits below the bowl where the seats of the pew meet, I have my grandfather's kente cloth stole and flag sitting with my grandmother's cake box. He was a deacon in the Catholic Church, and he wore the stole when he took his vows many, many years ago. I can still see the images of him in a white robe with that stole as the blast of color and a clear expression of Blackness around his neck.

My altar is also home to a photo of my paternal grandparents. And, while I really didn't have the same emotional connection with them, I acknowledge them and ask them for their guidance and protection as well. And, my ancestral altar is also where I speak to two dear family members who passed away most recently—my younger cousin who died in April 2018, and my sister-in-law's mother who died the same fall. She was always a beam of light and a resource for both my brother's family and for me. I loved her dearly. Losing her has been very difficult for all of us. But, I know, quite strongly, that she is with my brother and his family. And, when I ask for help for him and his family, I specifically call on Grandma Jackie on his behalf. I believe that she will always, as she did in life, show up for the ones she loves. And, now she can do so without pain or burden. Just pure love and light.

I feel more grounded knowing that I have a specific space where I can focus on and connect to my ancestors—that I have a ritual that connects me to spirit. And, it just makes sense for me to do this after moving to Senegal, in part because my grandmother is the ancestor to whom I have the deepest and closest relationship.

Having an ancestral altar, seeking my ancestors' guidance and protection reflects the fact that "connections to spirits, holy and ancestral, are taken-for-granted aspects of African life" (Holmes 24). In that vein, I just understand that my ancestors are all here with me. Hearing my prayers. Guiding my steps. Protecting me. How do I know to do this? Well, I just kinda do. I just trust my intuition, creativity and imagination. I know that they are with me. I have chosen to, like many of our ancestors and fellow diasporic souls, "to surrender to the realm of the unseen, the unknown, and allow it to reveal itself to us" (Parker 159). In order to put the energy, courage and heart back into my body, in order to heal and sustain my well-being and my capacity for resilience and resistance, I had to "let go of [my] attachment to the mind as the sole authority and open to spirit as [my] guide" (Parker 158).

In fact, I understand that while all my ancestors may not be at peace and may not mean me well, the ones who I engage with intentionally at my altar "are the 'living-dead' and compassionate spirits who are interested in my daily [life]" as their descendant who is still alive. I embrace the notion that my ancestors "are superior to the living and that because they have crossed over act as mediators between [me] and God."

Let me be very clear here. "This way of life is regarded as ancestor reverence, veneration or remembering, which is not to be confused with worship.... In traditional African religion, God is above and beyond the ancestors and is called the Supreme Creator/Being and the main pillar of the universe. This is one aspect that many people who do not subscribe to this belief system fail to understand: that the God that the traditional African religion subscribers worship is the same God that Christians and other religious groupings believe in. Because African religion reveres and holds God in the highest regard, worshipers do not speak directly to Him. Their prayers and wishes are communicated to Him through the medium of the ancestors. This is often aided by enlisting the services of a traditional healer or diviner," known here in Senegal as a *marabout*, "who can help interpret what the ancestors may be asking of us."[10]

As Arewa reminds us, we exist today because of our ancestors (48). They gave us life. Their love continues to nurture us. Yet, even when many of us are embracing many of the cultural sensibilities of the African diaspora unfortunately the fact that "much of the value and importance afforded the ancestors and the sacred have been lost in modern societies," which comes at a great cost to our well-being (Arewa 51).

Believing in the continuity of spirit and revering our ancestors means that the defiant declaration "I am not my ancestors," which has recently appeared printed on tee-shirts and shared in social media posts, does our ancestors a deep disservice. And, all that smug, know-it-all-ness and arrogance cloaked and draped in so-called wokeness gets in the way of our restoration and healing and our capacity for resilience and resistance—a capacity that our ancestors possessed, nurtured and fortified. Over and over and over again, in spite of white supremacy and anti–Black racism and the institutions built upon them. Power, in fact, that they passed onto us. Such a snarky, irreverent tee-shirt slogan is rooted in the faulty, ahistorical and ignorant assumption that our ancestors simply acquiesced and tolerated mistreatment rather than actually resisting in a myriad of ways. It is a flawed notion that in spite of its intention is actually rooted in hegemonic and dominant narratives that white folks have been giving us about our ancestors. It is actually a flawed notion that weakens our power to fight back, even if it is intended to be a declaration of resistance. As Dr. Gail Parker explained in her workshop on spiritual activism at the Amplify and Activate Summit, certainty is the only thing more dangerous than ignorance.[11] Such a declaration in this regard is certainly problematic when we need to be open to our ancestors' capacity to guide, love and support us. This requires us to possess some degree of humility and ongoing willingness to learn.

Thankfully, in spite of such foolishness, more of us are open to spirit and seeing our ancestors in the way that Arewa and Somé encourage us to. For example, Juju Bae,[12] a Black spiritualist and priestess in the Ifa[13] and Lucumi[14] traditions, passionately declares in her opening podcast that it is in fact "all about our ancestors." Juju holds to the truth that our ancestors are "ready to help us as soon as we recognize our earthly limitation, humble ourselves and seek guidance." There is nothing humble about a tee-shirt that dismisses our ancestors' proven capacity to be resilient and to resist.

In fact, we can find healing if we remember our ancestors and honor the circle of eternal life through prayer, celebration, meditation and ritual (Arewa 70). We can find healing and restoration and deepen our capacity for resilience and resistance if we understand, as Somé reminds us, that "death is not a separation but a different form of communion, a higher form of connectedness with the community, providing [the deceased] an opportunity for greater service." Somé also writes that knowing and understanding that "having journeyed adequately in this world ... [our ancestors] become much more effective to the community ... when [they] return to the world of Spirit" (53). Relating to our ancestors can be healing for us on many levels, offers Foor. Collectively, on a cultural level, connecting with our ancestors can transform our historical pain and traumas. At the personal or familial level, this connection—being open to it, nurturing it, sustaining it—can improve our well-being as we heal intergenerational patterns of family hurt and pain. At the same time, relating to our ancestors can feed our sense of confidence and personal and collective power.

How will you open to sprit, specifically to your ancestors? As suggested in chapter two, you might consider doing a genogram or family tree so you can begin to pay attention to your roots, to who you belong to. You might also consider spending quality time with family elders, listening deeply to them tell their stories about your family, those still living and those who are deceased. And, you might begin to consider the ways you can integrate ritual into your life that allows you to initiate and foster an ongoing connection to your ancestors. And, of course, you might be ready to notice the red birds and rainbows.

that recognize the mind-body-spirit connection and the connection of our bodies to the earth. As well nature's role in our healing." Rituals that connect us to spirit, our bodies and nature simultaneously are powerful ways for us to remove and release the energetic blockages in our bodies and minds that are in fact caused by stress and trauma, including race-based stress and trauma. We do so by remembering that "we abide in a vigorously and responsive cosmos, one where spiritual entities and energies are part of our [natural] world" (Holmes 26–27). The elements of nature are tied to the way we understand energy as defined and explained by folks like Arewa, Somé, Eden and others. Our energies, or our energy body, is associated with specific points of our physical bodies as well as with specific elements in nature. Each energy center is associated with specific qualities and characteristics—positive and negative—of its associated element. Each element has the power to create and destroy in some form or fashion. And, in astrology, each element is associated with the personal characteristics or qualities of three signs—those that can propel us forward and those that can limit us. Energetically, earth is associated with the root energy center or chakra in the body, which we associate with safety, security and belonging. Red is the color we associate with the root chakra. Energetically, water is associated with the sacral chakra or the energy center we associate with creativity, fertility, abundance and prosperity, and orange is its color. Energetically, fire is the element associated with Aries, Leos and Sags and the manipura chakra, which is aligned to our capacity to be courageous, confident and fully tapped into our agency and personal power. And, we associate air with the signs of Aquarius, Gemini and Libra and the heart or Anja chakra and the qualities of love, forgiveness, compassion and the capacity to extend grace towards yourself and others. Green is the color associated with the heart energy center in the body. The rest of the energy centers include the throat chakra, which we associate with the color blue and the element of ether. Your throat chakra is associated with your capacity to speak your truth. The third eye chakra, located between your eyebrows, is also blue and associated with your true and authentic self. And the crown chakra is associated with your connection to the divine, to the Source, to the great Spirit.

One of the energies is Mami Wata (water). In fact, Somé explains that "indigenous cultures identify with water," seeing it as a gateway to other worlds.[1] Water cultures are mostly peace and harmony seekers. Another energy and natural element is, of course, fire. In fact, "fire is an amazing and transformative energy that fosters our vitality, courage and personal power" (Arewa 174, 175). Like water, fire and smoke can be used to allow us to cleanse ourselves energetically or spiritually. It, like water and the other elements, can be put in service to help remove and release blocked energy. Fire has an important purpose in nature and in terms of how we put energy back into our bodies to heal. However, as Somé reminds us, fire can be quite dangerous; it, of course, can destroy everything in its path.

And, while Somé explains that water cultures are peaceful and harmony seeking, on the contrary, "modern cultures identify with fire" (Somé 169). In fact, a fire culture is a (violent) war culture. "[These cultures] see solutions in terms of fire and conflicts of fire that can be resolved with more fire." In cultures like ours, fire looks like our government declaring wars on drugs and crime, which most of us understand was and remains simply policies designed to commit state-sanctioned violence against Black people as well as other oppressed communities, including Brown folks and poor people. Fire this time, at this moment, looks like the New Jim Crow that Michelle Alexander outlines for us in the country that has just restored federal executions. Fire this time, at this moment, is a nation exploding this summer during a global pandemic in response to the fire of the state-sanction violence and white terror. Fire this time looks like massive fires destroying thousands and thousands of acres of land and everything in its way because we have refused to honor the earth and respond to the increasing threats of climate change. Fire this time looks like the biggest fossil-fuel producing and consuming state brought to its knees by snow, ice and freezing temperatures.

Fire cultures focused on increased production and consumption "require a lot of water to heal" (Somé 171). So, we must "wade in the water" if we wish to find some degree of healing and restoration, if we wish to unblock and release the energy in our bodies that is the result of deep racial wounding and racial trauma. We must consider ways that water rituals might allow us to experience healing and restoration as well as ways they might allow us to continue to be well and free from ongoing spiritual, emotional, psychological and physical dis-ease.

Milk. During our first beach vacation to the Outer Banks in 2004, just a year after we met, Eddy explained that we had to offer milk to Mami Wata to get her permission to enter. And, he seemed pretty adamant and insistent about it. Lovestruck and not unfamiliar with Mami Wata (at least conceptually), I took his word for it and completely what he was telling me. He has been telling me that ever since. He has insisted that we do not enter the ocean without giving her milk and asking her for her permission to enter. Each and every time.

Before Eddy introduced me to Mami Wata directly on the Atlantic Coast during our vacation to the Outer Banks in 2004, I first learned about Mami Wata in graduate school in my first and only Caribbean literature course. She appeared on the pages of Edwidge Danticat's *Krik Krak*, which is a collection of short stories, as a water deity who was, as I recall, a fierce female force to be reckoned with. Lasirèn, as she is known in Haiti, where Danticat hails from, "is deemed to be the protector of working women, faithful to those who have faith in her, she is as tough and demanding."[2] In Cuba, a few years later, Mami Wata came into my life again. There, I was introduced to Yomeja as the Santeria goddess for water or Mami Wata. "Often depicted as a queenly mermaid, *Yomeja* is considered the Ocean Mother whose strong and protective energy can be found virtually everywhere, but especially near oceans and lakes." Like, Danticat's Lasirèn, she is a "fierce, nurturing, gentle energy often associated with the moon and sorcery." As the "Mother of All," "she is said to help in matters of self-love, fertility, emotional wounds, trauma, and healing work. But if you cross her, disrespect her terrain, or hurt one of her children" and make her feel disrespected and angry, she will cut or destroy you with massive waves. "She's associated with the numbers seven and ten, the colors blue and white, pearls, silver, conch shells, and doves. Offerings for her [typically] include sweet things."[3] Here, in Senegal, in addition to milk, we have given her melon, oranges and beignets (donuts) and pastries drizzled with honey over the years, as well as flowers.

Reading Danticat and traveling to Cuba allowed me to accept Eddy's sense of caution, which is actually about showing reverence and deep respect for Mami Wata's power, her capacity to give and take away in a split second. Had I not been introduced to Larisèn or Yemeya, I am pretty sure, as a Westerner, I would have initially balked at and questioned Eddy's shoreline directive, not fully understanding the reverence and respect that I should hold for the ocean and her power. However, I understand clearly now that as a son of Senegal, Eddy, like many throughout much of the Black Atlantic, reveres and respects her, Mami Wata simultaneously. He fully understands very clearly that she is a force to be reckoned with. As a mother, she is a nurturer. Yet, she can be fierce and brutal. She can, as water, nourish life and take it away in one fell swoop. She is a mother, one who gives life. One to be cherished and respected. One with great power. She is a she. As the tide ebbs and flows with the moon, we associate her with the light of the night sky, which we associate with feminine energy and qualities.

Meeting, embracing and restoring our connections to our forebearers and ancestors—to Mami Wata specifically and nature as spirit more generally—is one way we might experience healing by, in this case, putting the energy that Walker calls on us to put back in our bodies with our own culture.

As noted earlier, having a ritual tied to my ancestors allows me to feel more grounded and balanced. It feeds my sense of well-being and ease. My daily ancestral practice reflects the fact that rituals offer us comfort.[4] Specifically, in this case, the comfort comes from the connection to my ancestors. Rituals can offer us the same reassurance and comfort. Rituals, as Holmes writes, are spaces where broken hearts and resilient spirits can heal.

As we consider how we can open to spirit and let it be our guide, we can also consider the fact that rituals help us to heal as they allow us to connect with spirit and to shift energy intentionally in a deliberate manner often at a specified place or time, and that they strengthen us and allow us to fortify ourselves. They allow us to put the energy, courage and heart back into our bodies. They allow us to take back or harness the power and agency we need to take action, to be courageous and confident. Rituals, Malidoma Somé advises us, "are the most ancient way of binding a community together in a close relationship with Spirit." Rituals, he offers, are tools that allow us "to maintain the delicate balance between body and soul." Rituals allow for the healing of the village, the collective, the community (141).

Rituals allow us to release and let go. They give us space for catharsis, for emotions. For feeling what we have far too often refused to feel. What we have repressed. Suppressed. Buried deep. What we keep running from. What we have hidden. Refused to see. Refused to hear. Refused to acknowledge. Refused to unpack. Refused to let go of. What we held onto under the guise of control in our tightly clenched hands attached to tightly wound bodies and closed hearts and rigidly made-up minds. Rituals allow us to make sense of our lives. They allow us to live forcefully as well as poetically, beyond rhyme, rhythm or reason. They require us to imagine that we are making magic, bearing witness to all that we know in our hearts and bodies as well as our minds to be true in a world that repeatedly negates our truths.

Ritual is a sanctifying action that allows us to make meaning— meaning of that moment, meaning in our lives, meaning in our hearts, meaning in our spirits. It is about reclamation, insisting that what our ancestors, our foremothers and forefathers knew to be true about spirit, about the sacred, about nature, about the world still, in some way, rings true. It is about giving order to our worlds that feel at times that it, us, we, you are literally unraveling, coming apart at the seams, coming untethered, untied, uprooted, ungrounded, floating aimlessly, belonging nowhere and to no one. Ritual is about remembering where you belong, who you belong to, what and who belong to you at a particular moment—big or small. Ritual is about slowing down, taking time out of the day to reconnect to yourself and to spirit. Ritual is sacred; it is not routine. It is a place where you are absolutely intentional and open to intuition and inspiration and spiritual intervention all at the same moment in time. Yes, open. Open to what your heart and spirit tell you when you let go and let them speak to you. Open to others. Open to light. Open to restoring balance in your life. Open to healing.

Just as our ancestors resisted imposed faith practices, we too have access to ritual, which affords us greater agency and authority over our own spiritual lives. In the spirit of our ancestors who practiced hoodoo, voodoo and Santeria, ritual is also about resistance and resilience, because ritual can allow us to be who we want to be even when the world tells us not to. And, ritual is powerful because ideally it is communal and collective in nature. It allows us to connect not only with spirit but with each other—another key aspect of African spiritual practice. And it allows us to connect with nature, which is an important conduit for energy and host for spirit.

In order to engage in ritual, you must be willing to surrender and allow yourself to be vulnerable and to feel what it is that you are feeling, even if it might be unfamiliar, new or a little unsettling and scary. You cannot practice ritual in a way that is healing if you stay in your head and remain bound to your Western notions of what is and is not possible. You must believe in and be open to magic, pure and simple.

For those who visit us here in Senegal, we open and close our visits with Mami Wata rituals, in part because we know that our ancestors are in the ocean as sand, as spirit, as energy, ebbing and flowing, caressing the shores of West Africa and the Americas where we traveled. And, died ... often resisting. And, while there are likely no bones of our ancestors to recover, as Haitian writer Edwidge Danticat reminds us, "the past is full of examples when our foremothers and forefathers showed such deep trust in the sea that they would jump off slave ships and let the waves embrace them. They too believed that the sea was the beginning and the end of all the things, the road to freedom...." (quoted in Sharpe 105). We know that "the atoms of [our ancestors] who were thrown overboard are out there in the ocean even today. They were eaten, organisms processed them, and those organisms were in turn eaten and processed, and the cycle continues.... Human blood is salty, and sodium ... has a residence time of 260 million years. And what happens to the energy that is produced in the waters? It continues cycling like atoms in residence time. We, Black people, exist in the residence time of the ocean's wake, a time in which 'everything is now. It is all now.'"[5] Thus, the energy, the spirit, the atoms of our ancestors reside in the ocean. They exist there now, in the ocean, amidst the waves, the sand, the organisms living in and with Mami Wata, who we understand to be a mother, a nurturer, while simultaneously a fighter, a force to be reckoned with. One that both gives life and takes it away.

As we understand energy in relationship to nature, specifically in relationship to water, we can also associate her with our sacral chakra, which is the second major energy center in our bodies. This chakra is the one we connect with creativity, abundance, prosperity, sexuality, fertility and sensuality.

As Diasporic Souls, water (the ocean specifically) also holds particular significance for us as we know that our beloved ancestors made their way across the Atlantic to the shores of places in the United States, the Caribbean and South America in bondage. And, as historian Ivan Van Sertima tells us, some of our ancestors arrived well before Columbus.[6] We also know that many did not make the crossing—some because they resisted and refused, jumping in the ocean to free themselves. Others were too sick to make the full journey. Others were simply discarded, thrown away like trash, when they were too ill or could not make weight in places like Goree Island. As reflected in the song "Bloody Waters"[7] by Kendrick Lamar on the *Black Panther* soundtrack, we exist in the watery wake, in liquid graves, oceanic tombs (Sharpe 38).

In fact, some say that the hurricanes that hit the United States and Caribbean are simply Mami Wata's wrath, her lashing out against those who took so many of her dear beloved children from their homes to be brutalized and dehumanized.

We go visit Mami Wata for permission, to express gratitude and for healing, cleansing, letting go of what no longer serves us. Therefore, we always start our visits here in Senegal with a Mami Wata ritual that gives our guests their first tangible experience with greater diasporic cosmologies that recognize nature as a spiritual resource. We do so with our first communal ritual at the seashore when they arrive.

With Mami Wata, oh, my goodness. I was able to be a child again. I grew up really fast so I didn't really get to experience childhood as long as everyone else may have. So being in the water and playing tag with her when it came to the seashells. I would drop one and she would get it. And then should would try to bring it back to me. It was just a whole back and forth thing. And to have that security which wasn't something I expected being by the water. For a long time I've been told to be afraid of the water, never to expect anything, that bad things would come from the water. But being with Mami Wata, being in her presence, it was so warm, like hugging my own mother, and it was, oh, it was amazing.

As this young lady's enthusiasm indicates, experiencing Mami Wata for the first time in this way is a powerful and transformative experience. For her, it meant overcoming some of the fear she had about the water, a fear that is sadly not that uncommon among Black Americans. She was able to let go of her need for control and be open to spirit. She was able to experience the energies of Mami Wata and all her nurturing maternal yet playful energy.

Another young man sent us a video account of his visit to the ocean after his visit to Senegal in June 2019 as he prepared to participate in the upcoming Olympics. In his video, he captures his offering to Mami Wata and the appearance of whales in the water. His excitement about having his offering accepted and the spirit sending him animals to affirm his journey is as palpable as the young lady who compares Mami Wata to her mom. He has learned that Mami Wata can serve as a spiritual resource for him as he pursues his dreams.

His close friend who was on the same June 2019 visit has retrospectively realized after our Mami Wata ritual that he had actually already established a relationship with the ocean, that he already had discovered her to be a resource who could help him ground, center and settle himself when necessary. But, it wasn't until after our Mami Wata ritual and an insight he gained from a divination that he actually noticed this connection he had previously established—a connection that offers him nurturing and affirming energy.

In fact, as he prepares for the fall semester that includes navigating another academic year with Covid lurking and looming about, he returned to Mami Wata to seek her support as he pursues membership in a fraternity. He understood very clearly that his relationship with Mami Wata is not just one of allowing her to support him when he needs to settle and restore, but that he also needs to seek her out in advance of a new pursuit that is important to him, similar to his best friend's visit in advance of the Olympic qualifying match.

These three young people exemplify the healing energies of nature, specifically with Mami Wata and of ritual. As the first student notes, some of our visitors leave their Diasporic Soul experience with a deep respect for Mami Wata that replaces a long-standing fear that they have had, which is certainly a sentiment that others have echoed, one that many of us know is deeply tied to our experience in the Middle Passage. That respect for her is due also in part to the fact that they not only enjoyed their first direct experience with Mami Wata both recreationally and ritualistically. During their time in Senegal, they also existed in a culture that deeply respects Mami Wata, as she is named in every major fishing community and city in Senegal and recognized by that name and part of harvest and other important rituals. Further, the healing also, of course, relates directly to the wounds of slavery and the Middle Passage. Our ancestors jumped from slave ships because they knew death was better than bondage, and a disturbing number of others were jettisoned as cargo into the sea for a variety of brutal reasons only the slavers and profiteers could have only rationalized. Thus, our Mami Wata ritual allows our students to connect spiritually to their ancestors, who remain in the ocean as atoms, as energy even today—their blood, which is salty and like sodium, has resided in the sea for millions of years, and their energy is in the ocean, existing, in residence time.[8] So our Mami Wata ritual and subsequent pilgrimage to Goree Island are both important opportunities for our students to reconnect with their ancestors, with their energy, with their spirits, both to mourn and celebrate them.

In addition to recognizing our historic relationship with the ocean as members of the African Diaspora, we also know that our bodies are made up of 75 percent (or more) water, which means that water can impact our physiology. Water conducts energy and is very transformable. It changes depending on what the offering or intention is, which our guests see when they offer Mami Wata milk upon arrival. They sense a shift in how she moves, the intensity of the waves. They sense that she is aware of and responding to their presence. They sense her strength, her capacity to both heal and to destroy. Most importantly, they recognize her as a resource for healing and restoration.

As our visitors' communion with nature suggests, the energies of nature offer us important healing resources that we can tap for our well-being and ongoing self-care, just like our ancestors, even if we are miles away from Senegal or Africa. Living waters are everywhere—our ancestors knew that as they "washed" away their sins in rivers as believers. Know it as you heal, as you restore, as you find a way to feel grounded in a world that seems to be consumed by fire, a world that seems to be unable to find enough water to heal itself.

CHAPTER VIII

#NatureHeals

This Land Is Our Land

In addition to connecting to nature's healing energies through water rituals to support our healing and restoration as well as our ongoing capacity for resilience and resistance, we can consider nature as a constant resource for us. We can allow nature to support us, particularly if we can open up to her with a sense of curiosity and delight, awe and wonder. Being in nature offers us solace and refuge for our bodies, spirits and minds.

In the essay titled "Turquoise and Coral: The Writing of the Temple of My Familiar," Alice Walker, in addition to explaining that the colors were her spiritual colors, speaks of our relationship with animals, of how colonization and conquest stifled the "wild" and the free in us and severed our relationship with nature, specifically animals (118). In fact, she describes that she found animals "suddenly everywhere in [her] life" at the same time she experienced synchronicity in her dreams, insights and intuitions that resonated with and guided her as she wrote (119). Walker's reflection confirmed for me the new relationship that I have now with nature, one that I don't fully sense that I had before, one that is connected to my spirituality and reflects my movement to a culture where nature, spirit and the divine coexist seamlessly.

Traveling home to North Carolina to see my family has, for quite some time, meant finding myself dressed in cargo pants and dirty, well-worn tennis shoes to find adventure in the woods with my younger nephews. My youngest brother David and his wife live in a housing development outside of Charlotte that straddles the NC-SC state line that was constructed on farmland. And, while there is so much to be said about the loss of open spaces and farm land, I will refrain from that. Instead, for now, I am more interested in considering how being there, with my nephews, in the woods feeds my SOUL. How being there helps me to feel grounded, centered, rooted and supported. How being there reflects our ability to find solace and restoration when it feels as if our lives or, at this point, perhaps, our world is unraveling. How being on an adventure in the woods with my nephews serves as a concrete example of our ability to put the energy back into our bodies so we can experience healing and restoration.

I appreciate the adventures my nephews and I have together. We giggle and shout as we climb gigantic rocks. We feel rugged and tough as we enter the woods and hear the sound that the leaves and underbrush under our feet make as we immediately venture off the asphalt walking and bike path in the community. We are excited as we pick our way in through the throned vines and climb over the fallen trees to get to the creek bed. We follow the length of the creek to see where it goes, as my nephews enthusiastically describe what is happening along the way. We play like we are scared and nervous, cautious, as we manage to cross the creek by figuring out how to strategically maneuver ourselves across the stones and fallen tree branches in the water. We pretend like we want to cross the creek without getting wet or dirty, which, of course, seems silly, because we always do get both wet and dirty in varying degrees as we play in the creek and around it.

And, let's be totally honest here, getting wet and dirty is kinda part of the whole point, even if their parents also pretend not to fully understand or appreciate this part. They play too much. As the apparent adult involved, for me going off into the woods means letting down my guard and allowing myself to relax, all while simultaneously being attentive enough to protect my nephews from danger. Being there means realizing that I can't control everything—my nephews, the fallen trees, the direction or the depth of the water in the creek. It requires me to be, like my nephews, open, willing to be vulnerable, curious and willing to take risks (at least the ones I know make sense for them at their age). Risks that build their sense of courage, confidence, agency and personal power. Their curiosity and sense of adventure. Their willingness to explore their sense of awe, wonder, curiosity and delight.

Being in the woods with my nephews feels very natural to me. Going outdoors into the woods to explore and seek some kind of adventure in nature is automatic for me because that is what my childhood consisted of. I do it with my nephews in North Carolina and with my sister's son (and I imagine eventually her now four-year-old daughter) in Durham. Oh, the challenge of getting them all to get from one point to another by crawling, walking, stooping to get under and through a section of evergreens on the perimeter of the woods overlooking a creek that seemed far, far, far down below. The thrill of the challenge. And, the joy of just being there filled with my own childlike curiosity and willingness to play and imagine. To be connected to nature is exhilarating and energizing in these moments of being open, curious and adventurous with the children I so adore.

And, if I'm being honest, this is a connection that I don't think I fully appreciated growing up. Or, perhaps, it was actually a connection that I am sure I took for granted (and scoffed at as well). Frankly, I know that I was not quite able to fully recognize or appreciate my father, his father and their relationship with the earth. Yet, now, I am so thankful that as the eldest child of five children growing up in the South during the '70s and '80s that the majority of my play involved being outdoors in nature. I spent most of my childhood in the yard, in woods just like the ones my nephews and I enjoy so much, and in parks like the ones my sister and I take her kids to when I visit. We spent hours and hours riding bikes, often along the greenway tucked away in the back of our neighborhood where we would stop to swing from vines across the creek that ran through it. Staying out until the sun went down. Chasing lightning bugs. Taking mid-summer camping vacations at Kerr Lake, which straddles North Carolina's northern border with Virginia. Being treated to weekend afternoons in parks, including Raleigh's Pullen and Umstead Parks.

At the time, it was such a treat for our dad to pack my two brothers and me up in the car and take us to a park just to eat a meal. I have vivid memories of eating dinner in the gazebo that overlooked Pullen

Park as the summer sun set. And, sitting at a picnic table eating sweetened cereal with real milk in Umstead Park before hiking down through the woods to the lake. These trips were special; they were my dad's way of treating us even if the meal we had was pasta salad with the elbow macaroni and canned tuna he put together from items he got from the food bank. Oh, and yes, to have sweetened cereal in lieu of store brand corn flakes or oatmeal was a treat that was made even better when we ate it in the woods. Fruit Loops. Apple Jacks. And, my favorite, Honeycombs. With whole milk in a jug with the red cap or in an orange and white Pine State carton instead of the far too lumpy and virtually tasteless powdered stuff my mom snuck in the empty milk jugs at home to make our ends meet. It is apparent to me now as an adult that my parents expression of love included giving my siblings and me more time to explore and experience nature, to be outdoors, to connect with the earth. To play freely without fear. Even though my Daddy was, I am sure, often tired and over-extended from working in a door and window factory loading trucks and part-time at a gas station and occasionally cleaning houses to make extra money. I imagine that in some way he, too, not only got joy in taking us to the great outdoors but also fed and restored some part of himself and his SOUL. I imagine now as I recognize my own relationship with nature as an adult that he must have felt grounded and centered and rooted as we trekked through the woods to get to the lake at Umstead Park. And, energized. Or that in some way he sighed out loud after his inhales and exhales deepened and his body relaxed as we sat outside our pop-up camper at Kerr Lake or in Pullen Park's hill-top gazebo. I hope that in the midst of supervising us and verbally corralling us that he somehow also found some peace and joy in nature as we did.

Yet, this connection I had with nature as a young child and that I strive to nurture with my niece and nephews is a connection that over time far too many of us as Black folks have unfortunately lost. This loss is tied to a variety of factors including aversion to the outdoors that we might easily blame on imposed servitude that included working the land. You know, the cotton, the tobacco, the sugar cane—cash crops that never paid out for us, for our ancestors. So, certainly, our aversion to nature (which, in some cases, is fear of it) might make sense. Yet, we know that in spite of our servitude our ancestors made great use of the land, stayed deeply connected to the spirit of nature, leveraged it, in fact, to be well. To be resilient. To resist. Saw her often as a healing resource in very concrete and specific ways—an understanding, a reverence we brought with us from the motherland. And, that was affirmed by our indigenous American brothers and sisters with whom we found community and built loving connections.

Yet, sadly, in our notion of advancement and being cosmopolitan, many of us came to reject or dismiss the value of working with our hands or in farming or other related fields. And, of course, the disconnect with nature can also be attributed to our existence in urban centers with parents and elders who, generations removed from the land (including gardening), filled us with fear about dirt, bugs and all things from the outdoors. And, our disconnect from nature and her gifts has also been exacerbated generation after generation in communities where there are few green spaces and where we exist disproportionately in food deserts, where access to fresh produce is limited or nonexistent unless intentional approaches such as a weekly farmers market and community gardens are available, which in some cases is happening. And then, of course, there is the fear of and failure to see the divine feminine of nature and how she feeds us in so many ways.

And, systemic and institutional white supremacy and anti–Black racism clearly have something to do with the ways that our ties to nature's healing energies have been so deeply severed and destroyed. The most recent report released by The Trust for Public Land tells us that not everyone has equal access to the kinds of parks that lower temperatures and allow for safe social distancing. Far too many of us continue to live in what is referred to as "park deserts." The Trust's "data reveals that across the United States, parks serving primarily non-white populations are half the size of parks that serve majority white populations and five times more crowded." Further, the Trust reports that parks serving majority low-income households are, on average, four times smaller and four times more crowded than parks that serve majority high-income households. In fact, The Trust for Public Land's 2020 ParkScore® Index, which ranks park systems in the one hundred most populous cities, shows, with the exception of New Orleans ... [that] the cities where we make up the majority of the population do not have adequate green spaces or parks. Take Detroit, where 78 percent of residents are Black. There, "the city devotes 6 percent of its land to park space, compared to the national median of 15 percent." The report also notes that "in Memphis, Tennessee, just 5 percent of land area is comprised of parks, while in Baton Rouge, Louisiana, only 3 percent of the city is dedicated to parkland."[1]

And, of course, connecting to nature's healing energies depends on whether we can access nature readily rather than feel out of place or unwelcome or even unsafe in parks and out in nature. The Central Park bird watcher incident that filled our social media threads during the summer of 2020 is a clear and cogent example, as are moments when we convene for cookouts or pick games of basketball in public parks only to have our joy and fun disrupted by calls to the police.

Further, our capacity to connect to nature's healing energies has been compromised by the ways that white supremacy has historically impacted federal agricultural and farming policies. The shit is deep, real deep. And, pretty damn disturbing. And, heartbreaking when you consider the loss and subsequent grief our people have faced as they have had their land as farmers taken from them because of our government. As Pete Daniel documents in his work *Dispossession*, between 1940 and 1974, the number of African American farmers fell by a staggering 93 percent, from 681,790 to 45,594. This decline, Daniel explains, resulted from the white supremacy that permeated the ways that "the US Department of Agriculture blatantly neglected, discriminated against and intimidated Black farmers. Black farmers were aggressively denied loans, information and access to programs necessary for the capital-intensive farming industry."[2] According to the Black Farmers Market, currently, of the over "3 million farmers in America, less than 2% are Black."[3] Clearly, land laws, discriminatory banking practices, and other institutionalized practices of racism have impacted a once thriving network of Black farmers.

In this case, the United States government and other entities by design have further severed our ties to the longstanding, earth-honoring traditions of our ancestors. This severing has resulted in consequences that include not only a disconnect with the land and nature, but food insecurity and poor nutrition as well. For example, as the Black Farmers Market notes, "in [North Carolina], there are far too many communities that have limited access to healthy and affordable food options. In 2015, 170,431 Wake County residents and 69,240 Durham County residents lived in neighborhoods with low access to grocery stores."[4] This is also the case in far too many communities across the country.

As Malidoma Somé notes, "the modern world is denaturalized, perceived to be in the way of progress. Western orthodoxies, often binary in nature, negate the body and see the earth as inferior to heaven. And, patriarchal religions mask the ancient cosmologies that recognize the mind-body-spirit connection and the connection of our bodies to the earth. As well nature's role in our healing." This reality is clearly evidenced by our current struggle with the deleterious impact of climate change and environmental degradation on the world around us. We see these effects as fires burn on the West Coast and flood waters rise as hurricane after hurricane emerges in the Atlantic Ocean, sending massive amounts of destruction to the places all along the Gulf Coast and the East Coast.

In recent months, I have dreamed of my paternal grandmother, which is new. I had not, until recently, begun to connect with her and subsequently see her in my dreams. In this particular dream, she is beckoning me across the yard of my grandparents' home to join her in the garden bed that for much of my life sat adjacent to the house. In the dream, she is there in the garden, and my aunts, my father's sisters, are under the huge Russian Elm tree located in front of the house. She is beckoning me to come to her with the support and guidance of my aunts, her daughters. I eventually go and find myself lying naked on the ground.

This dream is one way I have restored a connection with my grandmother. It also gives me the sense that I am to spend more time with nature, with the earth. That it will increase my sense of well-being. That it will allow me to feel even more centered, grounded, rooted and supported. That I will be connected more directly, perhaps, to her. What is most interesting is that my grandmother did not die this way, in peace, in a good place. She died in deep and ugly pain. Perhaps being open to her invitation and meeting her in the garden will actually offer her the chance to heal. Perhaps, even she and some of my other ancestors are on those roving adventurous hikes with my nephews, niece and me.

In her book focusing on healing Black women, *Sisters of the Yam*, bell hooks asserts that collective Black self-recovery includes renewing our relationship with the earth, remembering the way of our ancestors, recognizing that the earth and our bodies are sacred.[5] Therefore, we must recognize the fact that we come from a legacy of folks who understood the value of nature as a healing resource, one that allowed us to manage our well-being and self-care on our own terms.[6] That we come from a legacy of folks' bond to earth-honoring traditions. That in spite of the impact of slavery, our fathers and grandfathers, mothers and grandmothers still recognized the value of nature and the gifts that the earth gives us even as they pursued what they hoped were greater economic opportunities in the industrial North and out West.

However, I'd say that for most of my adult life I never fully recognized that the impulses that I had to wander off into the woods with my fearless nephews or to visit virtually every park in Cincinnati and Hamilton County, Ohio, are actually a reflection of my connection with nature. A connection that I certainly had to move to Senegal in 2016 to fully recognize. A connection that warrants me deeply respecting the connection that my father had, his father had and my ancestors over time had with nature. A connection that I have been able to deepen. Here, in Senegal, my relationship with nature is different. Senegal is a place where people are more connected with nature and all her resources than we typically are in the U.S. For instance, trees are called *garab*, which the term also used for medicine. They are also part of every "yard," courtyard or terrace you encounter here. Like many of our neighbors, the front of our home, which is also home to our café includes a flourishing mango tree. Her branches extended towards the sky, adorned in rich green fragrant leaves much of the year and offering shade to our café guests and foliage for those seeking respite on our balcony to enjoy. In January or February, her leaves are joined by stems of clustered small, delicate pink and white flowers on long deep fuchsia stems that offer the promise of the succulent and sweet fruit to come as spring becomes summer. Many of my neighbors have mango trees in their yards while others have *neem* or *nevedaye* die trees. And, in larger compounds and villages that have been here longer, dating back decades, there is almost always a baobab tree. And, along streets in Dakar, and as you walk up to the top of Goree Island along what is known as Baobab Row.

The connection with nature that I have now includes me being able to more clearly see how nature works in ways I never paid attention to while living in the States. In fact, the capacity to feel free to be curious and to experience awe and a sense of wonder is quite striking. It feels good and exhilarating to commune with nature and all that she is.

Partly, I assume I am having this experience, this deeper connection with nature and her energy, because I never seemed to have the time or the space to just sit and observe her with the same sense of wonder, awe, delight and curiosity as I do here in Senegal. Now, I am just beginning to understand the cycles of many plants and trees, including what is cultivated in the fields adjacent to our home. The red okra, the *nebi* or black-eye peas, the carrots, lettuce, cabbage, eggplants, habanero peppers, tomatoes, hibiscus, red and white, cassava. Not to mention the mangos, citrus and papayas. And, the living things, grasshoppers, frogs, crickets and dragon flies. Oh, and butterflies. And, song birds, and birds of prey. And, our beloved adopted dog Ginger, who chose Eddy and me after living in the street before we arrived, and who up until she died last year, lived on the café terrace. And, Jamie, named after my maternal grandfather, who lives in the house with us.

Another reason for my connection with nature now is because I live in a plant-filled oasis created by my husband along the national highway that rivals any outdoor terrace in the world. And, I live in a rural suburb outside the country's capital Dakar, a city where sheep are present in every neighborhood and plants are sold in nurseries on the highway exiting the city both on the national road and the busy freeway. My connection with nature is also the result of Senegal being a country whose primary economic sector is still agriculture.

My connection with nature is also the result of living in a place where the word for tree is the word for medicine. Where the *neve-daye* tree can offer you seeds and leaves that can help manage your diabetes. Or *kinkalaba*—high blood pressure. Or the *puftin's* milk can heal your scrapes and cuts better than neosporin. Or the dynamite tree seed can provide you with a natural laxative, and the baobab's *buoye* fruit, both the flesh and the seeds when powdered, can offer you fruit that, when made into a juice, can assist you with digestion. Or the antioxidants in limes, red grapefruit and soursop that have begun to arrive almost daily as summer segues into autumn.

In fact, the baobab tree is revered and considered sacred throughout Senegalese society and in other places across the continent. And, each year, I can see more of the subtle and nuanced changes she undergoes over the course of a year. In the late fall and at the turn of the new year, on our travels we can always find women selling the pulp of her fruit known as *bouye* on the roadside. In June, I can see her flowering, adorned with rose-petal soft and mud-brown speckled apple-shaped flowers that hang low. And, in fall in the midst of the rainy season, her previously bare limbs are filled with green leaves and the fruit that has been born of the flowers. During the rainy season, if she is in a more rural location, she is lush and often surrounded by green crops and ground cover. And, many of her fellow baobab trees. She, they, are awe-inspiring. In some cases, she may be centuries old. And, even today, in some villages, she marks the place where the community gathers to discuss important matters. In some homes or family compounds, she provides a safe home for the spirit of an ancestor who is not to be disturbed while he or she protects his or her descendants who dwell there. She is the tree of life. She is resilient; she is strong; she can withstand the torrents of most great storms and the season without rain.

Being in Senegal makes it very clear to me that nature has been and continues to be a valuable healing resource for us, like it was for our elders and our ancestors. Nature is healing in the sense that it gives me a feeling of well-being. Healing in the sense that it helps me to feel at times energized and vital, and at other times completely relaxed and calm—particularly this year, as I remained in Senegal for the full year due to Covid-19 and the 2020 cycle, during which white violence was certainly a possibility. Nature helps me feel grounded, rooted, centered and balanced no matter what challenges I face or upheavals I experience. I know that if I go out to her, on the balcony, underneath the mango tree on the cafe terrace, take a walk and find myself beneath towering *neem*, *baobab* and mango trees, I will feel better. It is as if some dormant part of what I know, what I value, what my ancestors must have known, what feeds me is more awake now than ever. And, as one who is holding space from Diasporic Souls, I continue to be quite curious and excited about all there is to learn about nature as a healing resource. These are gifts that Eddy and I want to share with everyone we hold space for here in Senegal.

This is why we intentionally hold space for each person who spends time with us in Senegal to restore their connection to nature. And, because when we understand SOUL as a healing resource, we recognize that our cultures traditionally were and still are in many ways earth-honoring, where the capacity to dialogue with the natural world exists. So we hold space for healing and restoration that allows individuals who have existed in toxic spaces so deeply poisoned by anti–Black racism and white supremacy, offering them the chance to connect with nature's powerful healing and restorative energies.

One aspect of understanding or recognizing how nature heals is the result of me restoring my connection to traditional or indigenous spirituality and wisdom traditions here in Senegal and West Africa that recognizes that nature is both matter and spirit. Restoring my connection to the belief that nature possesses life-giving energy that offers us healing. And, an unwavering sense of well-being. A restoration that goes well beyond the physical or medicinal. In fact, challenging dominant narratives about how personal and collective power means recognizing what Michele E. Lee reminds us in *Working the Roots*, which is that

> our ancestors observed nature; they felt the vibration of the earth and the heavens, the rhythm of day and night. They did not view themselves

as separate from their environment but as functional parts of a whole. They learned about themselves and achieved inner knowledge by seeing and sensing nature. The ancients built their religions, healing practices, mythologies and moral codes around the natural rhythms they observed. They recognized the interconnection between the elements—earth, air water, wood, fire and metal with our physical bodies. And, that their healing systems for healing the sick mind, body and spirit relied on nature.

I am, as I hope you might be, clear that nature certainly offers us a resource that reduces the spiritual and emotional dis-ease we experience. And, that feeds our ongoing capacity to flourish and thrive, to embody a sense of personal power, agency, confidence and courage. And that fosters our capacity to be resilient, and to, when need be, engage in resistance. A resistance that, actually, at this point includes reconnecting with nature and protecting her at all costs.

Further, connecting with the earth is an important step to healing energetically. As Donna Eden notes in *Energy Medicine*, not only is our root chakra imprinted with our early life experiences; it also is coded with our ancestral memories that include trauma going back generations and which are imprinted in our emotional DNA (160). Traumas that Resmaa Menakem and Joy DeGruy address in their work on healing racial trauma, which include the racially-marked wounds of our elders and our ancestors. In fact, our root chakra is the energy center in our bodies associated with our sense of safety, security and belonging. Thus, as we seek healing and restoration, we are addressing blockages in our root chakra. Because the root chakra is associated with the earth, one way to heal is to reconnect with the earth and nature's healing energies. Connecting with nature will allow us to feel more grounded, rooted and supported.

The easiest and most immediate way to connect with nature is to simply go outdoors and spend time in nature, particularly in a serene and quiet place where you can hear the leaves of trees rustle and birds sing. And, to absolutely make physical contact with the earth. Walk barefoot. Allow your feet to really reconnect to the earth. We have lost that key and important contact point where our energy and the energy of the earth that supports us is made. Place your hands on the earth. Sit in the grass under trees and the sun. Here are some other ways you can begin to restore your connection with nature and embrace her capacity to feed your sense of well-being and contribute to your self-care practice:

Many young people I know are now invested in having and nurturing plants. In fact, two young ladies who I have worked with send me frequent updates on their plants' progress. Another frequently posts her plants on IG. And, while I would caution you against making your social media accounts about the thrill of finding plants that are most obscure and thus expensive and somehow, oddly and tragically, a status symbol, remember that the point is to be earth-honoring and to foster a greater sense of well-being. That said, bring plants into your home, no matter where you live. Place them on window sills, on terraces and balconies or in your yard.

Stop, be still, and notice nature in small ways. Spending time consciously in nature nourishes us physically, emotionally, and spiritually. Russell Comstock, yoga teacher and cofounder of the Metta Earth Institute Center for Contemplative Ecology in Lincoln, Vermont, says that the source of that nourishment is the simple fact that we are, inextricably, a part of nature: "Our body is an animal body, governed by natural rhythms—planting and ripeness, daylight and night." He adds that much of the wisdom embodied in our oldest cultural traditions comes from sitting in deep stillness, observing the wild, and contemplating the human role in the natural world.

For instance, sit on your porch or in your yard or living room and just connect with your breath. From there, notice where light and shadow fall. Notice how the sunlight hits and illuminates certain places where you are, a specific leaf or section of grass. Notice where the shadows remain or where the sunlight contrasts with darkness cast in the room or wherever you are sitting. Be aware of the contrast and appreciate it. What do you see in the contrast, when light and dark meet and bump up against one another? Notice too how the light and dark shift over time as you extend your seated observation. Or as you do it at different points of the day or times of the year. How does light ebb and shift at the same time in fall versus summer, or winter versus spring?

Do the same with sound. What sounds do you hear if you simply sit with what may sound at first like silence? Or, just noise? Amidst the noise of cars and trucks and horns and sirens, what can you hear? Can you hear the wind or rain or birds singing? Dogs barking? Other animals calling out? Notice the sounds of nature.

Consider what and how you eat. Begin to examine where your food comes from and how your ability to have it impacts nature and her capacity to flourish. For instance, how does large scale farming to produce meat for us to consume impact the environment? How does deforestation impact the well-being of animals and plants as well as human beings? Consider ways that you can decrease the adverse impact of what you eat on nature. That may mean choosing to eat locally and seasonally rather than simply based on tastes that you have developed. Perhaps having Mexican avocados year round is not sustainable when you consider what it takes to ship and transport them.

Create a nature altar in your home that includes a variety of found items, such as rocks, shells, gourds, feathers, dried flowers, soil, seeds and nuts. You might be surprised what Mother Nature offers you if you are open to her gifts. My altar is ever evolving based on what piques my interest and curiosity as we see more of Senegal and as we spend time in the outdoors. Currently, my nature altar includes sheep horns, feathers, *bouye*, sand from Gorée Island, uncut calabash gourds, shells and rocks, as well as statues or carvings of specific animals or other living things. My husband and I also have similar items integrated into our home decor and my ancestral altar.

Get involved with a community garden or food program like the Fertile Ground Food Cooperative in Raleigh, North Carolina, in your own neighborhood or city. This will allow you to connect with what you eat in a whole new way. And, with community. Perhaps, you will enjoy finding new fruits and vegetables on the plants you put in the ground. Or, you will find solace when your hands are covered in dirt as you put the plants in a pot or in the ground. And, perhaps, as you plant and garden you will notice all that is around you, including your own breath and the people you are in communion with. You might consider reading *Freedom Farmers* by Monica White (UNC Press 2018), which chronicles the contemporary urban community gardening movement in the United States.

Spend time in local parks in your area. Many parks offer programs that allow you to better understand and connect with nature. For instance, the parks where I lived before moving to Senegal offered nature education programs as well as kayaking and canoeing classes. Take a class. Consider also taking a closer look at how racial politics and class impact parks and recreation access in your area. Who serves on your local park board? What cultural programs are offered?

Integrate essential oils and scents into your home. Consider making your own air and fabric fresheners using ingredients like lavender and peppermint oil. Or use dried herbs like lavender, chamomile, peppermint and basil to make small fabric satchels to sleep with or place in your dresser drawers.

CHAPTER IX

#GoingHome

Healing Where the Wounds Were Made

My husband Eddy and I traveled to Senegal in the summer of 2015 for a month-long vacation. Honestly, at the time, I really had no idea what to expect. I had been out of the country well before we ever met, which I attribute to my brother David, a true Aries, who gave me all his fire energy when he bluntly advised me to stop taking life so damn seriously and have some fun. So, thanks to him nudging me, I surrendered and got my passport. A few years later after my first hop across the pond (in my best British accent, of course), I went to Cuba for a month to set foot in what I believe is one of the most liberatory places I could ever imagine (read here a place that unapologetically and repeatedly rejects and challenges American imperialism, which includes allowing Assata Shakur to live in exile there) under the guise of learning Spanish, of which I still have a little left (*un poco*).[1] And, before that, it was Antiqua, where I traveled with my grad school colleagues and thesis advisor to deliver a paper about the ways that Jamaica Kincaid's novel *The Autobiography of My Mother* offered a compelling narrative of self-love and resistance. And, somewhere between Antiqua and Cuba was a nine-day trip to South Africa as the co-facilitator of a leadership development experience for Black and brown youth workers who the Washington, D.C.–based organization that I was working for was grooming to be critically conscious change agents at the same time that they provided necessary support and resources to the young people they served. Of course, it goes without saying, I learned a lot on my travels. As you already know, I learned some Spanish. I also learned how to salsa, which came in handy during my courtship with Eddy, but that is a different part of the story.

I learned in real time about the intersections of colonialism, conquest, tourism and privilege that Jamaica Kincaid speaks of so vehemently about in her book-length essay *A Small Place*. I also learned about myself; I deepened my self-awareness. To some degree, I engaged in *svadhyaya* or self-study long before I knew anything about yoga, yamas or niyamas, in part because I was drawn to the first C in the 7 C's (or what is known as the Social Change leadership model): consciousness of self. So, on my travels, outside my comfort zone, I saw some of my shadows and blind spots as I learned what happened when I was challenged and confronted with new and unfamiliar experiences. I learned how I reacted emotionally and physically at those times of uncertainty or when I felt uncomfortable. In the same vein, I also realized what brought me some comfort as I tried to navigate these spaces. And, to be quite honest, I'm really sorry to say but that comfort often came in the form of food and how it in some ways connected me to my routine and what was familiar.

In most places I traveled that comfort included drinking Diet Coke, which was my first addiction as an adult. Because of sanctions, Cuba only sold it in the Hotel National in downtown Havana; it must have cost like $5, but after weeks of not having one it was so good, especially paired with a cheeseburger, which I had also not had in weeks. In South Africa, I sought comfort in the Girl Scout cookies that one of our enterprising group members packed to sell to the rest of us. She was clearly a hustler, albeit one with a law degree. And, in this case, one slinging Tootsie Rolls and Thin Mints and Shortbread cookies. While I was pretty disgusted, I am sure I copped some treats as I navigated having a new and challenging experience as a professional working for what was a toxic organization and as a traveler. And, yes, there were the huge bags of Peanut M&M's that my friend Cleveland and I bought in Panama City's airport on our way back from the Dominican Republic to Havana, after we took a flight there just so we had access to cash at a time that well pre-dates PayPal, Wave, Wari and Cash App.[2] Which, I now know, ain't nothing but privilege, even for two Black southern folks with HBCU-conferred degrees on the proverbial come up from working class (perhaps even working poor) families.

So, yeah, it is pretty safe to say that I wasn't anxious about traveling to Senegal, per se. Besides, I could get some snacks if need be. Cookies, it turned out; shortbread with milk chocolate. At the same time, however, preparing to visit Senegal was definitely different than going anywhere else. And, I don't mean the fact that I needed real baggage that would allow me to exist elsewhere for a month and to take gifts for Eddy's large extended family. This trip was significant primarily because Eddy and I were going to Senegal as a couple for the first time, which meant I would be meeting his family, including his first-born daughter and oldest brother for the first time. It also meant, for us, as a couple, that we would, if possible, find a way to restore and heal ourselves, individually and together as a couple. That, in some ways, I was looking forward to, in part because I had begun the process of becoming well again.

Prior to our trip, I had returned to my yoga mat with great earnest. And, by earnest I mean sometimes taking three classes a day and holding monthly memberships at two studios in Cincinnati and exploring studios along the I-40 and I-85 corridors in North Carolina. This effort was about me responding to my own need to get and stay sober (alcohol and shopping became my addictions after Diet Coke), and to heal from being burned out and broken down from a job that I had given my heart and SOUL to for seven years. This effort resulted in me desperately needing to release what no longer served me so that I could eventually, God willing, find a way back home, back to me, to the best me I was capable of, to my authentic and true self who had lost her way. And, frankly, I felt beaten down and broken as a result. I felt like my teeth had been kicked in.

So, yes, going to Senegal needed to give me a chance to continue the healing and restorative work I had begun, and it needed to provide Eddy and me with something that would heal our union. That was my expectation. And, really, that expectation was not rooted in the notion that we were wounded spiritually, per se. I basically assumed that getting away together and having a shared experience was what we needed to get better, to be better, to do better. To get clean and sober. I mean honestly that I didn't have much to say in specific terms about healing and restoration back then. I just need to change my life. It was like Rolf Gates explained in his book on meditations. I found my way back to yoga, got a new therapist and traveled to Senegal with my husband because I was in pain, pure and simple. Nevertheless, I did not have any idea how healing our trip or our experience would actually be. And, I certainly didn't anticipate that the experience would be one that would go beyond that vacation and extend to my life today. I had absolutely no idea that going to Senegal that summer would result in Eddy and me ultimately coming to the place where we would decide to pack up our lives and move to Senegal. I had no idea that our 2015 vacation would result in the creation of Diasporic Soul so that we could hold space for Black folks to experience healing and restoration.

And, as we consider the experiences that deepen our capacity for self-awareness, healing and restoration by being contemplative, I honestly could not grasp at the time that going to Senegal would be healing in ways well beyond what I assumed and what I thought was obvious. In other words, I mean that I did not know that the trip would be healing in some way for me as a Black American in ways that were quite different than what Eddy needed or experienced on our trip. Unlike Eddy, who is Senegalese, French and American, I do not (and still do not) know exactly where I am from, where my ancestors are from outside of the United States, specifically in Africa. I have been a bit hesitant about taking the DNA test. I am not sure what knowing would offer me per se, particularly now that I am so deeply invested in being in and making my way in Senegal. In any case, yes, I am from North Carolina. And, as folks who know and love me will tell you, I'm real proud of that. I got mad love for the place, even though it has most certainly moved a bit tooooooo far right for my taste since I left in 1993 when Jim Hunt was still governing progressively. But something in me knows that I am from Africa. History tells me so. We are, as Burna Boy reminds us at the end of the track "Spiritual," African before we were anything else. Evoking singer Roy Hodge, my ancestors, now, that I am open to them, tell me so.[3] My blood, it tells me so. My body tells me so. I am from Africa. As, of course, yes, all of humanity is, ultimately. Even now, as I say so, my stomach curls in at my center, telling me, "Yes, Phyllis, you are from here. You got it. Exactly right. You are here." My tight jaw. My tight shoulders. Yes, my body continues to tell me I am from here. If I sit with those sensations, these feelings in my body, I know that I am connected to this place, going back and well beyond my own life and existence.

So, yes, coming to Senegal in 2015 was healing for me as a woman, not only as a wife, but as one who understands herself to be Black and a direct descendent of enslaved Africans. As a woman who was raised in what some like to call the "new" South, a place supposedly more progressive and more cosmopolitan and more sophisticated than the "old" South. Yet, the place where I grew up and the place where I was raised, in spite of how much I love it, was the same place where I experienced the lion's share of my own individual racial wounds, some of which were the result of all that was omitted. Omitted even for me, the Shut 'Em Down SGA president who hung out in a Black bookstore in high school and went to an HBCU during the 1990s when hip hop and popular culture (think Public Enemy, A Tribe Called Quest and Spike Lee) affirmed Blackness. As a result of omission and erasure and misrepresentation, my sense of being Black was muddied, made murky and blurred by notions of blackness that were still quite flawed, even though I studied more Black history than most as a student of literature enrolled at an HBCU.

Let me be clear here. Let me be more specific. I never learned much about Africa outside of knowing about the great kingdoms of Mali, Ghana and Songhai documented in John Hope Franklin's classic Black history tome, *From Slavery to Freedom*. At no time in my education was I introduced to contemporary or so-called modern Africa, which is kind of crazy since my best friend at the time was from Liberia. In fact, while she nicknamed me the Chef Boyardee kid to tease me about my American affinity for all the processed food that I consumed, typically drenched in tomato sauce that tasted like ketchup, never did she ever tell me anything about the place that was home for her and her family. Never ever. Yes, she could poke fun at who I was and the way I ate as an American of that era and that time, but she did not have the ability to tell me anything positive about the Motherland. And, to be honest, I probably, most likely, in spite of all that was unfolding around us, did not have the foresight to ask her to, either. My apparent lack of interest or curiosity about Africa, particularly the realities of modern Africa, was problematic because it contradicts the fact that Africa had captured my imagination and that of my peers. I mean, we were told about famine; we all knew the words to "We Are the World." We sang along with Michael, Lionel and the rest. But not much more. I still have the wooden Africa painted red, black and green that my father made hanging from the mirror in our truck, just as it has hung for over twenty-five years in every single car I've ever owned. The leather or pleather Africa medallions we wore. X Clan's declaration, "the red, the black and the green with a key sissy!" All mixed in with our love of brother Malcolm, made more cogent by Spike Lee's feature film. Informed by and bumping up against the murder of Yussef Hawkins and the beating of Rodney King. Oh, yes, and we can't forget the liberation of our beloved hero Nelson Mandela.

Yet, none of us knew really much of anything about Africa. Nothing concrete. Nothing specific. Nothing, most importantly, connected directly to who we were and are. Nothing tied to our specific families, lineages and ancestors. Instead, it was a cultural symbol we adopted and grafted on to that which might best be characterized as akin to, I would argue, our more recent adoration of a place named Wakanda. A place that exists in our Black futurist imaginations. A place that, in our deepest imaginings, hopes and dreams had somehow escaped all the wounding and scarring and carries no psychic, emotional, mental, spiritual or somatic baggage associated with domination, conquest and subjugation. Yeah, the 1990s offered me and my peers that—notions of our value and worth that went past where most of our parents could take us (unless they had happened to have an African-centered consciousness, which, in reality, few of our parents and elders did). There were my elder-mentors, the Dillahunts, and professors like Dr. Lydia Lindsey and Dr. Freddie Parker. And, I mean, one of my classmates had been to Senegal when she turned thirteen, which I did not know until a year or so ago when she brought her own thirteen-year-old daughter to us in Senegal for her Blackmitzvah. Like my girlfriend from Liberia and my elder-mentors, she never spoke of Africa as a part of her own experience or as informing how she saw or understood herself. Instead, her swag and her capacity to hold it down was attributed to being a New Yorker, not to her identity as a Diasporic Soul or a crucible life moment in Africa—a perception that was reinforced by the powerful nature of hip hop dominated by New York at the time.

So, in most cases our 1990s-era Wakanda was not located in any place specifically; it was not grounded or rooted to a specific place or places, culture or cultures. Instead, Africa served as a symbolic shield and a weapon. It did for us what it did for Kendrick Lamar at the 2016 Grammys when a large cutout of Africa adorned the stage behind him when he performed songs from his "critically acclaimed sophomore album *To Pimp a Butterfly*, which speaks directly to the modern day Black experience in America."[4] At a moment when we continued to insist that Black Live Matters, the image of Africa with Compton stamped on it allowed Lamar to convey that he was indeed invested in Black folks. It was a symbol of Blackness but not necessarily tied in any way, shape, or form to the actual continent itself. But, evoking Africa, like Lamar did at the Grammys, staking our claim to her tangentially gives us a way to bolster and strengthen our resolve as we set out to exist and occasionally challenge ongoing anti–Black racism and racial violence that serve the needs of systemic white supremacy. No, really more than that, concepts of our world, our lives that allowed us to continue to strive and survive even when the stakes seemed pretty much stacked against us. We not only had Yussef Hawkins and Rodney King; we were the generation of the Central Park Five and Bill Clinton's "Three Strikes and You're Out" and all that made up the draconian war on drugs in our fire culture. So, yeah, we needed something.

And, Africa, conceptually, along with our adoration of figures like Malcolm X and Assata Shakur, offered us the confidence and courage we needed to believe in ourselves and pursue our hopes and dreams against the odds. Because, in spite of the odds, we needed to be inspired and motivated so that we might live up to the expectations of our elders and make our ancestors proud. We needed, in some way, to feel good about ourselves. And we needed the self-love and self-respect it takes to push back and declare in the streets that Black Lives Matter (or actually, at that point, No Justice, No Peace!). Our understanding of Africa at that moment was in some ways certainly empowering and liberating, but it was limited and floating above, around something that needed to be anchored, tied down, connected, grounded and rooted in concrete and tangible ways to reality, one might argue. Even if there is deep healing value in creative imaginings about a place you were told as a people to loathe while simultaneously struggling to love yourself as someone from said place.

And, on my beloved HBCU campus with rolling hills and verdant greens, I was taught by truly bright, bold and brilliant Black people who changed my life. But, not one of them suggested that I should really want to know anything about Liberia, Ghana, the Gambia, Sudan, the Congo, Nigeria or Senegal. Anywhere in Africa. Oh, except South Africa—a place that in the narratives was framed up against the legacy of our civil rights struggle in the United States. We understood Mandela because we knew King. We understood Winnie because we knew Angela, Elaine, Katherine, and Assata. And, we knew that the Zulu were warriors and yeah, from Alex Haley's *Roots*, which we all watched with our families as children, we knew about the Mandikas, too. We understood Biko because we knew Medgar and Malcolm. We understood the ANC because we knew SNCC and the BPP. But not much more. We knew just a little bit, but, if you recall, the poet Alexander Pope advises us that a little bit of knowledge is dangerous. And, in this case, it was, for the majority of us, just a little bit dangerous because it simply was not enough, at least in North Carolina. And, we didn't know much more than that, and clearly what we thought we knew was seen through a set of lenses that was very deeply rooted in our own American experience.

Oh, and, by the way, nobody on my campus studied abroad (no shade intended). Nobody. No one. *Nada.* (See, told you that I learned Spanish.) So, for real, no one spent a semester or an academic year in Paris and came back from France the following fall telling us wild and exciting tales of a romantic tryst or one night stand they had with a 6-foot-five francophone West African brother with dark, rich sable skin who consumed rice (yes, of course, *Theibbu Jenn*) the way we scarfed down French fries and pizza. And, nobody went to Cuba and came back telling us about Santeria, the Orishas or the ways that Catholic saints allowed our diasporic cousins to mask the African spirituality that they practiced in spite of restrictions placed on them during slavery. Nope, none of that was part of what most of my peers and I knew or understood about Africa and the African Diaspora, including the Caribbean or Black people globally, much less about how that might have some value or influence on how I understood myself and other Black folks in my life.

So, coming to Senegal proved to be healing in part because it expanded what I knew to be true about Africa (or at least one country in it and a bit about the region) and, as a result, what I knew to be true about Black people, about myself, about us, about our capacity, our potential, our power, our worth.

A specific part of my visit that proved to be powerful and, upon reflection, restorative and healing, was my trip to Gorée Island. Eddy and I didn't leave for Senegal with a planned and hard fast itinerary outside of the fact that we were going for a month. We knew we would stay in the home he had built over the course of his time sending remittances home on a monthly basis over the span of ten or so years. We would stay there and with our daughter in Dakar and in his cousin's vacation duplex located in Somone, one of the cities on Senegal's *Petit Cote*, the small coast. I think I assumed that we would go to Gorée eventually, and we actually went twice.

My first visit to Gorée was at night for a concert that our son-in-law took us to. I felt a mix of emotions then. I was excited to be hanging out with Eddy's daughter, her husband and his friends who were all creatives. At the same time, I certainly felt some sense of dread then and I was a bit uncomfortable. I knew I was uncomfortable because I was talking too much and not saying nice things. I was grumpy and mean and judgmental. I was definitely mumble grumbling. A lot. I was critical of all that I saw that was different, "strange" and unfamiliar. I was sitting in complete self-protection mode and maybe some self-loathing with my nostrils flared and my nose turned up. "Yeah, these motherfuckers," I mumbled. But, why was I mad or angry? Why was I having such a visceral and embodied reaction to this place, to Gorée? And, who, in reality, was I mad at? What was I really reacting to? Why did my mood change so much from leaving the Daba and Malick's apartment to taking the boat to arriving on the island and the amphitheater where the show was held? Was I just hungry, or what? Perhaps, I had forgotten my snacks. No, I now know it was being there, in that place, that shifted my energy and my mood. The heaviness of knowing just a little bit about the place where I was sitting and being entertained by a live band affected me. Yes, now that I think about it, I am sure that to some degree being entertained in the same place where my ancestors were shackled, separated from their families and sold into slavery just really messed me up, pissed me off. Made me mad. Hurt. But, at the same time, I needed to sit there with my family, who I was just getting to know, and like, unable to share, at that time at least, what it felt like to be there in that place. I was trying not to be too upset with them for not seeing how being there might NOT be a good idea. Of course, I knew that Malick only wanted to have us meet his friends and see who he rolled with, talented and creative people, like the stylist for the band and the visual artist Laz who came with us to the show. In fact, my favorite bag and pants were made by that stylist who Malick calls the Dali Lama, and his friend Laz's works are mounted in the open gathering area outside the living room of our guest house, including (ironically, perhaps) a large *suwer* portrait of Gorée Island.[5]

Now, over six years later, I know that what I was feeling was what all my guests experience in some degree. Now I know that what I was feeling was tied to the trauma of being in a place where my ancestors were dehumanized and brutalized. Now I know that I was registering the weight of all that at the moment I was supposed to be enjoying a night out on the ocean under the moon and the stars, listening to live music.

For me, going to Gorée Island is not just some tourist attraction or a teaching tool, as one of the students from Xavier University who came to us in the summer of 2019 said. Gorée Island is a UNESCO heritage site that from the 15th to the 19th century is believed to have been the largest slave trading center on the African coast. So, for me, for Black folks, particularly those of us who can tie our family history to chattel slavery and who have elders and ancestors who experienced the terror and violence of Jim Crow America, Gorée is not a tourist attraction. It is, as she recognized, fundamentally a pilgrimage. A pilgrimage is a contemplative practice that in this case allows us to memorialize our ancestors and bear witness to an insidious and barbaric historical injustice and contemporary atrocities against Black lives and Black bodies that continue to be subjected to terror and trauma. We make this pilgrimage with the understanding that, as renowned and celebrated author-activist Alice Walker advises us, "healing begins where the wound was made."[6] Painful wounds that are certainly rooted in the fact that our ancestors were subjected to forced migration, kidnapping, colonization, and enslavement and that today we continue to experience the brutality of white supremacy, epistemic violence and anti–Black racism, as well as other intersecting forms of oppression.

And, because of the work that Eddy and I do, we absolutely make this pilgrimage knowing too that mourning and acknowledging our grief has profound and transformative healing power. Gorée Island is a concrete, consecrated and sacred place where we can individually and collectively recognize our ancestral soul wounds that manifest today as intergenerational trauma. Further, Gorée Island is one place where we imagine the remains of our ancestors exist even if only atomically in the water. In addition to their individual experiences with direct racial wounding, we know that our visitors carry the wounds of their families, their elders and their ancestors who they do not typically know by name. Ultimately, being on Gorée Island, specifically in the Maison d'Enslavement, is challenging but profoundly healing.

At the same time, our pilgrimage allows each person who comes to spend time with us in Senegal to restore their connection with their roots and ancestral heritage through ritual like I did. So, for at least an hour, we hold the space in the Maison d'Enslavement so that we can engage in a healing ritual that allows us to be fully present there in that space. We arrive and begin by forming a circle so that we can ground ourselves by connecting with our breath and one another. Then, we pour libations, declaring that we are present in the place where our ancestors passed, even if we do not necessarily know if they are those tied to us individually and specifically via familial bloodlines. We say our names, out loud, so that they, our ancestors, know we, their descendants, are there with them. We say our names because we do not know what their names might have been so many moons ago. And, we sing Ray Hodge's "I Am King" before we learn from, the curator of the house, Eloi Coly, or a designated tour guide the details of the damning atrocities that transpired in that space, in the holding rooms.[7]

Our visitors often experience intense feelings of loss and grief as they move through the house. And, they often report sensations that they have in their bodies such as headaches, nausea and burning feet that give them a sense that they are connecting with the energies, the spirits of the place, the spirits of our ancestors. The young men from the A2MEND mentoring program who joined us in June 2019 spoke about feeling a heaviness in the house—a presence, more than one. So have others. An energy, a sense that we are not there alone. That our ancestors' spirits, their energy is with us in that sacred, sacred place.

During our time there, each of our guests stands alone in the infamous Door of No Return, knowing that it represents similar doors dotting the coasts of Africa "out of which our ancestors were loaded onto wretched slave ships, ... a door of a million exits multiplied, a door that many of us wish never existed."[8]

For many, in that space, there is a catharsis that happens. A profoundly moving release. For me, on my first visit, it happened in the cell marked for the recalcitrants. As I entered that small crawl space, the same one, I later learned, that Nelson Mandela entered on his visit, I immediately began to cry, to weep, to moan out loud. I could not suppress myself or my tears. I know the whole house heard me, maybe even the whole island. I had never felt so much grief or wailed so loud in my whole life. It was like I was wailing for so much more,

more people, than I can fully understand or quite touch. Or know. All Eddy could do was hold me and let me cry when I backed out of the hole. But, it just happened. The need to grieve and lament was so strong and it was not something I could hold back or suppress. And, there was another time when I found myself in the back hallway of the house weeping and being held up by a pillar just outside the room where they confined children as Eddy, once again, moved in to comfort and console me. The grief is real and continues to need to be expressed, even if you have been to Gorée at one point already.

In fact, my experience is similar to those of many of our people who we take to Gorée Island. It just comes over you, the grief, the need to cry, the need to lament, to weep and wail. For some, it happens as soon as they enter the building. In some cases, they can barely stand as the grief and the pain take hold. Instead, they find themselves virtually in full collapse, needing to be held up by the wall at the entrance and caressed and comforted by the rest of us as we whisper reassuringly, "It's okay, it's okay." Or bowled over in clear pain as we attempt to pour libations, name ourselves for our ancestors and pray before we even begin to see the space in its entirety. All, by the way, at times, with folks looking at us in awe as if our grief is shocking or unexpected. A part of the experience that frankly makes being in the space that is haunted by the spirits of our ancestors even more difficult to be in. Which, in fact, is absolutely not okay.

But, it is okay for us to grieve, to mourn, to express the deep-seated sense of loss and pain that that space evokes in us. In fact, it would seem that doing so, feeling what we feel, expressing ourselves openly, being vulnerable there truly allows some part of the hurt and trauma we carry to heal, which is so clear in the reflection of one young man who experienced this catharsis during his Diasporic Soul heritage and healing experience:

I broke down. It took everything out of me. I broke down. It took whatever pain I came with. I didn't know I had it in me. I didn't even know. It was like all the systemic oppression. All the, you know, the belittlement of my character, from a systemic approach. You are not this you're this. Someone trying to guide my energy, my spirit to be something that I am not. No! This is who you are. And everything that I've been through in my life, you know, living in Los Angeles. We all can attest to that. We know. We know the stories. It was just almost like going through all that, all that trauma, it creates the energy; it became solid. It's like all this stuff was thrown into a pot and cooked until it became solid. All these years of my life. And, then once I go in here it don't matter how hard it was, how hard I think I am. How strong I think I am. It's like we gonna break this down. And we gonna leave this here. I just let it out. I just let it all go. It was the most enlightening thing I ever experienced. Just spiritually. It's like I didn't even know I felt that way. But I just feel things coming out of me. Oh, my goodness!

This young brother's words are powerful as he, unscripted, unprompted, ties his transformative experience at Gorée Island to the ways that his own personal experience with systemic oppression and white supremacy has adversely impacted him. How the pain and the trauma associated with racism has become this solid mass that burdens him as he carries it around day in and day out. What this young man so powerfully describes as a hard mass that is solid inside of him is what Parker and Menakem and I mean when we talk about racial trauma and racial wounding trapping energy in our body that we can't seem to get out. It is what we mean by adverse experiences that cause us emotional pain that gets trapped in our bodies and spirits. In this case, that trapped energy is both his and that of his ancestors. Be clear about that. No one before him in his family, it is fair to bet, ever had the chance to release this pain or experience this level of catharsis specific to racial trauma in a sacred, love-filled space held specifically for him to do so. And, he so cogently and clearly speaks to the ways in which being at Gorée offers him the chance to experience catharsis. How being there in tears and his body, literally racked with grief, inconsolable, allows him to release, to let go of some part of himself, of what has been imposed on him, of what no longer serves him or his well-being. This is significant because this reflection, this observation on his part is in addition to all the other observations he and his peers make about the impact of the history and the energy they all describe sensing and experiencing. And, the grief and sadness that he and his friends describe experiencing in the brutal and ugly, ugly place where our ancestors may have traveled through and stood in the door, never to return home or see the people they love and belong to ever again.

Interestingly enough, the way he speaks of how he is treated or imposed upon at home in the United States in his reflection on his experience at Gorée is echoed in the reflections of some of the other young men we have taken to the island. They, too, like this thoughtful brother, speak to how they are expected to move in the world because they are Black—how it feels to be expected to represent all Black people in their daily lives. How it feels to be treated as inferior or less than on campus and in classes. It is important to notice that a trip to the site where our ancestors were sent into slavery evokes these feelings, leads us to talk not necessarily only about historical wounds, but to name very immediate and recent ones. What one young man described as bumping up against bruises that you don't quite realize you have and that have not fully healed. Yes, going to Gorée in some ways is just like that—bumping up against bruises or scabs that need healing.

Embodied and energetic healing includes the bumps, the bruises, the scars and the solid masses of hurt, pain and trauma that have begun to grow inside of us. Those wounds are what he so eloquently describes as growing solid, calcifying in the pot, which is a metaphor for his body, hardening and holding us back and weighing us down. Finally, on a pilgrimage to a site of historical and intergenerational trauma, those wounds can begin to heal, that pain can be released and room, literally, can be made in our lives, in our bodies, in our minds and in our spirits for something bigger. What they all seem to experience, what he so eloquently describes, is in fact a transformative healing experience that is not in his head, but one that is fully embodied. One that clearly, in his own words, he understands to be spiritual in nature. And, his powerful and moving description of what he experiences on Gorée Island, on this pilgrimage offers us all the opportunity to understand how going back, going home, making a pilgrimage does in fact have healing value. The way that he and others describe the somatic, emotional and spiritual nature of their experience make it evident that such a journey can be transformative and life-changing for those of us who are members of the African diaspora, particularly those of us with ancestors who were enslaved and lived in Jim Crow America. And, while this level of vulnerability might be disconcerting and uncomfortable for many of us, what this young man experienced is not only about releasing the weight of the wounds of his life, many would suggest that what he released as he broke down adjacent to the Door of No Return is also the weight of his ancestors, those before him who experienced the ugly realities of living in America and the brutal realities of enslavement, domination and conquest. For certain, making a pilgrimage to Gorée Island provided me and provides others with the chance to begin healing their historic and intergenerational racial trauma as they allow themselves to grieve and fully acknowledge the pain that is in fact not something we can simply think about, but that is, in fact, trapped in our bodies.

The healing on this pilgrimage for Black people is also very much tied to the fact that going there also includes recognizing our capacity for resilience and resistance, which is not often what we associated with enslavement. That is not for many of us the way the story of slavery has been depicted or framed. We do not typically consider the ways we fought back or resisted. That is why that stupid tee shirt I mentioned earlier exists. And, if I'm extending grace to whomever came up with that tee shirt and the people who bought it, it is sometimes hard to see slavery in relationship to our capacity to flourish in spite of adversity, to be resilient. And, while Gorée curator Eloi Coly and the guides do not typically speak to either, Eddy and I do, insisting that in spite of the conditions our ancestors faced on the island in the home purported to have historically held African people in bondage, we were resilient and resistant. As a part of our pilgrimage there, we pay homage and express gratitude and give thanks to our ancestors, with gifts, tokens of our appreciation for their sacrifice, gifts for their spirits that deserve recognition and beauty in a place steeped in ugly, ugly, ugly, distorting pain and anguish. In this sacred place, on this pilgrimage, in obvious grief and with deep reverence, we collectively convene below the Door of No Return in silent reflection where we watch the waves crash as we pray and commune with our ancestors, knowing that "they are with us still, in [the holds and waves]" that are crashing against the foundation of the house below where they stand. There, our guests cast their gazes at "the bottom of an ocean [that] already holds millions of souls from the middle

passage the holocaust of the slave trade that is [a part of] our legacy, [considering] the past sacrifices that were made for all of us,
so that we could be here."[9] Here, they recognize our resistance. As
Haitian-born author Edwidge Danticat reminds us, "[our] past is
full of examples when our foremothers and forefathers showed such
deep trust in the sea that they would jump off slave ships and let the
waves embrace them. They too believed that the sea was the beginning and the end of all things, the road to freedom and their entrance
[to the next life]." And, before we leave, we pray again, out loud to our
ancestors in spite of the press of visitors entering the sacred ritual
space we intentionally created for ourselves and our ancestors as our
time in there comes to an end.

A pilgrimage to Gorée Island can be healing as it offers us not
only a chance to experience a deep and powerful cathartic release,
but it can also deepen our resolve. As one student offers, her pilgrimage to Gorée Island was "such an emotional and powerful moment
and it broke my heart at the same time. But it made me realize that
I'm here—that my ancestors went through hell and back to have me
here. And, now it's my duty to do more, it's my duty to do more, to
embrace the beauty that I have, that I have to show my brothers and
sisters that we are more than what the narrative says we are."

It can also, as her peer observed, deepen our sense of interconnectedness. "Going to Gorée Island was so emotional but at the same
time I felt so much closer to everybody after bonding over the pain
of being on the island and being in the house of slaves. For me, dinner felt even more communal after visiting Gorée Island despite the
fact that we had been eating communally before going to the island."

Our pilgrimage to Gorée Island, which one student described
as mystical, was healing. As one student noted, it "made me more
open spiritually and emotionally. I felt a sense of gratitude and connected to my ancestors and to spirit." As another student stated, "I
found a piece of myself that was missing, that helped me feel whole."
A wholeness that speaks to the healing and restoration that intentionally restoring our connection to our ancestors and a heritage of
both resilience and resistance offers us.

Yet, the healing that we experience on this pilgrimage does not begin or end with expressing our grief in the Door of No Return, or in any of the similar venues dotting the coast of West Africa. First of all, knowing and acknowledging that we are experiencing grief is very significant. And, recognizing that we must grieve and giving ourselves permission to do so is important. This I understand more deeply as I allow myself to recognize our collective loss and our collective grief in places like Gorée, places where we were wounded. Places where spirit or energy impacts the way I feel immediately. Where I sense a presence or where I am moved to tears.

In the fall of 2019, I attended the Universities Studying Slavery (USS) symposium that was hosted by Xavier University and the University of Cincinnati. One of the institutions in the consortium is Georgetown, which, like Xavier, is a Jesuit institution with ties to slavery—ties that mean the institution could not and would not exist had it not been for the free labor of enslaved Africans. At the conference, two Black young men, Georgetown students, read the names of the 272 Africans who the university sold in 1838 to stay financially solvent.

Then, something hit me. All I could do was cry out the same way I had done at Gorée Island during my visit in 2015. All I could do was wail the same way I have at Gorée Island. All I could do was weep out loud for all to hear and witness. Some part of me needed to cry. It wasn't something I thought about. It just happened. And, really, it needed to—not just for me, but for the other folks in the room. Those who, unlike the young people and friends who consoled me, have yet to make such a pilgrimage but who most certainly carry the same type of grief and residual trauma in their own bodies and spirits. A collective grief, one not to be ignored. And, it needed to happen for the onlookers, who might not understand that our enslavement and the subsequent injustices we have experienced and continue to fight do in fact impact us deeply. Further, weeping there, at an academic symposium, meant I was taking up space with my body and my voice, with my sobs, not so much for myself, but for the 272 plus ancestors sold in 1838 by Georgetown, deemed to be one of our nation's most respected institutions, and their descendants. I feel that my lament there in that space at that moment allowed our ancestors to be heard, too, to be more than a mere list of names, but to be real people, who experienced and continue to experience pain and suffering because of America's most peculiar institution. Further, as they do at Gorée and similar sites where we experience a public catharsis, my tears, my wails, my audible laments forced folks to get out of their heads, even for just a few minutes, in this space where folks insist on only studying slavery, rather than considering embodied ways to heal the emotional, spiritual, physical and psychological wounds from it that continue to persist today. The wounds that trap energy in our bodies and spirits that restricts our capacity to flourish and thrive as fully and as humanly possible.

So, will you be able to travel to Senegal or Ghana or Benin? If so, please do. Please allow yourself to visit a door of no return like the one we visit on Gorée Island. I promise that doing so will be powerful and transformative and healing, even if it is uncomfortable, unsettling and challenging. Go to what might be referred to as trans-Atlantic sites where African people were held captive prior to traveling to the so-called new world, but which are actually places where you might find ancestral energy. Connecting to that energy, noticing it, recognizing it, directly acknowledging it, is healing. And, it is a healing that not only includes catharsis and the chance to truly release some of the pain and grief you have been carrying for so long, but that also allows you to deepen your capacity for resilience and resistance. Of course, doing so will be an emotional experience. And, it is one that will be embodied as it impacts you physically. And, as noted here, in many cases it will impact you spiritually, in part because your ancestors in some way will be part of the experience with you, either as spirit in those spaces or with you as you find yourself physically there. This may be healing and restorative for them as well. And, for the members of your family perhaps who could not travel with you there. They will see something quite different in you when you return, I promise you that. This sacred pilgrimage is healing because it adds to what you know about yourself, others and Black folks, all important parts of how we foster our sense of well-being and capacity for self-love.

Certainly, consider how such an intentional approach to a

pilgrimage to Africa more broadly might be of value to you. You do not need to have done your DNA tests or know what countries you might have genetic ties to. You might consider that if you cannot yet travel to Africa, then maybe visit a market where we were sold, like the one in Charleston, South Carolina, or New Bern, North Carolina, or Richmond, Virginia. Or, perhaps, your pilgrimage will be to a museum like the Equal Justice Memorial that opened recently in Alabama, or the Smithsonian Museum of African American History and Culture in Washington, D.C., or the Charles Wright Museum in Detroit. Or maybe the site of a race massacre—Tulsa, Atlanta, Wilmington—a place where you can acknowledge what happened to us collectively and how it might impact you specifically. Making a pilgrimage to these sacred places can offer you what my friends and I experience at Gorée—a chance to release, to get out of your head, to let go, to move some of the grief and pain out of our bodies so we can pursue our heart's desires and make room in our lives for bright, bold, brilliant and beautiful Black futures that we imagine. Wherever you decide to go, just go, knowing that doing so will heal you on many levels, but only if you go with your whole self, body, mind and spirit, with an open heart and a willingness to be vulnerable. To surrender. And, with people who can support you and understand what you are experiencing. When you are ready, go in your own time. There is no hurry, there is no rush. There is only a chance to heal some wounds and to open up to the energies that will allow you to be more resilient, to live more fully and engage in resistance when necessary.

CHAPTER X

#CultureHeals

Bold, Bright, Brilliant and Beautiful

I have four nieces; the youngest one just turned four. I adore her. She is radiant and full of energy. Right now, her capacity for joy and happiness is limitless, as is her capacity for love. She is strong, fierce, carefree and tenacious. I can see her power and her light. And, I love it. My impulse is to protect her, fiercely, like a lioness, who is her Aunt Phyllis. I want to protect her from anyone or anything that intends to do her harm in any way, shape or form. Yet, I am cautious about not allowing my fierceness to impede or block her innate sense of wonder. I in no way want to instill fear, timidity, or trepidation in her. I never want my desire to protect her to crush her organic curiosity and natural inquisitiveness. I want her to be fascinated and awestruck by all the world has to show her, from butterflies to balloons, from flower buds to blueberries, from bright blue summer skies to the beaming starlight of dark, cool, autumn nights. I want her to play, explore and get mud on her favorite shoes, sand in her frilly shorts and leaves in her kinky, curly hair. I want her to feel safe, secure and supported. I want her to always feel loved and free, bright, brilliant and beautiful. I want her to thrive and flourish. I want her to boldly take up space and shine unapologetically, always. I want her to have an unwavering sense of her innate dignity and worth. I want her to love herself, always.

This impulse to protect my sweet Madelaine is echoed by anti-racist scholar and educator Ibrahim Kendi in a Summer 2020 interview that is part of NPR's *America Reckons with Racial Injustice* when he speaks to how he protects his daughter Imani.[1] What he offers is profoundly instructive for all of us, not only as we protect our children, but also as we consider the ways in which we heal and restore ourselves from racial wounding, and as we foster our capacity to flourish, thrive and be well in the first place:

> [There is] a need for us to [i]f it's a Black child, if it's a child of color, it's critically important for the parents of Black children to—even long before they go and experience another child telling them their hair [or skin, nose, etc.] is ugly—to be constantly sharing with them and telling them that their hair is beautiful, because when they receive that type of racist idea from another young child, they may not internalize it. They may not see themselves as the problem. They may see what the child said is the problem.

Kendi goes on to say that he has explained to Imani as she processed hearing from George Floyd's daughter "that there was nothing wrong with Black people to protect her." With the hope that "if one day she is rejected because of the color of her skin and she doesn't have awareness of racism, who is she going to blame? Herself. And there's nothing worse for a very young child to be struggling with their own sense of self and their own confidence in themselves."

Last Christmas, my niece received Lupita Nyongo's book *Sulwe*. I remember the day it arrived at my parents' house where my sister was having all of her holiday packages sent to avoid negotiating deliveries with her ever curious children. I can hear my sister's eldest, my nephew, asking, "What's that mommy, what's that?" The book arrived in a box with nothing else. When I opened it, my heart filled up with joy and I got a little teary-eyed. I knew immediately that it was for my niece.

Sulwe's face was surrounded by the starry, deep rich eggplant purple night sky on the cover. I saw her and I saw my niece at the same time. My niece, like Sulwe, has rich dark skin and, as Sulwe is described in the book's promotional copy—"she is darker than everyone in her family. She is darker than anyone in her school." And, of course, like Sulwe, my niece is most certainly "beautiful and bright." And, like Sulwe, I know that she, as Kendi offers, must continue to be reminded to recognize her own unique beauty. She needs to have many books that feed her SOUL—whimsical and heartwarming stories that affirm all that she is and all that she can be. So, at four years old and beyond, she can clearly and consistently see herself in the world, knowing that it is certainly okay to boldly take up space and shine unapologetically always. Additionally, ensuring that my niece and all the children in my life see themselves this way is, as Kendi suggests, a form of protection. Protecting their spirits and hearts while simultaneously celebrating and affirming them. Fortifying them so that they might flourish and thrive for a lifetime.

Perhaps you remember, in spite of all the thousands and thousands and thousands of images you have probably seen since then, the photo of two-year-old Parker Curry that went viral in March 2018. In the photo, Parker is standing awestruck beneath the portrait of former first lady Michelle Obama painted by artist Amy Sherald that was unveiled at the Smithsonian's National Portrait Gallery. Parker's adoration for Michelle Obama, a Black woman who has a complexion much like her own, is so apparent. A woman who is beautiful, bright, brilliant and bold. An image that, of course, is not very common in the National Portrait Gallery.

I draw your attention to Parker and my niece because it is important that Parker and my niece can locate and see themselves in characters like Sulwe and women like Michelle Obama. It is critical for their well-being to see more books and other forms of media and art that feature Black children who can help them understand that they are beautiful, brilliant, bright and bold. That they will be able to see themselves in what they read and in the world in a far better light than many of their elders ever did.

Unlike my niece, as a child, I never had a book with a child in it that looked like me. The closest I had was a book, *The Sunflower Garden* that was a young Native American girl who planted sunflowers and saved her younger brother from a snake one day in the fields. I loved that book so much. I checked that book out of my school library weekly for all of third grade. Luckily, my niece will not have to wait until third grade to see a girl in a book who looks like her.

For those of us who are not two- or three-year-old little girls growing up in an era that includes books like *Sulwe* and *Hair Love*, our well-being is also tied to recognizing that we are beautiful, brilliant, bright and bold. And, when we haven't and are wounded by a world that tells us otherwise, we owe it to ourselves to be intentional about seeing what it is that Parker saw that day in the National Portrait Gallery, and what my niece gleefully found under the Christmas tree. Or to engage in self-talk that echoes what Kendi said to his daughter Imani. Telling ourselves that there ain't nothing wrong with Black people.

While Parker, Imani and Madelaine have not begun to see themselves as inferior, some of us have, for quite some time. Many of us (if we are being honest with ourselves) have, to some degree, internalized white supremacy. Some of us—far too of us in fact. As Gay Wilentz describes in *Healing Narratives: Women Writers Curing Cultural Disease*, in spite of vehemently denying it, we still suffer from cultural dis-ease and self-loathing. We struggle with shame and self-hate that is the result of being subjected to anti–Black racism and epistemic violence. A reality reflected in the insights of two of the young people who had a chance to spend time with Eddy and me as a part of the students who came from Xavier University in the summer of 2019:

> I believe I unconsciously told myself that I would never be as beautiful or find myself as beautiful based on colorism or Western standards. Going to Senegal gave me so much confidence. I am beautiful. Senegal taught me that I am beautiful.

> Before I went [to Senegal] I always thought we were the minority. That we are not as talented as the majority. That we weren't as smart as them. I was completely wrong. We are constantly told that we are less, that we are not valued. We have limitless potential to do anything we set our mind to. We are stronger than we think we are. It took going to Senegal to realize that.

These two young people's words are chilling. As young adults, they have absorbed damning, destructive and deleterious notions about themselves as Black people. As talented and smart as they are, they need to be reminded and shown that there is nothing wrong with Black people. They need to locate images and narratives that affirm that they are in fact beautiful, brilliant, bright and bold. Doing so, as they did here in Senegal, is powerful and transformative. Thus, doing so is profoundly healing and restorative. And doing so protects and fortifies us as we continue to grapple with the ways in which anti–Black racism, epistemic violence and systemic white supremacy operate in our minds, hearts, bodies and spirits.

As these young people indicate, quite honestly, Parker's awe in the National Portrait Gallery is what it feels like to be in Senegal for many of us. It felt that way to me the first time I visited in 2015, and it often continues to feel that way. And, while Senegal is certainly not free from the influences of white supremacy, it is a place where young people of all ages, including Black girls like my niece, Kendi's daughter and Parker, can see themselves and their beauty everywhere.

Such an experience is not to be taken for granted. Clearly. Seeing ourselves this way explains why Seinabo Sey declares in "Breathe" that she loves it here, in Senegal. As she explains, "I don't gotta to explain to them why I'm beautiful; Cuz, I am beautiful." Sey recognizes that one of the most powerful aspects of the trip to Senegal is that coming here allowed her to realize that she is beautiful. Beautiful. Like Sulwe. Like Michelle Obama. Like Parker. Like my niece. Yet, it is striking still at this moment in time that she, as the Xavier students point out, ultimately had to come all the way to Africa to see that about herself much more clearly. To see and recognize that she is, in fact, beautiful, brilliant, bright and bold.

Of course, *Sulwe*, like any children's book, is compelling not only because of the story it tells but because of the way that the illustrations speak to us. These books remind us that wherever it exists, in whatever form or medium, art can prove to be healing and restorative. It is a resource that reinforces our capacity to see that we are indeed bright, brilliant, beautiful and bold. That we do, in fact, have unlimited potential. That we can, in fact, do anything we set our mind to. That we, in fact, are stronger than we think we are.

For example, in Senegal, the Museum of Black Civilizations, which opened in 2018 to great fanfare throughout the Diaspora, is home to extensive, awe-inspiring art collections and exhibitions that impact visitors the way Parker is impacted when she looks up at Michelle Obama in the National Portrait Gallery. While the exhibits change over time, they consistently reflect the beauty and brilliance of Black folks across the Diaspora.

For example, I will never forget the way Dr. Kyra Shahid's face lit up with pure childlike joy and wonder and with awe like Parker's at the sight of Oumou Sy's breathtaking installation *The Forest of Africa Across the Universe,* which was an original display located in the hall that primarily featured works by Senegalese artists who had won Dak'art Jury Prizes.[2] Sy's eye-catching, visually-stimulating installation that takes up quite a bit of space in two places in the hall consists of seven Black female mannequins with rich, dark Black complexions like Michelle Obama's and Sulwe's. Three of the women are elevated overhead along the back wall of the hall, and the other four are mounted on a high, wide round pedestal—an aspect of the installation that is certainly part of its power. Reflecting the fact that Sy is considered to be the Queen of Senegalese Couture, all seven of the women are dressed in gowns and robes made from a variety of rich textiles, natural materials and adornments. The installation is breathtaking and awe-inspiring as you take in what is clearly a celebration of Black women and Senegalese culture, which is reflected in the use of small *jimbe* drums and miniature *koras* stitched together into the regale attire worn by one of the women.[3] They are all adorned in headdresses (one of rich green fabric, another from rope) that make them feel important and proud. They feel like magic, because in all their splendor they truly remind us that we are bright, brilliant, bold and beautiful. And, for some of us, their physical, life-size presence declares in vehement and striking silence, radiating confidence and pride, that there ain't nothing, not a damn thing, nothing at all wrong with Black people. Nothing.

Yet, what I have found here in Senegal to be so moving and inspiring and what I know is so compelling for women like Sey and Shahid is that the beauty and brilliance they see goes well beyond museum walls. Such celebrations and affirmations of who we are as Black women are not hidden and saved for Sunday afternoon visits or intermittent school field trips to a museum or art galleries. Nor are they saved for when we are murdered by the police in our beds or killed because we do not conform to limited notions of gender. No, here, there are no murals for Black women like the ones done by Yetunde Sapp in Washington, D.C., of Breonna Taylor or OLU-WATOYIN SALAU, who are dead at the hands of unwarranted and state-sanctioned violence. No, here, there are no murals where grieving families, friends and communities leave candles, flowers, gifts and protest signs. No, here, in Senegal, there are no murals marked by hashtags that are demanding justice, insisting that the system work in a way that assumes out of the gate, from the jump, at the very beginning that Black Women Matter, that our lives matter.

Here, in Senegal, instead, we can see images of Black beauty and brilliance all over the country. Everywhere. Public murals across the country often include images of beautiful Black women with dark black skin, colorful head wraps and gorgeous faces who I imagine Sulwe, Parker and my niece can look up at and see themselves so clearly in. Faces and images that evoke such a sense of awe as they see themselves rendered so beautiful, brilliant and bright across massive walls that have become canvases for Senegal's graffiti artists.

And faces that remind us to take up space, to be bold and, when necessary, to resist, to fight, to demand freedom, justice and liberty. I have seen Angela Davis rendered in numerous places. And, then there is the powerful mural of female freedom fighter and warrior Aliane Diatta that was completed in 2019 as part of the 11th annual Festigraff gathering organized by Docta Wear, that is located on the side of a single-story colonial-style building adjacent to the sea at the edge of where the corniche, the road that runs along the ocean where the Medina and Soumedione neighborhoods in Dakar meet. It is an area with heavy foot and vehicle traffic, where you cannot miss her face.

Aline Diatta (also Aline Sitow Diatta and Alyn Sytoe Jata; 1920–1944) was a Senegalese heroine of the opposition to the French colonial empire, a strong young female symbol of resistance and liberty. A Djola leader of a local religious group living in the village of Kabrousse, Basse Casamance, Aline Sitoe Diatta was one of the leaders of a tax resistance movement during World War II. Since her death after being arrested and exiled to Mali by the French, Aline Sitoe Diatta has become one of the best known symbols of resistance in West Africa, and a national symbol in Senegal, especially in Casamance. In fact, she was crowned "queen" as the result of the former king of Casamance's death in part because his successor could only be a person endowed with supernatural powers, reflected in her capacity to perform miracles, including, it is said, ending a drought.[4]

Her powerful image in the Festigraff mural presents her with skin that is rich, dark and beautiful like Sy's regal mannequins. The look on her face is peaceful, confident, proud and knowing. It is powerful because in this image she evokes defiance and resistance. She is beautiful, bright, brilliant and bold. She has gravitas and garners respect that this culture associates immediately with age and spiritual guidance, with which comes, it is understood implicitly, great wisdom. And, it is a reminder that there is nothing wrong with Black people. Or our need to resist. Nothing at all.

Beyond the artwork of graffiti artists (including those rendered by Zeinnex, who is considered Senegal's first female graffiti artist), couturiers and sculptors, there are the billboards across Senegal that also include images of beautiful Black people. There is the red and gold ad for Shell gasoline that features a Black woman and her husband dressed for *Tabaski,* which is the Eid that marks Abraham's sacrifice. Or the ones featuring a voluptuous, beautifully-dressed woman who has made her family what appears to be the tastiest, most well-presented *Theibbu Jenn,* Senegal's national dish, using whichever of the flavor cubes is being advertised that go in most Senegalese cuisine. Her smile is warm and welcoming; she is proud and confident as she creates an amazing meal that nourishes the ones she loves. She is certainly not Aunt Jemima in any way, shape or form. She is not the product of an advertiser's limited racist imagination; instead, while in a food product ad, she reflects core Senegalese values and the beauty of Black women. And, yes—the cynic would say, "Of course she does. That is how advertising works." Yes, it is. But, understand that it also tells us who we are, even if only as consumers. And, for those of us who have not seen ourselves enough, ever, these images also matter. They also serve to feed our sense of worth. They also offer us the protection that Kendi wants for his daughter and I for my niece. They also offer young women like those who have spent time with Eddy and me here in Senegal a reminder that they do absolutely matter and that they are in fact beautiful, that their faces are worthy of being on huge billboards and public murals.

Coming to Senegal and being surrounded with such images is truly a joyful experience. And, it is an experience that is healing and restorative, as these images and depictions of Black beauty and brilliance offer compelling and inspiring counter narratives to white supremacy and European standards of beauty that have, frankly, caused us great harm, generation after generation, and all over the world.

During the same time that *Sulwe* arrived at my parents' door to be hidden away until Christmas for my niece, I tagged along, somewhat begrudgingly, to the City of Raleigh's annual Christmas parade with my sister, my mom, my niece and my nephew. I went because I love my sister and I understood the way that parades can evoke awe and wonder in children. I refused to let my cynicism and alleged wokeness get in the way of the joy of my niece and nephew. Plus, I am a huge fan of the marching bands from places like the Helping Hand Mission that bring it like an HBCU band at halftime. I knew I would find some joy there, too. However, at two years old, my niece was not very interested in standing still on the parade route to see whatever high school marching band, civic group or local business gallivanting in the street or atop a float pulled by a pickup truck was coming next. And, you could forget about getting to the point when white Santa rolled through with two of the city's fire trucks escorting him down the route. She was so not interested.

That was okay. As the aunt that goes off in the woods with my nephews and brings them back wet, dirty, tired and happy, I was good with her refusing to stand still amidst the crowded curbs filled with people who reflected the city's problematic population shifts since the days my siblings and I attended the parade as spectators and to help my dad sell coffee in later years. So off we went to the grounds of the state capital, which is a place to play that I was familiar with from my childhood. My brothers and I had enjoyed playing in the grass and figuring out how to scale the massive statues that dot the lawn around the building. However, that day, as I maneuvered my niece around parade goers and puddles, hoping to keep her off the concrete and in the grass, I noticed those same looming statues that were simply climbing walls or jungle gyms for me as an adventurous, thrill-seeking, fearless child. They looked very different that morning with my two-year-old niece beside me. I no longer had the innocent, unknowing eyes of a young child. At that moment in the late fall of 2019, they struck me in quite a different way. I realized how menacing they actually were, and I understood the message they sent to me and my forebearers, who would have been directly subjected to the violent norms and expectations rooted in a society that demanded their ongoing deference and compliance. I felt something shift for and in me. I felt myself not only wanting to keep my sweet niece from stumbling, falling and skinning her knee. I felt an urgent need to protect her spirit. That energy had me teary eyed and holding my breath as I realized that we were actually in a space that we were never meant to be in as Black people. I now simply wanted my niece to stay away from the statues and away from what felt like tight, cold, unwelcoming energy that they and many of the parade goers seemed to radiate. And, frankly, it was an energy that didn't feel that warm and welcoming to me as far as the Christmas festivities were concerned. Some part of me felt like an outsider at a parade in a part of town where I had actually spent a lot of time as a kid and young adult. I had come to see those statues for what they actually were at the same time that I realized that the town I grew up in had lost so much of its SOUL.

The Confederate statues that loomed over my beautiful and bright niece at play that late November day were, as I am sure you know, erected well after that war ended, to speak so loud and clear (to scream, actually) threats of violence, suppression and imposed subjugation. Stern stone monuments to white supremacy and anti–Blackness. Insisting on us knowing and staying in what some deemed to be our place. In Raleigh. In Durham. In Chapel Hill. In Richmond. All over the country. And, as they begin to be torn down, we have the chance to erect and stand beneath new ones that evoke the same awe that Parker had when she looked up at First Lady Obama. And, the way Kyra and other visitors to Senegal admire Sy's *The Forest of Africa Across the Universe* installation at the Museum of Black Civilizations and the public art dancing on and draping across the walls throughout the country. Statues that, like my niece's picture book and Senegal's graffiti, remind us that we are, in fact, beautiful, bright, brilliant and bold. Statues that make us feel proud and remind us that there ain't nothing wrong with Black people. Nothing at all. Statues that can actually contribute to our healing and restoration.

Dominating Dakar's skyline at 160 feet, sitting on top of a 100-meter-high hill sits the Renaissance Monument, a copper sculpture of a man, woman and child that is seen as a symbol of defiance and future prosperity and represents Africa taking "its destiny into its own hands." It was unveiled in 2010 during the presidency of Abdoulaye Wade to commemorate Senegal's 50 years of independence from France. Unveiled in 2010 and standing 49 meters high, it is taller than New York City's Statue of Liberty and Rio de Janeiro's Christ the Redeemer. According to former Senegalese president Abdoulaye Wade, who commissioned the project, the monument is a synonym for the continent's "greatness, stability and durability" after centuries of colonization and conquest.

The monument evokes a sense of awe and pride for Black folks who visit Senegal, who, like me, for much of our lifetimes have rarely, if ever, seen us rendered artistically in such a grand fashion. In contrast to the statues I grew up seeing like those on Raleigh's capitol grounds, this statue does not make me cringe or angry or want to protect myself. Instead, it makes me feel a great sense of pride and joy. The same sense of pride and joy that our visitors describe feeling when they see it. Like one of the sisters who attended our Calm in the Chaos retreat. In a FB post encouraging a friend to visit Senegal subsequent to her visit, she emotionally described the monument as majestic and explained that she cried at the top when she made it to the hat on top of the man's head.

Like a young man from California who came with a group of his peers and their mentors, who saw the statue as a highlight of his visit, in part because it exposed him to an aspect of Black culture he wasn't familiar with. He explained that such an experience was a huge eye-opener because it allowed him to see the gaps in what "we are taught in school versus what's real." He explains that seeing the monument "was a huge eye-opener for me because it is bigger than the Statue of Liberty. Yet, I never heard of it ever, which is ridiculous. So, for me, it was a big eye-opener and it made me want to dive deeper into learning about my culture and the different customs."

Put another way, the African Renaissance Monument (and much of what he saw in Senegal) was powerful because it reminded him of our potential and capacity to do what we dream of. Of our beauty, brilliance and boldness. It reminded him that there just ain't nothing wrong with Black people. Nothing at all.

Thankfully, there are statues, finally, in the United States that, like Sulwe and Obama's portrait and the Diatta mural, are truly awe-inspiring. That take our breath away at the moment we see them. That open our eyes and allow us to truly behold our beauty, our brilliance, our brightness and our boldness. That offer us a challenge and push back against the still disturbingly pervasive notions of white supremacy.

For example, there is *Rumors of War*, the work of highly-regarded artist Kehinde Wiley, which he first unveiled on September 27, 2019, in New York City's Times Square, where the statue remained on view for several weeks. The statue serves as "a direct response to the Confederate statues that have historically lined Monument Avenue in Richmond, including the recently removed 61-feet-high Robert E. Lee statue that loomed above the street on a granite and marble base reminiscent of a shrine honoring a *Roman emperor*," made of bronze, which Black Lives Matter activists have insisted be taken down after toppling the statue of Confederate President Jefferson Davis, which they drenched in bright pink paint during protests that erupted in the weeks immediately following the murder of George Floyd in Minneapolis. Wiley conceived the idea for *Rumors of War* when he visited the city in 2016 for the opening of *Kehinde Wiley: A New Republic* at the Virginia Museum of Fine Art. *Rumors of War* takes its inspiration from the statue of Confederate Army General James Ewell Brown "J.E.B." Stuart created by Frederick Moynihan in 1907. As with the original sculpture, the rider strikes a heroic pose while sitting upon a muscular horse. However, instead of a Confederate, Wiley's sculpture features the figure of a young African American dressed in urban streetwear. Proudly mounted on its large stone pedestal, the bronze sculpture commemorates African American youth lost to the social and political battles being waged throughout our nation. In the statue, which was unveiled December 10, 2019, at the

Virginia Museum of Fine Art, "Wiley draws from a series of paintings he created in the early 2000s [which were] inspired by the history of equestrian portraiture, in which he replaced traditional white subjects depicted in large-format paintings with young African American men in street clothes." The VMFA explains in its press release about *Rumors of War* that it "offers an exquisite example of how to imagine and develop a more complete and inclusive American story."

Certainly, that is the case, but this statue is about far more than quaint notions of diversity and inclusion as we work to center and celebrate Black folks. And, that push back against narratives that center whiteness, as do the monuments that have existed in cities like Richmond for some time. And, like First Lady Obama in the portrait gallery evokes nothing but great awe and the sense that we do indeed matter, as do our lives, our beauty, our brilliance, our brightness and our Blackness. That simply stop my nieces and nephews in their tracks because they see themselves in ways that are simply awesome.

There is also the statue of Frederick Douglass that was unveiled in 2015 on the University of Maryland campus, where he is over seven feet tall and in the middle of delivering a fiery oratory, "with one arm outstretched, and a copy of his storied autobiography under the other arm [as] his coat/cape billows out behind him in a swath of bronze." Here, he is rendered as such a powerful force to be reckoned with. This striking statue adeptly captures the fervor of his commitment to our liberation and freedom. As such a central figure in our freedom struggle and American history, of course he of all people warranted a statue of great stature. It most certainly reminds us of our power and capacity to be bold and courageous. Like the Sy installation and the African Renaissance Monument, the Frederick Douglass statue fills you with pride and joy as you see Black boldness, brilliance and beauty in such a dramatic, larger-than-life fashion that cannot simply be ignored or passed by with some recognition of all that we have been and all that we have the potential to be. The statue effectively conveys our capacity to take up space and demand freedom, liberty and justice.

In *The Healing Wisdom of Africa,* Malidoma Somé reminds us

of the critical role of the artist. He explains that "the connection between the artist as a sacred healer and the community is undeniable." He goes on to describe the traditional role of an artist in African culture, where an artist was not focused on commodifying her work, nor did she have to worry about what works to show or how to gain stature through her work. Instead, her focus is on healing. It was understood traditionally that the art was the result of a connection to the spirit realm and that her work is to be deeply revered and respected (Somé 95–98). Such echoes and extensions might be seen in Wiley's body of work, which is focused "on addressing and remedying the absence of Black and brown men and women in our visual, historical, and cultural narratives." As is the case with his paintings, which include the portrait of Barack Obama that hangs in the National Photo Gallery, adjacent to the one of his wife that Parker fell so deeply and immediately in love with. And, with the graffiti artists of Dakar and muralists in Washington, Charlotte and Cincinnati.

At this point, at this moment as we grapple with the stark realities of our nation and the pain and suffering it has caused and continues to cause us as Black people, thankfully there is art that offers ways to heal simply by looking up and seeing ourselves. When we look up at art that reminds us that like Sulwe, we are bright, brilliant, beautiful and bold. When we look up like Parker in awe. When we see ourselves in statues, books and canvases of all forms and fashions and squeal in delight like Shahid in the Museum of Black Civilizations. When we cry at the magnificent sight of the African Renaissance Monument overlooking the whole city of Dakar. When we understand in our very fiber that there ain't nothing wrong at all with Black people. Nothing at all. Not a thing.

CHAPTER XI

#LoveHeals

Self-Love and Being Your Authentic Self

You were born to win
Don't let them make you colorblind and not adore your skin
—"Shine," Tobe Nwigwe

Yes indeed, as Tobe Nwigwe tells us, "the world can be toxic (toxic); especially when your skin look like chocolate (chocolate)." And, unfortunately, as he reminds us, that toxicity can result in a degree of self-loathing and shame that reduces our capacity to shine, to flourish, to adore ourselves. To be comfortable in our (chocolate) skin. To love ourselves, individually and collectively.

And, by love, I am evoking the work of well-regarded Black feminists like bell hooks, Alice Walker and June Jordan. In her book, *All About Love: New Visions*,[1] as well as her book on Black women and healing, *Sisters of the Yam*, bell hooks cites M. Scott Peck's definition of love—"love is the will to extend one's self for the purpose of nurturing one's own or another's spiritual growth."[2] In her earlier work, *Sisters of the Yam*, hooks explains that such a definition is important because the focus is not on material well-being, but instead the focus is on emotional needs as well as spiritual well-being.[3] In fact, love like this, according to hooks, should be thought of as an action rather than simply a feeling, which allows us to insist that anyone using the word love will assume and accept a fair amount of accountability that goes along with such a definition. Subsequently, understanding that love is an action requires us to accept that the actions we take, the choices we make in the name of love have consequences that we must take responsibility for.

149

Feminist poet and activist June Jordan offers a complementary definition of love in her essay entitled "Where is the Love?" In this essay, Jordan states, "I am not talking about sexuality, I am talking about love, about a steady-stated caring and respect for every other human being, a love that can only derive from a secure and positive self-love."[4] She goes on to say, "when I seek to evaluate the potentiality, the life-supportive commitment possibilities of anyone or anything, the decisive question is, always, where is the love."[5] Moreover, Jordan asserts that "I cannot be expected to respect what somebody else calls self-love if that concept of self-love requires my suicide to any degree. You cannot expect me to respect what somebody else identifies as the good of the people if that so called good (often translated into manhood or family or nationalism) requires the deferral or the diminution of my self-fulfillment."[6]

Much like hooks, Jordan's notion of love emphasizes a commitment to ensuring the well-being of both the self and others. At the same time, her notion of love rejects any behavior that restricts and restrains either individual's self-expression, self-determination or self-fulfillment. For both hooks and Jordan, love includes a commitment to do no harm, a commitment to affirm life. So when Eddy and I say that the work we do includes holding space folks to be more loving, we are referring to the willingness to extend oneself for the well-being of self and others. This is what I mean when I use the term love as we explore the ways that we can collectively deepen our capacity for healing, restoration, resilience and resistance.

However, let's be really clear here. Loving ourselves, individually and collectively, is not always easy as Black folks with a variety of intersecting and oft times conflicting identities. Loving Black people is not easy—no more than loving anyone else is. It takes work. And as Jordan notes, you can't love anyone else unless you truly love yourself. Or to evoke Alice Walker, loving us takes courage, heart and energy. Sometimes, honestly, lots of energy. Particularly in light of all that we have been told over and over and over again about our value and worth, or perceived lack thereof.

Even now, at a moment after having a two-term Black president, a Black female vice-president, and Black people out front and "on top" in the public eye seemingly driving and influencing so much of who and what America is culturally and economically, self-love is still hard. And, when many of us are still vehemently and passionately declaring that Black Lives Matter. Even now, with all this, some of us are still experiencing varying degrees of what Gay Wilentz characterizes in her work *Healing Narratives* as cultural dis-ease that includes, in some cases, levels of self-loathing and shame.[7] Or put another way, at the 2020 Amplify and Activate Summit, Dianne Bondy, well-respected yoga inclusivity and accessibility leader and author of *Yoga for Everyone: 50 Poses for Every Type of Body*, explains that before we get to self-love, many of us actually struggle with self-loathing, which is followed by self-acceptance.[8] Our culture, which is hellishly materialistic and deeply racist, as Bondy and Wilentz explain, does little to have us accept and adore ourselves. It is a culture, you will recall, that is quite toxic when your skin is like chocolate (chocolate). And on this journey to self-love that forces us to deal with the self-loathing we may have been taught is not simply our own. In fact, many of us are still carrying the scars and bruises of our racial wounding and hurts, our own and those, frankly, of our elders and our ancestors who did not have the chance to move from self-loathing and shame to self-acceptance and self-love.

However, we do have the capacity to love ourselves more. We must if we are going to experience healing and restoration, be resilient and engage in resistance. Self-love is an important part of our capacity to flourish and be well. If we are going to collectively and individually heal, we must be able to love Black people, unapologetically and as deeply and tenderly as possible.

So, when we speak of putting the heart, courage and energy back into our bodies with our own culture, as Walker advises us to do in order to heal these wounds, we must consider love, self-love in particular, albeit not exclusively. In that vein, we must recognize the relationship between knowing, accepting and loving ourselves. Part of the struggle we face, the struggle to love ourselves as Black folks, individually and collectively, is tied to the ways we as human beings fail to remember our true and authentic selves. As spiritual leader and educator Parker Palmer explains in *Letting Our Life Speak*:

we arrive in this world with birthright gifts—then we spend the first half of our lives abandoning them or letting others disabuse us of them. As young people, we are surrounded by expectations that may have little to do with who we really are, expectations held by people who are not trying to discern our self-hood but fit us into slots. In families, schools, workplaces and religious communities, we are trained away from true self toward images of acceptability; under social pressures like racism and sexism our original form is deformed beyond recognition; and we ourselves, driven by fear, too often betray the true self to gain the approval of others. We lose sight of who we are and allowed social expectations and norms.[9]

This includes, Palmer notes, those norms that are deeply rooted in white supremacy and anti–Black racism that inform how we see and understand ourselves. What Palmer describes is echoed in Dr. Gail Parker's explanation of acculturation as "the adoption of dominant cultural values and beliefs and behaviors and adapting to cultural norms and physical characteristics [we] may not share" (124). Continuing to adjust to such norms that require us to deny who we are is a form of racial wounding that affects us "psychologically (anxiety and depression) and physically (diabetes and hypertension)." Parker warns us that giving up yourself, moving away from your unique and authentic self is "stressful and wounding" (125). Indeed, "the world can be toxic (toxic); especially when your skin look like chocolate."

In yoga, we also recognize what Parker and Palmer describe; we understand that our suffering, our pain, the sense that we are out of balance, the dis-ease that we experience is tied to the fact that we have lost sight of and the connection to our authentic and true selves. One way to understand that is in relationship to our SOUL, our spirit, how it is we are here to express all that is divine about. A relationship that offers us the opportunity to be at peace and comfortable with ourselves, even when we face obstacles and challenges related to race and other issues.

Well-regarded yoga teacher and author Rolf Gates explains that "we are in a state of imbalance when it comes to over-efforting because we are still living from the logic of fear. Fear of not being worthy. Fear of not being enough" (155). We know that fear of not being worthy, of not being enough, the struggle to love ourselves and our over-efforting is what yoga therapist and author of *Restorative Yoga for Ethnic and Race-Based Stress and Trauma* Dr. Gail Parker describes in relationship to race-based stress injuries, when she references high-effort coping, specifically "John Henryism" and "Sojourner Syndrome" (67–69).

Another way to understand our struggle to love and embrace our authentic selves looks like us ignoring our dharma, which Gates explains "is the recognition that each of us is born with unique gifts and that it is our path to discover these gifts and share them with others." When we are able to share our gifts, we live most fully. When we are able to share our gifts, we give others permission to do the same. Further, Gates reminds us that "chances are we already know what makes our heart sing." And, that "when we reflect on the millions of smiles of our lifetimes, we see our dharma looking back at us with love." Trusting and embracing our dharma, expressing our true and authentic selves is far more rewarding, fulfilling, sustaining and healthy than "fuel[ing] our dreams … outside ourselves" and forcing "our unique gifts … in truncated notions of success or distorted notions of what makes us valuable, beautiful and lovable."[10]

As Gates, Palmer and Parker remind us, we are conditioned to ignore our inner voice and deny our true selves, our authentic selves or our dharma, our calling, our purpose. Unfortunately, all too often our culture does not allow us to take the time to be still and know ourselves. At least it does not encourage us to sit with and explore who we are and what makes our light shine as we strive to be productive at all times (at, often, our own expense). Instead, far too often we are focused on surface-level appearances and maintaining the status quo. Or we focus on materiality and dreams of being the next Instagram sensation, or achieving some sort of distorted celebrity status, even if only in our minds. Or as hooks notes in her definition of love, we get far too focused on material gain. Or as Gates notes, we force ourselves to exist in ways that do nothing to feed our spirit or fully express our dharma or our true selves. We are often too scared to take risks, be courageous and be our authentic selves. Or challenge the systemic ways we are conditioned to see and understand success that looks a certain way. Or question the order of things that tells us what we should value the most, including the value of our Black lives. Our love. Our joy. Our capacity to hope, dream and imagine something more fulfilling, more life-affirming for ourselves, collectively. Our well-being.

So, what then, if we are going to experience healing by putting the heart back into our bodies and practice self-love, if loving your Black self is important? So, what then, if you have lost sight of your true and authentic self in a world that "can be toxic when your skin looks like chocolate (chocolate)?" If you have been racially-wounded, then what options do you have for healing and restoration? How do you arrive at a point in your life when you feel like you do in fact love yourself, even if you still have parts of you that will continue to heal? When will you be able to let your guard down, open up and be vulnerable? When will you be able to stop holding your breath and feeling all balled and bound up in your Black body? How and when can you heal yourself, in this case, love yourself and be fully aware of your worth and value, even as we face recurring experiences with various forms of racial stress and wounding? Not to mention other forms of oppression and marginalization. How do you fortify and protect yourself, your well-being?

We got SOUL! You got SOUL! SOUL is a "transformative healing resource that reflects the cultural sensibilities from across the African Diaspora." Further, I offer that culture and contemplative practices are the resources that allow you to deepen your capacity to love yourself and love others, specifically in this case, Black folks. Which is still today, at this moment, sadly considered an act of resistance.

My only Mecca was, is, and shall always be Howard University. This Mecca, My Mecca—The Mecca—is a machine, crafted to capture and concentrate the dark energy of all African peoples and inject it directly into the student body. The Mecca derives its power from the heritage of Howard University, which in Jim Crow days enjoyed a near-monopoly on Black talent. ... I first witnessed this power out on the Yard, that communal green space in the center of the campus where the students gathered and I saw everything I knew of my Black self multiplied out into seemingly endless variations. There were the scions of Nigerian aristocrats in their business suits giving dap to bald-headed Qs in purple windbreakers and tan Timbs. There were the high-yellow progeny of A.M.E. preachers debating the clerics of Ausar-Set. There were California girls turned Muslim, born anew, in hijab and long skirt. There were Ponzi schemers and Christian cultists, Tabernacle fanatics and mathematical geniuses. It was like listening to a hundred different renditions of "Redemption Song," each in a different color and key. And overlaying all of this was the history of Howard itself. I knew that I was literally walking in the footsteps of all the Toni Morrisons and Zora Neale Hurstons, of all the Sterling Browns and Kenneth Clarks, who'd come before.

Ta-Nehisi Coates, truly, in this stirring passage, writes a love song to Howard University, his Mecca. A love song that I believe that so easily and effortlessly extends to Black folks more broadly. He so lovingly identifies our diversity, our brilliance, our creativity and our pure genius, actually. He makes so clear that we are not a monolith, that we are not all the same. That we are all of that and so much more. And, that we are no doubt dope AF. I get chills and so excited when I read this passage. I get chills and so excited when I hear the passage narrated by Susan Kelechi Watson, a Howard alumna and star of *This Is Us*, as part of radio interviews and promotions for the HBO adaptation of Coates' *Between the World and Me* for the screen.[11] My heart fills with pride and joy as he names the greats in whose footsteps he walks as he names our legacy. He so accurately captures our SOUL. He so clearly explains that Howard, as an HBCU, offers us an antidote, a vaccine, the protection Kendi speaks of, a cultural cure to any way that we might not be loving ourselves as Black folks. There, at the mecca, you can get injected with our culture(s), with SOUL. With history and heritage to affirm who we are. With constant reminders, in a communal space, on the yard, in every class, in every dorm room, that we are simply extraordinary and more than worthy. And, it is at Howard where Coates is able to deepen his capacity to love himself, to be comfortable in his own skin. To know that there is absolutely nothing abnormal about Black folks being smart, no—brilliant, creative, and sensitive. In fact, beyond preparing him to achieve and be an accomplished journalist, the legacy of Howard makes Coates who he is by teaching him to love himself on that campus, on "the yard" of Howard University. And, it is there at his beloved HBCU where he begins to deepen his love for Black people, a love that as a writer has led him to extend himself for our well-being.[12]

Like Coates, in what I now define as an act of self-love, an act of affirming and celebrating some part of myself, I also packed my bags (and a big six-foot black foot locker), oh, and my red, black and green afghan and bed sheets, and headed to the rolling hills and verdant green of my beloved alma mater, North Carolina Central University (NCCU). In an act of what, at the time, was "fuck this shit; I ain't doing it no more," I chose NCCU because I needed what Coates got at Howard. More specifically, I needed to heal from the nasty bumps and bruises I got in high school. I needed to heal some of my own racial wounds. Ask my mama, she will tell you, that I was emphatic about it. Emphatic, you hear me. Going to an HBCU was absolutely the only option I was willing to consider. It was either North Carolina A&T State University (which I still like saying) or North Carolina Central University. I chose to attend my alma mater North Carolina Central University because I needed to be in a place that affirmed my value, worth and magic. I needed to go to college where I would be loved and celebrated as a young Black woman who was sensitive, smart, creative, free-spirited, rebellious and loving. A place where I did not have to apologize for being my authentic self, particularly after my high school experience, where systemic white supremacy, epistemic violence and anti–Black racism informed the ways that my peers and I were treated. And, that love just got fed over and over and over again during my college years and early adult years in what was then known lovingly as Chocolate City, Washington, D.C. My time on the campus of NCCU and in Chocolate City in the early 1990s was a powerful, self-affirming experience that reflects the beautifully striking picture that Ta-Nehisi Coates paints of his alma mater.

Choosing to go to an HBCU was an expression of my love for Black people and my desire (even if at the time only sub-consciously) to know and love my Black self. And, I flourished and excelled in college. Academically, I was the top English major for three consecutive years and recognized annually at our spring honors convocation. I came in as an honors student. Socially, I had a blast. I turned up and turned out, particularly during my sophomore year, even with a course load of 21 credits. I hung out with honors students and hip hop heads. I managed to balance my studies with going to games, going to parties and working part-time. Oh, yeah, and I organized my first protest with my peers as a freshman. That, however, is another story. And, I served on our newspaper staff and as editor of our literary magazine. I did honors research on the poet Gwendolyn Brooks. And, during my final year, I served as the Shut 'Em Down student government president. I had a blast, and I am certain that the ways that I fed my SOUL on the campus of my alma mater made me who I am today—someone who loves herself and Black people. And, all that we are.

For Coates and me, along with hundreds of thousands of others who matriculated to a university like Howard and walked those communal campus grounds (aka "the yard"), HBCUs gave us a place to both heal and fortify ourselves. Put another way, we found our Wakanda. (And, yes, Chadwick Boseman is also a Howard graduate.) At our alma maters, we found a powerfully strong antidote to shame, self-hate and self-loathing. We learned how to love and celebrate ourselves, unapologetically. And, while I am more than tempted to write a lengthy encomium for HBCUs, I am fully aware, as others have noted, that HBCUs are not immune from white supremacy, and they often perpetuate problematic notions of respectability that many seek to disrupt, reject and replace with a deep embrace of all that we are without such limiting standards applied.[13] Somé would say that Kamala Harris, a Howard grad, has not adequately extended herself for the well-being of others, particularly Black folks impacted by the prison industrial complex. However, even as we bump up against notions of respectability and individuals driven by their own ambition, there is absolutely no doubt that attending HBCUs allows Black folks to deepen our connections to and appreciation for the culture that Walker speaks of, our SOUL. We learned that our culture(s), our SOUL, will most certainly deepen our capacity to love ourselves, fully and without apology, even as we navigate a world that is quite toxic when your skin is chocolate (chocolate).

As 1990s–era HBCU grads, Coates and I developed the capacity to love ourselves and express our authentic selves in part because we were steeped in SOUL for at least four years. Experiencing SOUL can foster our capacity for healing and self-love, which is evidenced by the young Black people who Eddy and I host here in Senegal for their Diasporic Soul racial healing experiences. When asked to talk about the best or most powerful aspects of their experience with us, what we hear very clearly and repeatedly in a number of ways is that these young people find some sense of themselves and see themselves in far more affirming ways than they had previously. What we clearly hear is that coming here to this place, to Senegal, offers them a chance to restore their connection to their true and authentic selves.

One graduating senior stated, "I reconnected with a sense of myself that was lost before I even knew who I was. When I say lost I mean like generations kind of lost. I feel like I reconnected to generations of myself that were lost." Also, in our discussions she noted that her trip to Senegal allowed her to better appreciate her family members who are Rastafarian, which is a sentiment similar to what I heard from another young man who came to us with a group from California who now feels compelled to visit Ghana, where he has not been since he was a young boy. Like this young lady who felt like she restored a connection to generations of herself, he, too, can see the value and worth of his diasporic roots. And, his own diasporic SOUL.

Another young lady planning to attend dental school stated:

I think I was kinda forced to realize that I had a Western view of what exactly talent and culture is and what creativity is for myself. So, during my time in Senegal, I was able to realize and embrace the fact that I am talented and I can use my creativity to express myself the way I want to. And, not using the guide and standard that the Western, you know, America, uses for who and what is talent.

And, while she is struggled to find balance and to stay grounded in dental school, she now recognizes that she has talent, that she is creative. That she is worthy because she has SOUL.

A young man majoring in biology and a member of a Black Greek-letter organization explained that coming to Senegal gave the group the chance "to authentically be [them]selves without any

belonged in the place where he lives, in his city, in his country and on his campus. These realities are damning. But, what is compelling and moving is that in spite of the struggles these young people name, they find that they have had a chance to have a transformative healing experience in Senegal. And, while there are a number of ways that this experience offers them the opportunity for restoration and healing that are addressed elsewhere in this book, here it is important to note that they speak specifically to being able to (like in the case of the first young lady) restore a connection to themselves, one lost long ago, evoking, of course, the nature of the Diaspora, that includes our movement from the continent. The second reminds us that how she sees her worth and value, specifically her talent and gifts, has expanded because of her time here with us in Senegal. I know that this is because she has seen SOUL, including creativity, resourcefulness and ingenuity expressed in a myriad of ways during her time in Senegal, including the aspects of heritage and history that she is introduced to and the artistic works she has seen all throughout her sojourn to Senegal. At the same time, the young men spoke to being able to express their true selves in ways they cannot back in the United States (or so they came to believe prior to their trip). Yet, as the elder cohort member notes, he, they, have the power to change these realities. They actually have the capacity to love themselves, to see their worth and express their true and authentic selves.

It is particularly interesting that they use these terms—the same terms used by the likes of Parker, Palmer and Walker, hooks and Jordan. It is important to see that they speak of being able to be their true and authentic selves. I did not spend much time going in depth into yoga philosophy and discussing at length that the goal of yoga as a spiritual practice is to restore our connection or union to our true selves and the spirit or the source. Yet, these are the terms they use as they speak to the ways in which a sojourn, a pilgrimage to Senegal, to West Africa, to the motherland offers them ways to see themselves differently and to love themselves and to embrace their true and authentic selves. For them, as PWI students, most of whom have attended predominantly white schools for much of their lives, coming here offers them some of the same affirmation and healing that Coates and I achieved as HBCU students. And, while the experiences are certainly not the same, particularly in terms of the depth and duration of time directly reveling in SOUL, both do offer safe, brave, affirming, love-filled, validating spaces where we all feel safe, secure and keen, and an unwavering sense of belonging. Both offer us the resources that allow us the chance to put the energy, courage and heart into our bodies with our culture. Both offer us the chance to feel the love—love for ourselves as Black folks, individually and collectively.

Reflective Journal Prompt

So, where will you go to feed your capacity to love yourself in spite of white supremacy and other forms of oppression? How will you deepen your capacity to know and be your true and authentic self? What ways will you seek out cultural restoration and engage in practices that offer you opportunities to experience healing so that you can remain resilient and engage in resistance as we fight for social and healing justice, as we create a world where we can flourish, a world where, in fact, Black Lives *do* Matter?

CHAPTER XII

My SOUL to Keep

Self-Care and Resilience

Angela Franklin, a native of Cincinnati, Ohio, and owner of Chez Alpha Books in Dakar, is a well-regarded multimedia artist who served as the 2019–2020 Artist-in-Residence with Xavier University's Stained Glass Initiative. Her works evoke and capture our history and our culture, including our capacity for resilience and resistance in spite of oppression and life's hardships. While her commissioned works for Xavier tell a visually compelling and rich story about the institution's disturbing and unresolved relationship with slavery and white supremacy, her 2018 series *My Soul to Keep* is a riveting and striking collection of multimedia art textiles that she created to express and process her grief after losing her sister. The series consists of multiple pieces, all of which deeply resonate with me, including *When Feeling Blue, She Reaches for the Redbird* and *Pour First from a Full Cup and a Full Heart*.

Pour First from a Full Cup and a Full Heart is a beautiful piece that features a female subject with dark skin who is standing in front of a tall shelf of cups that look like pastel-colored Easter eggs. To me, they look like hot/cold style travel cups without their lids. In the subject's hand is a cup turned upside down being emptied of its contents, which pour out and over to the opposite side of the canvas where you can see a more vibrantly blue person who seems to be adorned in a crown with their hand extended to receive what is being poured out. The contrast in colors on the piece read as if the pourer is draining out her vitality, as the colors on her side are pastel and light. In contrast, the one who is being poured into or receiving what is in the cup is being fortified, filled and enriched, as he or she consists of much richer, deeper patterned tones and textures, deep blues, reds, blacks and oranges. The soft, pastel blues and lavenders (the kind you might find on a line of baby product labels) on the left side of the piece behind the pourer seem to reflect a soft angst for the pourer's constant care for others at the expense of her own vitality and well-being. The fabric of the deeply colored red, black and green scarf on the pourer's head, which contrasts with the lighter hued energy behind and around her, repeats beneath the receiver as if to say that she is virtually giving her life force away. The strand of black, red and green fabric feeds up from the bottom of the textile into the rich, vibrant energies of the one who is receiving. It is as if you can feel the energy being shared in this red, black and green wave of shifting colors that serves as specific visual connections between both sides of the piece. And, knowing Angela, I can hear her voice; I hear her scolding her sister, fussing rather than simply expressing her own raw grief or lament. There is disapproval and frustration with her sister being expressed for not finding some way to keep something in her cup for herself. It is frustration that her sister has found herself left only with an empty cup, one with nothing left to give herself. Actually, a whole shelf full of empty ass cups that like the one in her hand are that way because she has repeatedly extended herself over and over and over again and done little in the way of refilling her cup or cups. Little in the way of self-care.

Pour First from a Full Cup and a Full Heart resonates with me quite deeply. I can understand how Angela might have been feeling when she created it. What I sense are her mixed feelings of frustration and grief and worry, care and concern reflected in *Pour First from a Full Cup and a Full Heart* and in the conversations we have had over the last year. The proverbial empty cups and the ones that threaten to spill out and all over the place, making a huge mess, look quite similar and feel in such an embodied way quite familiar, I imagine, for many of us, but the ways that the cup got there, empty, most certainly vary.

An empty cup looks like a college student juggling a part-time course load, family caretaking, and a full-time job in the service sector, which are all bumping up against her deep sense of unworthiness,

fear and self-doubt. An empty cup looks like a student affairs practitioner in her early thirties working on a small private college campus in the Midwest during a global pandemic at the same time as
she continues to show up and attempts to hold space day in and day
out for her students because she is one of few Black staff and faculty on campus to support multi-cultural students, particularly Black
ones who are disproportionately impacted by the pandemic yet
who are still up in arms at the end of one of the most racially volatile summers in decades. An empty cup looks like a working mother
approaching forty trying to work from home with two young children ages three and six who are homebound due to a global pandemic and who is deeply anxious (terrified, actually) about the ways
in which racial violence might impact her husband, three brothers,
her parents (who live in a more rural part of a bright red state) and
other loved ones during the most volatile and racially charged election cycle in decades. An empty cup is a dynamic, bright and creative
fifteen-year-old student living in an under-resourced community
whose school's front office serves not only as the administrative hub
for the building but is home to a food pantry, a resource center for
emergency aid and where she and her fellow students find solace
and sanctuary with their overextended school counselor as they
grapple with all their fear and anxiety about post-secondary plans,
family poverty and living with the threat of both street and police
violence, tentatively hoping to pursue their dreams while simultaneously avoiding getting swept up into the school-to-prison pipeline and subjected to anti–Black and anti-transgender violence. An
empty cup looks like an unemployed twenty-three-year-old brother
who just invested the lion's share of his savings to start a new fitness
business while finishing his undergraduate studies just weeks before
a global pandemic locked the world down, deferring his dreams
and cutting off the income he needs to live. An empty cup looks
like a brother who is booed up with his college sweetheart who had
planned to be in graduate or professional school this fall but instead
finds himself as the primary caregiver to an ailing family elder while
simultaneously maintaining two jobs only to find out that his immediate family all have been stricken with Covid. An empty cup looks

like an essential worker in his late forties stocking grocery shelves in an affluent community as he grapples with his own worthiness while raising two children under the age of six at home with his wife, who is dealing with her own debilitating depression that one might argue is rooted in her own doubt that she might actually be enough. An empty cup looks like a recently retired couple living hand to mouth on a limited retirement income because they do not have pensions or robust retirement accounts because they used the little bit of money they were able to squirrel away to respond to major emergencies for the last two decades of their working years. An empty cup looks like a creative, artistic, fifty-two-year-old HBCU grad who has had the same employer for over twenty years wondering if her job will be cut as the profit margins plummet to all-time lows while simultaneously navigating serving as a caretaker for her aging grandfather and having her racially wounded nephew who recently graduated from college living with her as he tries to make his way in the world, while facing a global pandemic at a time when it is more than apparent that the verdict is out on whether or not he lives in a city, in a community, in a nation where in fact Black lives do indeed matter. Yeah, the cup can absolutely get full pretty fast, especially when faced with such a massive challenge as two pandemics in a world that is toxic when your skin is like chocolate. And, God forbid the shit in the cup is hot.

Yes, full cups. Overflowing at times. Hot contents trickling down the sides, burning your fingers and hands as you try to move about in spite of the burn and the pain. And, then, all of a sudden, before you even notice, empty. With nothing, not a single drop for anyone. Nothing left to give. To them or to yourself for that matter. But continuing to push, grind and hustle hard as hell anyway. That is the way, the American way. With the exception of some "conscious" artists, the hustle, the grind, the deep affinity and devotion to it is quintessential hip hop ethos in many respects. John Henry and Sojourner remixed to a dope ass beat you can dance to. That is our way. In part because this way is tied to a promise of advancement and mobility. A real fine line between our capacity to be resilient and making things happen and hurting ourselves in ways we can't quite always see or sense. Yep, you are right—there is that damn high-effort coping again. And, in part, we roll like this, we exist this way because failure to do so, realistically, for most folks, does mean facing the terrifying risk of falling through the cracks and not having our basic needs of food, clothing, shelter and love met in our selfish culture. This is the story, the reality we have been given and that some of us continue to buy into, particularly as Black folks. The notion, the belief that we absolutely cannot take time out to care for ourselves because there is just way too much to be done. At home, in the streets, for the family, for the community, for my people. As a result, we have, of course, understandably struggled to practice self-care.

Of course, as Black folks we have consistently been quite proud of our work ethic, generation after generation. Yet, now, while many of us continue to do what we must, we are beginning, finally, to understand that this way, this aspect of our culture is deleterious, destructive, dangerous and the root of far too much of our dis-ease. Dis-ease caused by stress that has taken us over the edge, stress that has burnt us out, stress that makes it seems that we, the world, life as we know it is simply unraveling at the very seams. Stress and suffering, normal aspects of life, yet still perhaps more than we should accept, more than we should take on, more than we should tolerate and simply bear as some sort of noble burden to drape over our shoulders and proudly carry around like a damn cross. Stress and suffering deeply rooted in the soil of a culture built on our backs, a culture that with all its richness is tied to our exploitation and oppression. Stress and suffering that is far too often tied to race, class, gender and other ways we are marginalized. Stress that is tied to having no real safety net, even during a global pandemic, particularly when our elected officials do not have the capacity to come together to support those who are facing dire economic and financial circumstances, including looming evictions and foreclosures; illness and death; and hunger and deep food insecurity.

And, in spite of having a cup that is about to spill out and make a mess all over the place (or one that is empty because the spill has already happened), we refuse or cannot truly take time to care for ourselves and to rest. To restore, reflect and renew ourselves. Partly because of the social, economic and political realities tied to white supremacy, anti–Black racism and other deeply entrenched systems of oppression. At a systemic level, we do not have adequate ways for the collective to find and take rest. Our collective devotion (or, perhaps, addiction) to work is constantly bumping up against our ongoing effort to demand justice, when many of us feel like we are, in fact, engaged in the fight literally for our very lives.

Then, of course, there is the fact that, like me, you may have aunties and uncles and elder-mentors who are much like Angela's sister. For me, yes, it's absolutely my father and his elder sisters who have just now, later in life, begun to care for themselves in ways that as children of the Jim Crow South was denied to them. Or, perhaps, most people in your life, like you, are overwhelmed by the stress and pressure they face. So, maybe, like most of us, you have not really seen or been a witness to what a healthy and robust practice of self-care, one that might, in fact, be radical and collective in nature, looks like. You may not have seen most people in your life practice it.

Then again, perhaps, self-care looks far different than the way we have been conditioned to see it. Perhaps you have gotten so far away from your people and who you belong to that you cannot see sweet, simple, communal self-care right under your nose. Maybe you don't recognize that your uncle's visits to the barber shop where his face lights up and he laughs out loud and banters with the elder barbers, the younger ones, and the other patrons for hours even after they are shaved and cut is self-care. Or, perhaps you don't realize that the solace your grandfather finds out back in the free-standing garage blasting Miles and Coltrane or Isaac Hayes' *Hot Buttered Soul* while he tinkers on his Cadillac or cuts and stains pieces of wood for his most recent art project is self-care. Or then maybe you ignored the fact that his trips with a few buddies down to the river to fish on the third Friday of every month after meeting up for a sausage, egg and cheese biscuit and coffee at Bojangles is a form of self-care. (These brothers do NOT drink Starbucks, okay.) Or, maybe, like the "educated" sister who comes home to get the family quilt she sees as fine folk art to be framed and mounted on the wall in her home that she shares with her standoffish and aloof husband who absolutely no one likes in Walker's "Ordinary Things," you might be too damn full of yourself and your notions of what parts of Black culture are valuable to see which ones you should actually stop and recognize, you know—to see how restorative it is for your mother to kneel on the back deck with rich soil all over her hands humming church hymns as she repots flowers and sows seeds for baby tomatoes, greens, basil, and oregano for your auntie, mama or meemaw is self-care. Or maybe you have been too busy, running, running, running, being self-important, people pleasing, to stop and notice how simply restorative it feels for your elder cousins, including the play ones and the ones twice or three times removed, to sit on the front porch in rocking chairs overlooking the front lawn and the pebbled country road or on the stoop, with the neighborhood kids sitting beneath them staggered down the concrete stairs, laughing out loud and touching one another intermittently in absolute and utter glee as they recall some crazy stunt their twenty-year-old selves pulled off without ever getting caught by grandma and granddaddy. Yes, maybe it takes a shift in perspective to fully understand that these gatherings, these convenings, these spontaneous moments of joy and pleasure that are free and easy like Sunday morning, that are unplanned, feed us. That they restore us. That they, in fact, offer us the chance to be well, to practice self-care without even trying. Maybe it is hard for you, for us, all of us to fully recognize and appreciate these deep connections of love and support as self-care because they do not look like self-care that is focused solely on pampering and indulgence.

If that is the case, if you struggle to see the value in your people gathered together in simple ways to feed one another, then, perhaps, like so many of us, you have been holding onto what BLM activist and change agent Alicia Garza describes as "one of the biggest misconceptions about self-care, [which] is that self-care is for white people who are rich or wealthy. That self-care has to involve buying something to make you feel better." Maybe you have "bought" into the idea that you have to be able to go get a massage at a high-end spa or take a twenty-dollar-per-session yoga class in some cold, unwelcoming yoga studio where you are one of two Black folks. You may just be operating under the "huge misconception that if you can't afford to do that that you also are not able to take care of yourself."

Seeing self-care that way reflects the way that the concept of it, the practices of it have "been really bastardized." Bastardized as Tricia Hersey of The Nap Ministry observes, where "there's a stigma around caring for yourself. Unless it's attached to capitalism, then it's okay. You can pay $200 for a facial, and then you're taking care of yourself. Bastardized, appropriated and commercialized in that it is marketed and promoted today in a way that self-care feels out-of-reach and inaccessible rather than being empowering and focused on attending to our individual and collective own health and emotional needs."[1]

So, then what do we mean when we speak of a self-care practice? What does that look like exactly? According to Alicia Garza, one of the three founders of Black Lives Matter and head of Black Futures Lab, "what self-care actually means is having a practice of putting yourself in front in a world that doesn't encourage us [as Black people] to be alive, to stay alive, to take care of ourselves, to feel okay about stepping back or stepping aside so that we can nourish ourselves [in order] to be in this world another day."[2] According to Azania Heyward-James, a member the 2020 Amplify and Activate Summit Self-Care panel who advises Congress on matters of public health, self-care means recognizing your need to be seen and to allow others to actually see and support you and your worth as a fellow human being.[3] As Anana H. Parris, founder of SisterCare Alliance and long-time social justice organizer and advocate, outlines in her groundbreaking work *Self Care Matters: A Revolutionary's Approach*, self-care means making sure that your critical needs are met. That you consider the ways you can fully meet your own needs before constantly moving to take care of the needs of everyone else. By critical needs, Parris is speaking to being intentional and strategic about the ways we take care of what we need in these areas or aspects of our life: spiritual/emotional, economic, artistic, physical, educational, and social. Self-care means coming to a place where you understand that you must meet these critical needs if you intend to be well, to flourish, to survive, and to be resilient as we co-create a world that we imagine and as you face life's challenges.[4]

Garza's insights, and Parris' comprehensive strategic self-care framework approach reflect the fact that our self-care is part of the

Black radical tradition. This tradition is reflected in the declaration of feminist Audre Lorde who asserted that "caring for myself is not self-indulgence, it is self-preservation, and that is an act of political warfare." This declaration is, as Garza explains, rooted in Lorde's understanding that "we, [as Black people] weren't ever meant to survive" what Angela Davis explicitly names as "the most unimaginable forms of violence, including slavery, colonization and torture, that Black people all over the world have been subjected to."[5] In fact, Lorde's declaration shows us that the roots of self-care are radical and deeply tied to our efforts to create change in the world. Or put another way, "Audre Lorde's words in 1988 and now today are a rally cry for liberation." Her words, then and now, invite us to consider where our power lies and how we might use it in service of our well-being and our values. The idea that she—a Black, queer woman—had the right to claim space, identity and bodily autonomy in a world that was hostile to her very existence was truly revolutionary. For Lorde, self-care wasn't a measurement of social equality; it was an insistence that she mattered and was worthy of care. Self-care, as she saw it, is an act of resistance. To care for oneself—to rest, recover, and restore—was (and still is) essential to doing the hard work of social change. Practicing self-care, by insisting that our bodies belong to us, choosing to rest in this way disrupts capitalism, pushes back against white supremacy and other systems of oppression and forms of discrimination that work to cause us dis-ease.

In fact, caring for ourselves, practicing self-care and insisting that our bodies belong to us as Lorde declares is actually work that is absolutely part of our Black radical tradition, one that declares that holistic health care is not a luxury, but rather an act of resilience, survival and disobedience—a necessity.[6] However, we have "stripped away its radical political roots by commercializing of self-care that is depicted as personal responsibility, underscored by concepts of productivity, self-worth, and deservingness as defined by a capitalist market. The core concept—that rest is an essential part of resisting against oppression and fighting for social change—gets lost. This neutralization of self-care as a tool of political warfare is not an accident." When self-care is framed as little more than "me time," "collective survival becomes an individual responsibility. And that's a problem. It makes it much harder for people who experience multiple systems of oppression to care for themselves without community support. Framing self-care as a simplistic replacement for integrated systems of social care, takes governments and organizations off the hook for a greater responsibility for the wellness and healthy functioning of communities. Shifting responsibility for well-being onto already vulnerable people is a strategy of divide and conquer." It weakens the power of the collective, and the moments we spend together caring for one another. It weakens the power of how we gather to find joy and comfort, solace and security with one another. It ignores the moments we share over kitchen tables, in barber shops and beauty salons, on porch swings, in church pews, at HBCU homecomings and over communal plates of *Theibbu Jenn.*

Self-care is also about choices, ones that contribute to the well-being of others, ones that by their collective nature might be seen as radical and revolutionary. It is also about making choices that are not always easy. Ones that allow you to put yourself first in the context of existing in a thriving and nurturing community of care. Doing so sometimes means refusing to do what no longer serves you. And, when you do decide, when you make the choice that you aren't doing it anymore, emptying your cup at your own expense, then you, hopefully, will commit to a self-care practice, a life that will sustain you and your well-being. And, the well-being of others.

As Lorde's declaration suggests, and as the work being done by Anana H. Parris and other women implies, self-care, in fact, is directly tied to our activism and our fight for racial and social justice. Efforts that are deeply tied to the collective, to the communal, to a clear understanding that we are, in fact, interconnected. Put another way, self-care is collective in nature. Collective self-care requires us to be humble when we are in need so that we are willing to reach out to our community, those with whom we are in a relationship, for help. At the same time, collective self-care requires those of us who can give to have the generosity of spirit and willingness to do so, to meet a call for help with compassion, grace and love. As Alicia

Garza offers, collective care or radical self-care means being intentional about how we incorporate radical self-care into our organizations and communities.

For example, Garza explains that "at the Black Futures Lab before [we] start [our] meetings [by] ask[ing] each other how are you doing, what is something amazing that happened to you this week and what is something that's causing you anxiety; what's something that disappointed you. [We] move through different questions to check in because we're so used to having to leave our authentic selves outside of our workplace to be able to cover up any pain or grief or rage or happiness or elation that we're experiencing just to get the job done." And, Garza acknowledges that talking about radical self-care, talking about their feelings may be off-putting to some when there is work to be done. Yet, while agreeing that we do have lots of work to do, Garza believes, in the spirit of her predecessors and elders, Davis, Jordan and Lorde, that "sometimes the work can't move unless we allow people in their three dimensions to be present."

Not practicing collective self-care adversely impacts us individually and those we are in relationships with, our families, our communities, our organizations. Unfortunately, as individuals, far too many of us only learn about the value of self-care when we crash and burn, when our cups are empty and crash to the floor, breaking into small pieces that have us down on the floor sobbing over the shards as we try to clean them up before someone comes in and cuts their feet. We end up in the hospital with chest pains thinking we are having a heart attack when we are only twenty-one years old. Or at the doctor's office or the pharmacy because our skin has broken out in an uncontrollable rash on our first "real" job, or as we pursue a graduate degree right out of undergrad. Or we have unbearable migraines that make doing virtually everything impossible in our first administrative position while we raise our children and manage our households. Or our hair is falling out in what feels like lumps, clumps and patches. We end up with high blood pressure, scared shitless that we will not "sing all the songs we were meant to sing in this lifetime."[7] We end up unable to get up and go because we are stricken by debilitating depression. We burn out and find ourselves barely able to meet our obligations and responsibilities. We find ourselves feeling a fatigue that goes down to our bones that no amount of sleep seems to fix. We find ourselves snapping at and breaking off people who mean us no harm but our fuses are short and our patience is virtually non-existent. We find ourselves erupting in tears unexpectedly and wondering, "What the hell am I crying about?" We find ourselves curled up in a ball on the couch binging on Netflix and not-so-good-for-us foods. Over and over and over and over again. We find ourselves disinterested in others, in staying in relationships, in enjoying the company of those we love and adore. When it truly feels like we are losing our ever-loving minds. Yes, often, we drop the empty cup and find it virtually beyond repair before we recognize how much we have not done to care for ourselves. Often we "hit the ground" before we realize the value of self-care. Those are unfortunately the moments that eventually allow us to fully see that we must reconsider how we treat ourselves, our bodies, our minds, and our spirits if we, in fact, intend to do the important work that must be done to create and flourish in the world we imagine. And, when you don't manage your cup. When you don't recognize that self-care does indeed matter. When you fail to have your critical needs met over and over and over again.

And, our failure to practice radical self-care collectively means that—based on Garza's observations during her twenty-plus years doing social justice work—institutions, movements, and organizations crumble because we haven't prioritized collective care. What it means to build radically few relationships with each other and with ourselves. As she explains, "if we study who [and] where we've come from what we know is that the government has created programs to create chaos and discord inside of organizations that have the potential to really change the status quo. They created government programs [like] Cointelpro [that] were deliberately designed to infiltrate organizations and to play on their strongest weaknesses." Weaknesses that are exacerbated when we don't practice collective and radical self-care. Which results in our communities not having the institutions we need to help us collectively be "healthy and whole." Not practicing self-care collectively means not having "the ability to move our communities in a direction that is hopefully towards freedom because our communities won't trust each other and we won't trust ourselves. And fundamentally we will lose the ability to not just build power but to transform it." Not practicing and investing time and energy, making and keeping a commitment to collective self-care, as elder foremother Angela Davis tells us, hurts our movement work. In addition to reminding us that "anyone interested in making change in the world also has to learn how to take care of herself, himself, theirselves," Davis reminds us that "for a long time, activists did not necessarily think that it [was important] to take care of themselves in terms of what they eat, in terms of mental self-care, corporeal self-care, spiritual self-care." Although there were some people of that era like "one of the members of the party, Erica Huggins, who began to practice yoga and meditation in the seventies and encouraged many people including Huey Newton and Bobby Seale, founders of the Black Panther Party for Self-Defense to join that practice." However, as Davis recalls, they only "did a little bit of it." And, she knows now, that "the movement would have been very different had [they] understood the importance of that kind of self-care." And, by different she means that, in spite of the government intervention that Garza names explicitly, the movement and its members may have fared better, at least in terms of their spiritual, mental, physical and emotional well-being, even while being directly and constantly attacked by the powers that be. Taking such important lessons from and embracing the wisdom of our heroes like Davis will allow us to pour from our reserves rather than an empty cup.

Following Davis' advice ultimately allows us to develop greater resilience, which, as Julie Lusk explains in *Yoga Nidra for Complete Relaxation and Stress Relief*, is the ability to withstand stress, rise above it, and bounce back stronger than ever (Lusk 37). On both an individual and collective level, self-care allows us to sustain ourselves. To survive, to thrive, to flourish. According to Dr. Gail Parker, "resilience is our ability to remain flexible and to adapt to situations and circumstances, as required. It is essential for recovery from life's inevitable hard knocks. Resilience allows us to bounce back from stressful and traumatic experiences, [including those related to race].

Being resilient involves being able to tune in to the hidden energy that hides inside each betrayal, loss, heartbreak, and disillusionment we experience. It keeps us from getting stuck in suffering and allows us to use the pain of ethnic and race-based stress and trauma as catalysts for growth" (179). It allows us to continue to engage in the work that serves the collective in ways that are healthy with all of our critical needs met.

Practicing self-care and feeding our capacity for resilience is absolutely about liberation. At the end of the day, it is about choosing freedom. The freedom to honor and care for ourselves, individually and collectively, unapologetically. But, it is, be very clear, about making choices, a series of them, over and over and over again, for yourself. And, with the collective—your family, your friends, your communities of care. Of course, having a full and robust cup of a hot beverage along with a full pot of it that we pour our cup from that we might at some point share with others is about our capacity to recognize the need to care for ourselves without guilt or apology and our capacity to be connected to others in community doing the same and supporting us in ways that make self-care possible. Making sure, as we have always done, that "No One Cries Alone." Reminding one another, as we have always done, that we will be "Fine Again." Reassuring each other, as we always have, that we will be "All right."[8]

Chapter XIII

#YogaHeals

Being at Home in Our Own Bodies

"We arrive at our mats with devalued bodies" (Gates 181) that have experienced varying degrees of race-based stress injury and racial trauma. And, with broken, grief-stricken hearts and deeply wounded spirits. In part, because we have heard the cries of George Floyd and Eric Gardner. The cry, "I Can't Breathe" continues to haunt many of us. Their murders are a cogent example of how expendable Black lives still seem to be in our society, one where we still remain fearful (terrified, actually) of dealing with the police or white vigilante violence at the hands of men named Travis and nicknamed Roddie (hear my sneer here, please), as in the case of Ahmaud Marquez Arbery. And, as noted in earlier chapters, it is the pain and grief associated with traumatic deaths like theirs and the fear and anxiety that we experience in our lives as Black people that have such deleterious effects on our health and well-being. On our capacity to flourish and thrive. On our capacity to love and value ourselves without apology. On our ability to dream big dreams and imagine magnificent futures. On our capacity to feel grounded, rooted and supported. Our capacity to, at a really basic level, feel safe, secure and a sense of belonging. Our capacity, yes, to breathe.

However, yoga can be a source of healing and restoration; it can help us develop a greater sense of well-being. Yoga is a powerful and effective method for stilling the mind, healing and restoring the body, and awakening the spirit (Lusk 10). As Bessel van der Kolk offers in his seminal work *The Body Keeps the Score*, "yoga offers us a vehicle for noticing and befriending the sensations in our bodies, which can produce profound changes in both mind and body that can lead to healing from trauma."[1] Our healing must be embodied. Yoga allows for an embodied healing. Yoga is an embodied practice.

As a contemplative practice, yoga allows us to deepen our awareness, including our self-awareness as well as our bodily and emotional awareness. Yoga offers us a practice where we can break through "the layers of falsehood, the sense of disconnection" and "experience the power of connection" (Gates 181). Through yoga, we can more deeply experience our connection to and communion with spirit, with one another, and with our authentic selves. Yoga is a practice that can contribute to us restoring our connection with SOUL, the transformative healing resource that reflects longstanding cultural sensibilities of the African Diaspora and that supports our capacity to be loving, courageous and connected to spirit so that we can practice self-care, experience well-being and be resilient and resistant. In that vein, yoga is a contemplative practice that helps us restore said connections, and that when done with SOUL offers us the space we need to "disentangle dehumanizing and fragmented ideas of [our] true selves individually and communally."[2] And, when done with SOUL, yoga can offer us the space to affirm our "communal and transcendent identit[ies] that extend beyond the masks so many of us create and wear in the service of survival, coping, adaptation, and to be palatable and 'acceptable' to the world." Put another way, yoga with SOUL can be a contemplative practice where we are able to let down our defenses so that we are able to be vulnerable, surrender, let go and open up. So we can let go of the trapped and blocked physical and emotional and spiritual energies that no longer serve us. So we can make room for more SOUL, more joy, ease and peace of mind.

But, I often have Black folks balk and tell me that yoga isn't for them. Or they don't quite understand why I insist on it being integral to the work we do, why my husband and I include yoga in every healing-centered experience we offer. I know that in many ways this resistance occurs because yoga feels and is presented in a way that is not inclusive in most places around the country. And, let's be clear, as warm and fuzzy as yoga might appear on magazine covers at Whole Foods or Trader Joe's, there are far too many yoga spaces that have very cold (read: frigid), unyielding, tight, constricted energy that does not feel warm or welcoming to our SOUL. Places where yoga is fitness—just a physical practice that feeds egos as folks literally and figuratively contort themselves to standing on their heads. And, while there ain't nothing wrong with a headstand, there is much more to yoga than how well you stand on your head.

In fact, like everything else in this world, Covid-19 and the summer of 2020's racial reckoning forced us to reconsider how we practice yoga. The year of 2020 pushed folks in the yoga community (both BIPOC and white) to begin to address the ways in which the yoga "community" perpetuates, maintains and contributes to white supremacy. How the true meaning, purpose and cultural roots and history of yoga have gotten whitewashed as the practice has become commodified and sold at prices that often make it inaccessible to many of us, making it what some now call the "wellness" or "yoga industrial complex" (which is meant to evoke feelings you might have when you hear the term "prison industrial complex"). Some folks are focused on confronting the ways in which anti-blackness and white supremacy play out in yoga communities. And, others have been investing their time and energy and emotional labor on exclusively holding restorative and healing community spaces for Black folks as well as Indigenous people of color. Both strands or approaches are necessary as Black folks and other people of color need opportunities for healing and restoration that are free from the energies of white guilt, white fragility and white privilege. That said, the other strand offers white folks the space they need to do the work they must do— the work to dismantle the system that has benefited them most. It has been exciting, fulfilling, and quite powerful to see these efforts offered since, really, around the time we saw George Floyd breathe his last breath while he cried out for his fucking mother. And, as the streets filled with protestors of all races who decided we ain't doing this insane, violent, anti–Black, anti-immigrant, white supremacist racist ass shit no more. In the yoga world, that's what I'm calling it. For healing artists and teachers, this work, the work of unpacking the racial reckoning in a way that centered Blackness included the seven-session series the State of Union Yoga organized by J. Miles and Shankari Goldstein, and the Hotter than July program by Jasmine Hines, and the dope ass Black women of Amplify and Activate. In some spaces, those that welcomed white people to sit with BIPOC folks explored the question of how those of us who practice yoga and its eight limbs might hold more welcoming spaces, ones that consider racial justice and truly reflect of the tenets of the sutras, including the ahimsa, the yama that calls on us to do no harm.[3]

However, when Eddy and I have the chance to explain why yoga should be a part of the work that we do, we tell folks we are invested in holding space for Black people to experience healing and restoration so that they can deepen their capacity for resilience and resistance. And, certainly, yoga contributes to our ability to do just that.

Another major reason we offer yoga is because it helped me manage my own dis-ease over much of the last fifteen years of my life. I left my beloved Chocolate City—Washington, D.C., where I moved after finishing my undergraduate degree at NC Central University, to relocate to Cincinnati in 2005 in order to begin a new chapter of my life. Leaving my favorite riverfront weeping willow tree, my extended community of friends and family as well as being even further away from my family in North Carolina left me feeling off balance, disconnected and uprooted in one of the nation's most segregated cities, with far less SOUL than Washington, D.C.

In search of so(u)lace, I went to yoga within the first year after my move. I found that practicing yoga brought me some degree of peace. It helped me get my footing, literally, and to ground myself in a city that did not fully resonate with me as an HBCU grad who started her career in spaces where being Black and educated was the norm rather than not. However, two years after moving to Cincinnati, I sought out SOUL at the only public HBCU in proximity to where I lived. I decided to work. Sadly, my yoga practice rapidly went on the back burner because my job required extremely long hours, an hour and a half commute each way and extensive travel. I loved working there; I loved my students. I felt that the work I was doing as I passionately served and fought for predominately first-generation, low-income Black students as their Ma Dean mattered. I knew I was making a difference every day. But, at some point, the stress became overwhelming, particularly after the game changed in 2008 after the economy tanked. In response, I was beginning to drink heavily and engage in other self-destructive behaviors to numb what I was feeling.

Eventually, I burnt out and my cup was very, very, very empty as I worked harder and harder to create ways we could support our Black, predominately first-generation students, who were disproportionately impacted by the consequences of the recession and meet the truly unrealistic metrics set by the state education authorities who some believe never cared much about the success of the institution (see civil rights case) or our students. And, this all happened as my professional responsibilities conflicted with my need to be one of my brother's caretakers after his catastrophic swimming accident, albeit temporarily. Ultimately, my own well-being and self-care suffered and I eventually hit rock bottom. It took hitting rock bottom for me to be aware of what was happening, what I was doing that fed my dis-ease and find my way back to the mat.

Like my father, my personal spiritual journey began when I was down, lying on my back, broken and unable to recover on my own anymore. Or, put another way, after a journey into THE darkness. It took being on the ground, broken and burnt out, to revisit how yoga might allow me to heal and to regain some degree of well-being. After losing my job, I had to get myself together. In addition to getting clean and sober, I had to restore my sense of personal value, confidence, courage and worth after experiencing the loss of a job that I truly loved and enjoyed doing in spite of being burnt out, not to mention becoming a problem drinker or alcoholic, something I had always insisted would NEVER happen to me.

When I eventually reconnected to my own yoga practice, I reveled in the fact that it gave me permission to be my authentic self again. Practicing yoga gave me a path to peace and serenity. It gave a place to rest after high-effort coping for years. It gave me a chance to lay my John Henry hammer down. And, it gave me a place to take off the burdens I had cloaked myself in like Harriet and Sojourner trying to save, I mean serve, my people. Yoga gave me room to surrender and submit to spirit. It gave me room to renew, settle, rest and heal. And, to nurture and sustain my connections with my authentic self and spirit. Put another way, yoga offered me so(u)lace.

Yet, at the same time, the space I needed to express my bumped and bruised authentic self, including the pervasive grief, hurt, fear and anger that I carried in my Black, female, working class, size sixteen, completely stressed out body, didn't always feel available to me, at least not at my studio, partly because I was typically the only Black person in my classes. And, having a Black teacher was completely out of the question.

Thus, I eventually came to the place where I realized that hitting rock bottom gave me the chance to see another way to hold space for Black people, particularly Black young people. I could start my own business so that I had the opportunity to be a yoga teacher who passionately, vigilantly and at times defiantly holds space for Black folks to take up all the space they need to heal and restore. That I could be a teacher, a guide, who is deeply invested in yoga that, as revered Black feminist Alice Walker offers, recognizes that "healing begins where the wound was made."[4] A wound for us that is rooted in the fact that we come to the mat in Black bodies that carry varying degrees of stress and trauma, including race-based stress injury and racial trauma. I teach yoga with the understanding that "healing means putting the heart, the courage and the energy back in our bodies with our own culture."[5]

So that is what I do. My husband Eddy and I develop and lead healing and restoration experiences that include practicing yoga with SOUL. I teach yoga in a way that celebrates and affirms the fact that we come to the mat filled with SOUL—with creativity, vitality and resourcefulness and much more in spite of being subjected to the brutalities of white supremacy, epistemic violence, anti–Black racism and other intersecting forms of oppression. I welcome Black folks to the mat knowing that they live in the world that is in fact toxic because their skin is like chocolate (chocolate). Thus, I teach yoga in a way that celebrates and nurtures my students as I remind them that they can indeed take up all the space they need and can with their bodies, voices and spirits. That they are indeed beautiful, valuable and magical as they put energy, heart and courage back into their bodies.

Seinabo Sey, who is a Swedish-Gambian singer, wrote "Breathe," which is an orchestral string-backed song about self-love and self-acceptance, while on her first visit to Dakar, Senegal.[6] Sey explains that "she felt at ease in Senegal, but couldn't quite pinpoint why until she realized that she loved it in Senegal because she didn't have to explain herself to people. She realized that as Black women, so much of our time is spent explaining obvious things about our culture or ourselves, when we would rather just be." In other words, in "Breathe" Seinabo Sey speaks of Senegal being a place where she can do just that—breathe. A place where she can express herself authentically as a Black woman. It is interesting that she ties her insistence that we breathe with her own journey to her authentic self. She adeptly ties our breathing beautifully to our capacity to be resilient and to see our own worth and value. She too connects our breathing to being able to move forward, ever, towards our collective future where are indeed magical, valuable and beautiful. Sey's insistence that we breathe reflects the importance of pranayama to our yoga practice because a pranayama allows us to release what no longer serves us and improves our connection to the life force, to others, to the energies that serve our best interest, to prana.

> *Breathe you gotta believe me*
> *It's gonna be all right*
> *Everything gonna be all right*
> *Remember to breathe*

Similarly, R&B artist Laylah Hathway, daughter of soul singer Donny Hathaway, reminds us of the power of breath.[7] Power that she claims offers us far more than any good luck charm we might cling to. In fact, it is the breath that will heal us, the breath that will anchor us, the breath that will restore our connections to our authentic selves, to spirit, to our well-being, even in a few short seconds. We only need to remember to breathe.

By practicing pranayama and reconnecting to our breath, we are able to restore our connection to our life force, spirit and divine energy. And restore our connection to SOUL. A pranayama practice also allows us to calm our fight-flight reflexes and trigger our parasympathetic nervous systems so that our bodies understand that they are indeed safe and secure. In fact, when I have asked the students I have worked with which contemplative practice resonated the most with them, they identified pranayama practice. As one student explains, I "learn[ed] to handle my breathing in different ways, which is something that I truly appreciate from this experience." Another states, "I did deep breathing practices that allowed me to be aware of my body and allowed me to ground and to center myself as I grappled with the wide range of feelings and emotions that I experienced during the trip." And, another has declared that "it is more than okay for me to stop and take a deep breath when necessary to relax or center myself," which he has indicated he continues to do as he juggles his academic and leadership responsibilities.

Pranayama practice is an important part of yoga; it is one of the limbs of yoga, along with asana and meditation. It is actually the fourth limb coming after asana, which is preceded by the yamas, the first limb, and niyamas, the second limb. Pranayama activates and regulates prana, fostering our awareness of our own body, other beings and the cosmos. Prana is energy, it is the vital life force; it is found in everyone and everything—people, air, all things in nature. It exists after we die. This concept is reflected in this culture when we understand the ongoing presence of reverence for ancestors. As well in cultures like the one I live in in Senegal, where nature is respected and revered and consulted as an integral component of one's notion of well-being and wellness. Prana is not the breath we breathe; instead, it rides on our breath. Within our bodies, prana can become blocked when we engage in harmful behavior or experience pain, trauma and stress. And, when prana gets blocked, we can experience physical discomfort, ailments and dis-ease. Yet, we can practice pranayama to restore balance and cleanse and release what no longer serves us.

We actually do pranayama each time we practice yoga asana, or the physical postures most of us associate with yoga, when we align our movements with breath and breathing when we enter, hold, and exit a pose. And, during a restorative yoga practice, we take great care to focus on our exhales being longer than our inhales in order to deepen our relaxation and foster restoration and resilience. However, we can practice pranayama without asana or posture sequence.

Pranayama, as T.K.V. Desikachar explains in *The Heart of Yoga: Developing a Personal Practice*, allows us to make space in the body so that prana can come in.[8]

Pranayama Practice

To practice, you can begin by finding your way to a comfortable seat on the floor, with your legs crossed or underneath your hips in hero pose. You may wish to elevate your hips on a blanket or give yourself support by sitting against the wall. You may also practice seated in a straight back chair that you find comfortable. And, there may be cases when coming down onto your back and lying down will facilitate an effective pranayama practice.

Begin simply by taking a deep inhale and sighing it out loud. Breath in through your nose and exhale out of your mouth—audibly so we can hear you exhale. Repeat that twice more, inhaling deeply and exhaling out loud. Don't be self-conscious about exhaling out loud for others to hear you. Part of our healing and our resistance is to remember that we are taking up space, unapologetically—in this case, with our breath.

Now, we will begin to deepen our breath. We will breathe using our nose with our mouths closed. Inhale and exhale. Inhale and exhale. Notice your belly and chest filling each time you inhale. And, notice them relax and release each time you exhale. Allow yourself to focus on your breath to quiet your mind and your thoughts as you continue to simply breath in and out, inhaling and exhaling. Allow yourself to do so for three cycles of three. Breathe in and breathe out a total of nine times, aware of the practice as sets of three. Try it again and do seven rounds. Try it again and do three rounds of seven. Notice your body, notice your mind, notice your energy. Be aware of how connecting to your breath intentionally makes you feel. It should feel relaxing, but it may take time for you to feel comfortable, so be patient with yourself.

Now, let's continue by deepening our breath. We will begin by inhaling to a count of four and exhaling to a count of four. Inhale 2, 3, 4. Exhale 2, 3, 4. Inhale 2, 3, 4. Exhale 2, 3, 4.

Inhale 2, 3, 4. Exhale 2, 3, 4.

You may increase the number of inhales and exhales over time, but for now, let's continue as we were, completing four more rounds of 1:1 breathing. This is the way you may be using your breath during an active vinyasa yoga practice, connecting your inhales and exhales to your asanas and movement. It is called four count, or 1:1 breathing. Yogic breathing, however, is slightly different. In yogic breathing, you pause slightly at the top of your inhale and at the bottom of your exhale. Inhaling, 2, 3, 4, pause; exhaling, 2, 3, 4, pause. Repeat.

You may want to combine your 1:1 breath or yogic breath with a mantra or internal chant with your breath. For example, you might repeat "let go," saying "let" silently on your inhale, and saying "go" silently on your exhale. Inhale "let." Exhale "go." Using the breath and a mantra can deepen your capacity to quiet your mind and experience greater relaxation and stillness.

This four count or 1:1 breath can be used during our asana practice, particularly in vinyasa flow. However, we typically use extended exhales during a restorative yoga practice. We do so because the extended exhales make it possible for our parasympathetic nervous system to allow us to relax.

We want to always be attentive to our breath during our yoga practice. But, when we speak of pranayama practice, we are speaking more specifically of focusing our attention on our breath. We are following our breath, being conscious of it, noticing the subtleties of it, paying attention to it, being mindful of it. Each time we breathe in and each time we breathe out. Keeping our attention on the places in the body where we feel or hear the breath. Or following the movement of our breath in our bodies. The inhalation from the center of your collarbone down through your ribcage to your diaphragm. Following your exhalation upward from your abdomen. Or noting the sensation of the breath entering and exiting your nostrils. Or noticing the sound when you constrict your throat, contracting your vocal chords in when we practice ujjayi breath.

Ujjayi/victorious breath and nadi shodhana/alternate nostril breathing are two additional forms of pranayama you can practice.

Ujjayi or throat breath consists of even exhales and inhales while creating a "hah" sound in the back of the throat. You will inhale and exhale as you constrict your throat so that you sound like the sea, or the *Star Wars* villain Darth Vader. To create the sound, we constrict our throat or contract the larynx slightly, narrowing the air passage. This produces a sound when we breathe. I really like this breath because it allows me to imagine the ocean with waves coming in and out. That is the sound I hear when I use ujjayi breath. I also appreciate the sound of it because it allows me to stay attentive and fully aware of my breath, thus keeping my mind from taking me off of my mat.

Try three rounds of ujjayi pranayama. Now, do it four more times being fully conscious, combining it with 1:1 breathing, so we inhale to a count of four and exhale to a count of four. As you can see, ujjayi is not a quiet breath. It makes a noise. That might make you uncomfortable. It should not. Like sighing out loud relieves stress, breathing this way is helpful as you seek to let go of what no longer serves you—your stress, your anxiety, your doubts, your fears, as you work to connect with yourself, your true self, the divine, the life force, others. Let me say it another way: it doesn't matter what other people think. Be comfortable taking up space on your mat, in the studio, in the world. Just as I have encouraged you to stretch out and let go, I'm telling you to breathe in and breathe out using ujjayi if that is what allows you to make the best of your practice and your life.

Nadi Shodhana/Alternate Nostril Breathing

Here again, you want to be in a comfortable seat.

Begin by lengthening your spine. Your head and spine should be upright.

Bend your left arm over your belly so that your right elbow can rest on your left forearm.

Bring your right hand up and hold the fingers in front of your face. Rest the index and middle fingers gently on the center of your eyebrows. Both fingers should be relaxed. Position your thumb next to the right nostril and the ring finger next to the left nostril. Your pinky finger should be comfortably folded.

Inhale, then close your left nostril with your ring finger and inhale though your right nostril. Unblock the left nostril and close your right nostril with your thumb. Exhale through your left nostril. Inhale through your left nostril.

Unblock your right nostril and close your left nostril with your ring finger. Exhale through the right nostril and inhale through the right nostril. Continue alternating between your left and right nostrils. Repeat this sequence seven times. Now, take a minute and bring your hands to your lap. Be aware if you feel as if one of your nostrils is blocked, or that air is not flowing easily.

Practice again. See if you can do so for five minutes for the best effect. You can set a timer on your phone (with the ringer off, of course) to let you know when you reach five minutes so that you can do this at your own pace and observe your breath.

Once you have practiced nadi shodhana/alternate nostril breathing for five minutes, you can bring your hands down and place them in your lap. Close your eyes and scan your body. See how the pranayama practice has left you feeling. Make a mental note of it, but don't get too focused on it. Just observe how you feel. Do you feel calm? Did you feel like your breaths were balanced, or did one side feel like it was carrying more or less air than the other? Or did you feel as if the air movement between your nostrils was balanced?

The left nostril carries more air when we are depressed or depleted. The left side of the body (thus the left nostril) is connected to the moon, femininity, passivity, receiving, nighttime, introversion, spiritual life and resting. The right nostril is more engaged when we feel or experience anxiety. It corresponds to the sympathetic, energizing branch of our automatic nervous system.

And we associate the right side of our body (thus the right nostril) with masculinity, activity, giving, daytime, extroversion, social life, partying.

We seek an equilibrium between our two sides, our masculine and feminine sides. And, this pranayama practice can help us do so. We can also use single nostril breathing to impact how we feel. If you need to be energized, use the right nostril. When you need to calm yourself, use your left nostril. Grief will often result in a prevailing left nostril. Noticing, being aware of these subtleties in our breath and emotional states, fosters our self-awareness as we pursue wellness and engage in self-care.

Restorative Yoga

While there are a variety of approaches to practicing yoga, we primarily practice restorative yoga as a contemplative practice. Restorative yoga, Dr. Gail Parker explains in her book *Restorative Yoga for Ethnic and Race-Based Stress and Trauma,* is "an ideal self-care strategy" that offers us opportunities for healing and restoration, that fosters our capacity for resilience and resistance. In her book, Parker explains that "restorative yoga is an important self-care strategy that supports physical, psychological, emotional and spiritual health. It is ideal when we feel depleted or overwhelmed or are recovering from an illness or physical or psychological injury. It offers physical revitalization and psychological renewal and fortifies us spiritually. It can be a buffer against secondary trauma and trauma in general, including race-based traumatic stress. It helps us self-regulate, restore resilience and establish physical and emotional balance" (39).

Amber Burke explains that a

restorative yoga practice is one that is comprised of poses in which the arrangement of your bones, the support of props (blocks, bolsters, blankets and eye pillows) and the gentle pressure of gravity work together to re-channel the breath. Every tissue in the body, from the soles of the feet to the crown of the head, can and should receive movement from the breath. Restorative yoga can be healing if the poses in the practice are pleasurable and you would like them to continue, and they allow the vibrations of the breath into previously unreached, blocked, constricted, closed and tightly-held places.[9]

Tightness and constriction are caused by stress and trauma (including racial trauma) when our fight-or-flight reflex is triggered and we feel constantly on guard. And, look—we all know that we are often on guard as we move in a world where it feels like we are not safe in our own skin.

One young man who spent time with us described his experience with restorative yoga this way:

> Restorative yoga was the first new method of healing introduced to me. On the first night I famously said "I'm not very bendy." By the end of the trip I had set up a permanent Legs Up the Wall in the living room. Now that I am back in the United States, I miss the moments we shared and the way my body felt after our yoga sessions. I was at peace in Senegal. My body did not ache; I did not have any stress in the world while I was there. I may go back to the same place but I will never return the same person. I have never felt more spiritually whole yet incomplete at the same time.

This brother truly captures why restorative yoga is integral to the work that we do.

Practicing restorative yoga allows us to release some of what no longer serves us, including the wounds of racial trauma. In this vein, restorative yoga practice allows us to engage in what Dr. Gail Parker refers to as low-effort coping, which is the opposite of the high-effort coping that can best be understood through the condition known as John Henryism, which reflects the strain and stress of seeking validation and acceptance in a culture that repeatedly tells Black people that we actually do not belong.[10] Further, a restorative yoga practice allows us to feel rooted, grounded and centered by being deeply and intentionally aware of the connection of our bodies to the earth, to the mat and other props as well as the sensations in our bodies. Grounding and rooting through yoga asana focused on the root chakra contributes to our sense of belonging that stress and trauma, including racial trauma, short-circuit. Restorative yoga also offers us stillness for extended stretches of time as we stay in each posture much longer than we might in an active or vinyasa yoga practice. This extensive stillness allows those of us who are typically constantly on the go, striving, being John or Johnetta Henry, operating underneath the masks we wear, to rest, renew and restore.

In a restorative yoga practice, we focus on stillness and being in poses for an extended amount of time. In those poses, you are fully supported, which means that you bring the floor to you and create support for yourself with props. Our materials include large pillows known as bolsters, blankets, blocks and our mats to create that sense of feeling safe and supported. And, there are never too many supports in a restorative class. In fact, I am deeply invested in making sure my students have access to two bolsters if possible and three or four blankets. You can use as many props as you like. Using an eye pillow can also help us to relax, be still and let go.

You can practice restorative yoga at home on your own or in a studio. You can find a pre-recorded restorative yoga practice on my website, www.diasporicsoul.com. There are also a number of organizations that offer live classes online for free or a reasonable price. I enjoy taking my yoga classes with Octavia who particularly appreciate that she is Black, female and Southern, and committed to helping us find peace in this world. Her approach resonates with me because we have some of the same experiences and sensibilities. And, of course, she has mad SOUL. Sanctuary in the City emerged in the summer of 2020 as another resource for practicing yoga online. They offer a variety of BIPOC only yoga practices that are free. I particularly enjoyed J. Miles' Breath is Key pranayama session on Saturdays. Like Octavia, I feel connected to him as my teacher; in fact, he actually reminds me of a college friend in many ways, including the things he enjoys like hip hop and his sense of humor. He too has SOUL, and for me that connection is important as I seek to find refuge and restore myself on a regular basis. Tracee Stanley, who just released her book *Radiant Rest*, and Michelle Cassandra Johnson, who just released her book *Finding Refuge*, are well-respected Black women teachers to learn from and practice with. I have also begun to take Kriya yoga classes with a teacher who really resonates with me, Keisha Battles founder of I Am Yoga in Charlotte. In fact, she and Candace Jennings also provide yoga teacher trainings. I have just completed my advanced 300-hour teacher training with them. Being in community with them and the other members of my cohorts has been a balm during these ongoing months of Covid-imposed separation and isolation. The community that I have with them warms my heart and SOUL. And, I am not saying I do not practice with non–BIPOC teachers.

But for now, I offer you a practice to try on your own, at your own pace, in your own space. Begin your practice by setting up your mat. Once your mat is rolled out and you have placed your props around it, including folded blankets, a bolster(s), yoga blocks and an eye pillow, stand at the top of your mat.

As we do with any yoga practice, you want to begin your yoga practice by connecting with your breath. Yoga is all about connection. Connection with our breath. Others. The divine. The sacred. Spirit. Your authentic self. You can do so either in a comfortable seated position on the mat or in tadasana, mountain pose. Both offer you room to connect to your breath and to be aware of your body's connection to the earth, which can allow you to feel rooted, centered and grounded.

Tadasana/Mountain Pose[11]*/Standing Pose*

Stand with your feet together or hip-width apart, whichever is more comfortable for you. Your legs are parallel. And, you may or may not have an ever so slight bend in your knees. Bring awareness to your feet. Press down through all four corners of your feet—inner and outer heels, inner and outer balls of your feet. Lengthen your torso and side body. Allow your tailbone to lengthen to the floor as your pelvis lifts toward your navel. Notice if your shoulders are relaxed, and move your shoulder blades down your back.

Your arms are extended with your palms facing your thighs and fingers toward the floor. Your chin is parallel to the floor. Your ears, shoulders, hips and ankles are aligned. From here, take a deep breath in and release it with a loud sigh. Take another deep breath in and exhale it audibly. Do this again with your eyes closed. Let go of all

191

that happened before you got here with your exhales. Repeat three more times. Notice the rise and fall of your hands as your belly rises and falls with each inhale and each exhale. Continue to be aware of your breath, as your belly fills with air. Begin to notice as your chest rises and falls as your breath moves in and out. Notice the rise of your belly and chest as you inhale. And, notice how they fall with each exhale. From here, begin to count your inhales and exhales, noticing if your exhales are a bit longer than your inhales. Work to make them equal.

Continue to breathe here, remaining aware of your inhales and your exhales. Now, bring your hands down to your belly. Continuing to breath here. Feel the rise and fall of your belly in your hands as you continue your 1:1 breathing. You may practice ujjayi breath as well by contracting your throat so you can hear your exhale much more audibly like the sound of "haa" when you blow on a mirror with your breath, or like the sound of the sea or Darth Vader. Allow yourself to remain in tadasana, mountain pose, for seven more breath cycles, inhaling seven more times, exhaling seven more times. Once you have reached your seventh exhale, you can prepare to set your intention.

Setting Your Intention/Sankalpa[12]

Relax and return to your natural breath. No need to count or control it. Before you continue your practice, you will set an intention. We often start a yoga practice by setting a specific intention for the class. You might understand an intention as a dedication. Or vow. Or resolve. Or a heartfelt prayer. You might dedicate this particular session to yourself, someone you love or something larger that you would like to see in the world. Or, you might simply commit this class to the sankalpa or vow you have set previously. A sankalpa is a broad vow or heartfelt prayer that can serve you extensively and be used during your yoga practices. Close your eyes. Take a few moments and set your intention or recall your sankalpa. Now that you have decided what you want to dedicate your practice to, you can continue. From here, reconnect to your yogic breath, inhaling and exhaling, as you prepare for uttasana, standing forward bend.

Uttasana/Standing Forward Bend

On your next inhale, raise your arms up over your head. Allow yourself to exhale with your hands extended towards the sky. On your next exhale, bring your hands back down to your sides. Inhale up, reaching for the sky. Exhale back down. Inhale up, reaching for the sky, stretching up, with your shoulders relaxed. Exhale down, bending at your hips and allowing your hands to reach to the ground. Hanging here for a minute, allow yourself to relax. To let go. Your hands may or may not touch the ground.

Your knees might be bent slightly, particularly if you have tight hamstrings. Just dangle here, continuing to breathe. On your next inhale, come up halfway to a flat back. Your hands may rest just above your knees. Exhale back down to the mat. Bring awareness to your core. Pull your navel in, contracting your abdomen with each exhale. Inhale back up to a flat back, hands resting on your thighs. Stay here inhaling and exhaling. Push your hips back. Exhale your torso and hands back toward the mat. Remain here, breathing. Remain here for three more breath cycles, relaxing a bit deeper with each exhale.

Tabletop/Hands and Knees

After your standing forward bend, you will want to find your way down onto your mat. To do so, on your next exhale, slightly bend your knees enough to allow you to bring your hands and knees flat to the mat. Once you are on your hands and knees, make sure that your palms are flat with your fingers spread wide. Your hands are shoulder-width apart. Lift out of your wrists so that you don't collapse into them, and allow the eyes of your elbows to face each other. Your knees are hip-width apart. And, your hips are stacked over your knees. Press the tops of your feet to the floor.

Your shoulder blades are firm against your back and spread away from your spine—don't round your shoulders forward. Engage your core, draw your navel in. Keep a neutral spine, and your tailbone is lengthened straight back. Keep your neck long, aligned with your spine, with the crown of your head forward. Your back will be flat like a tabletop. Gaze into the space in front of you. Bring awareness to your breath, inhaling 2, 3, 4 and exhaling 2, 3, 4. Stay here for three breath cycles. Once you are done, you can find your way to a comfortable seat on your mat. It is a good idea to sit on a folded blanket so that your hips are slightly elevated.

Child's Pose/Balasana/Forward Bend

Create a support of firm pillows, blankets, or a bolster lengthwise in front of you. Find your way back to tabletop, on hands and knees. Slide the bolster between your knees so that they are on either side of the support, your big toes touching. Sit back on your hips and, without lifting your hips, lay or fold your torso over the length of the support. Your head and torso will be supported on the bolster. Rest your forearms on the floor alongside the support, and turn your head to one side (or rest your forehead on the support—whatever is most comfortable). Let gravity pull the hips toward the earth as you extend your lower back and release the tailbone toward your heels. Halfway through the pose, turn your head to the other side as the body continues to settle into the pose. Hold this pose for 2–5 minutes on each side. When you are ready to come out of the pose, take 2–3 deep breaths and gently press both hands into the floor to lift up to seated on your heels. Once you are comfortable, return to your breath. Inhale deeply and exhale. Continue to focus on your breath, working to deepen your inhales and exhales, which should be twice as long as your inhales. Breathing this way signals to your parasympathetic nervous system that you are safe, that you do not have to fight or flight. When you are ready, after you exhale three more times, find your way up to a comfortable seated position.

Reclined Butterfly/Supta Baddha Konasana Backbend/Heart Opener

Bring your bolster or a set of blankets (three is typically ideal) behind your back with the short side aligned with your lower back. The lower edge of the blankets or bolster should come directly into contact with your buttocks to support the lower back. Bring the soles of your feet together and spread your knees apart, each knee supported by yoga blocks, blanket rolls, meditation cushions, or bolsters. From here, lie back on a bolster or your narrow stack of blankets, with your head supported on the bolster or an additional blanket. If you experience strain or lower back pain, consider placing another bolster or blocks behind your bolster so that it forms a ramp to support you. Also, check that your sacrum, your lower back, is flush with the bolster, because space between the two can create strain in your back. You might also enjoy an eye pillow and a blanket on top of you. Once you are settled, return to your breath, allowing your inhales and exhales to be deep and slow. Stay here for 7–10 minutes. You can extend to 12–15 minutes as you deepen your capacity for stillness. When you are finished, you can find your way up to a comfortable seated position. To come out of the pose, put the soles of your feet on the floor with knees bent and roll to your right side, coming into fetal position. Pause there and enjoy your breath before lifting yourself using the strength of your arms.

Legs Up the Wall/Inversion

Bring your mat to a place in the room near a wall so the short end of your mat is touching the wall and the length of your mat is facing back toward the center of the room. You may also want a block, bolster or blanket. After you are seated on your mat, bring your right shoulder, hip and thigh against a wall. Keep a bolster within reach, and exhale as you lower your back while swinging your legs up onto the wall. Press the soles of your feet into the wall, lift your hips, and slide the bolster underneath them. Extend your arms out to the sides or place them in cactus position (upper arms perpendicular to the torso, elbows bent at 90 degrees, palms facing up). If extra support is needed, place a small roll with a blanket under your neck to support and lengthen the cervical spine. You may also be more comfortable with a blanket underneath your shoulders and folded blankets under your lower arms and hands. And, of course, your eye pillow. You might also enjoy a block, bolster or blanket under your hips. When you are ready, after being in this pose for 7–10 minutes, find your way up to a comfortable seated position. You can exit this inversion by pressing the soles of your feet against the wall and lifting your hips to slide the bolster, blanket or block out from under you. Gently lower the pelvis to the floor. Roll to the right side, coming into a fetal position, pause, enjoy your breath, and use a hand to press yourself back up to a comfortable seated position.

Savasana/Corpse Pose

Savasana or corpse pose signals the end or "death" of a yoga practice. Seated on the floor with your legs slightly bent, slide a bolster or blanket roll beneath your knees and slowly lower the back, neck, then head onto the floor. Let the arms rest comfortably by your sides, palms facing up. To make this posture deeply restorative and to feel even more supported, I encourage you to prop your hands and arms with folded blankets and to consider rolling a blanket up to support your neck, or simply placing a folded blanket under your head like a pillow. This is also an optimal posture for using an eye pillow and to cover up with a blanket.

Savasana is also an ideal posture to practice yoga nidra in order to deepen your capacity for rest, relaxation and stress relief. Yoga nidra is a combination of "specialized relaxation exercises, breathing techniques, meditation and guided imagery [that] are utilized for becoming extremely relaxed and to replenish energy." Known as yogic sleep, yoga nidra allows us to let go of "every day tension" and "healing deep-seated stress" (7). At its best, at a deeper spiritual level, yoga nidra, as is the case with yoga in general, allows us to find our way home to our authentic selves; it offers us a "direct experience that our inner core is stress-free and that unshakable peace and joy really exist within rather than outside ourselves" (Lusk 8). You can use a pre-recorded nidra by Lusk or Stanley as you rest in savasana. In other contexts, you might also choose to devote a full yoga practice exclusively to a longer nidra practice as well as integrate yoga nidra for sleep.

Once you have all your props arranged so that you are comfortable, allow yourself to relax into the posture. And just bring awareness to your body's contact with the mat, the floor, the earth and to your breath. Being aware of your body and breath will allow you to calm your mind and settle into a deeper, more relaxing and restorative savasana. Ideally, you will be able to practice savasana for 15–20 minutes. However, as a beginner, 7–10 minutes may be more realistic for you.

After 7–10 minutes, you can begin to bring awareness back to your breath. Wiggle your toes and fingers. Perhaps, extend your arms overhead and stretch your whole body as if it is the first stretch of the day. You may open your eyes or keep them closed. When you are ready, roll onto your right side, coming into fetal position. Pause here, take 2–3 breaths, and gently press your hands into the floor to move back up to a comfortable seated position.

Once you have found your way back up to a comfortable seat where you feel supported, bring your hands toward your heart center in prayer position, bow your head slightly toward your heart. Take a moment to restate and reflect on your intention for your practice. And, silently express gratitude for the benefits of the practice to spirit as you understand it. You have completed a restorative yoga practice. Take your time getting up. Allow yourself to drink plenty of water and to stay relaxed. This is an ideal practice for the evening so that you can stay relaxed.

While some prefer to practice yoga without it, music is one way that we bring SOUL to our yoga practice. You will find a variety of music and ambient noise played in classes that you might take. However, as you begin to practice yoga on a more regular basis, you will develop a better sense of what songs or artists you find support your practice. Over time, you may develop a range of playlists that reflect various themes based on seasons, moon and astrological cycles or specific motivation or inspiration that you may find yourself needing. I have a standard playlist I use for my restorative practice that reflects the tone and energy I want to have in the space where I practice, which includes female vocalists like Laylah Hathaway, Maimouna Youssef, Erykah Badu and India Arie. When I do a more active practice, I use more energetic music and artists like Michael Franti, Janelle Monae, Sampa the Great and Kendrick Lamar. And, of course, you can always let your streaming service help you create a playlist that works for you. The options are endless.

As you consider ways to improve your self-care practice, restorative yoga is an ideal choice. You can start with a pranayama practice and then eventually try a restorative yoga practice. You can do so at home or at a local studio that feels welcoming and comfortable for you. Practicing yoga continues to keep me balanced and centered no matter where I am and what I am doing. You can practice pranayama and restore your connection to your breath anytime, anywhere. You can find stillness anywhere. You can take time to care for yourself anywhere.

CHAPTER XIV

#XEEX!

Resistance Is Healing

Robin D. Kelley, scholar and author of *The Black Radical Tradition*, reminds us that "resistance is our heritage," and that "resistance is our healing." He explains that "through collective struggle, we alter our circumstances." Resistance, he offers, altering our circumstances, means "containing, escaping, or possibly eviscerating the source(s) of our trauma." Yet, he cautions us that "managing trauma does not require dismantling structural racism," which ultimately is at the root of much of our trauma. Therefore, at the end of the day, resistance fundamentally means challenging institutions that interrupt and undermine our individual and collective abilities to heal and continue to injure us and do us harm, that are the sources of our stress and trauma. Altering our circumstances, our healing, in this regard, includes "recovering our bodies that carry generations of trauma; reclaiming and redeeming our dead; and making ourselves whole."[1] Put another way, this means that our healing can include providing healing and restoration, recovery for our people, our ancestors and our elders and ourselves, who, as Black people, have had our bodies, individually and collectively, sold, exchanged, violated, vulgarized, undervalued, brutalized, negated and neglected over and over again. Healing means finding our way back to feeling and being whole and well, able to feel joy and peace, and experience ease, instead of feeling broke, broken and broke down. This includes recognizing our capacity to heal inter-generationally and give our ancestors the gifts of reclamation and restoration. Yes, indeed, resistance is absolutely healing. Resistance, altering our circumstances, has been and continues to be our heritage, our history and our legacy.

199

Resistance, altering our circumstances, is our legacy, as Patrisse Cullors, Black Lives Matter co-founder, reminds us when she states that "we're a part of a long legacy of organizers and human rights workers and civil rights workers [who] have tried to change and pushed for change for the material conditions of Black people." As Charlene Carruthers, a Black, queer, feminist organizer who is a founding member of Black Youth Project 100 (BYP100) reminds us that at "this moment—both the resistance and what people are resisting to—is a part of a long history in this country." Echoing Kelley and Cullors, Carruthers reminds us that "this moment [reflects] the work that our [elders] and ancestors did first and we are building on that."[2] Resistance is our heritage. Resistance is our healing.

Shawn Ginwright offers in his essay "Radically Healing Black Lives: A Love Note to Justice" that altering our circumstances, engaging in resistance and subsequently healing, means "disrupting and rejecting hegemonic notions to justice, particularly in regards to race." It means confronting and interrogating injustice. Disruption looks like direct action, protesting, organizing and movement building. It looks like members of the Movement for Black Lives bringing the BART transit system to a halt in December 2014 by forming a human chain in a train car and locking themselves to the BART platform in West Oakland. Disruption, resistance, in this way, looks like them using and reclaiming their bodies to assert power and control and authority over their own well-being and to make it explicitly clear that the murder and over-policing of Black people is not acceptable.

Resistance looks like Bree Newsome using her body to assert power and control over our collective well-being when she courageously removed the Confederate flag at the South Carolina State House following the massacre of nine congregants at Mother Emmanuel church in Charleston in June 2015. Like her California peers, Newsome disrupted injustice when she (with the support of a community of organizers) scaled a 30-foot flagpole and took the flag down.[3] And, while Newsome's bold action might be perceived to be in direct response to the Charleston massacre, in actuality, as Newsome herself explains, "the massacre in Charleston brought a refocus on the flag."[4]

Newsome's resistance was healing because her "ancestors, [whose names she knows,] were enslaved in South Carolina." While done on behalf of the collective, this action was deeply personal for Newsome, as a native of South Carolina, who grew up with her grandmother, who was raised in Greenville and told Newsome stories about "seeing the Ku Klux Klan beat her neighbor and [white violence] like that." Through this act of resistance, this direct action, Newsome offers her family, her ancestors, and all of our ancestors, redemption, restoration and healing. In light of what is "represented by the Confederate flag," Newsome resisted the state and the institutions that did nothing to protect her grandmother, her grandmother's neighbors, her ancestors, our grandmothers and our grandfathers, our ancestors, from the ever-present fear and threat of racial terror and violence. In fighting back, she reclaimed and restored for them the sense of power they may have felt they never had living in Jim Crow America, a place that explicitly sanctioned the terror and violence that her grandmother recalled. By acting, Newsome reclaimed and restored for them and us our humanity, our right to dignity, agency and self-respect. For those in deep shock, grief and mourning after the massacre, Newsome took action against that same state and the same institutions that allowed a young white male terrorist to exist with hate festering in his heart and easy access to firearms. Done "very much in the spirit of the history of civil disobedience and the history of the civil rights movement in this country, with that historical awareness," Newsome's direct action, her act of resistance, was part of our legacy. Pulling down the Confederate flag was healing because she took down a racist symbol, that "was raised in 1961 really as a statement against the civil rights movement that was going on at the time." A flag designed (like those Confederate statues in Raleigh and Richmond and across the country) to put us in our place, to tell us to be docile and subservient. Pulling down the flag allowed us to heal by saying to our country that the state-sanctioned murders of Black people that happen far too often and far too regularly are not acceptable. Her action allowed all of us, our ancestors, our elders, us, to directly reject a symbol of white supremacy and what it was designed to do. By doing so in a communal fashion with a collective of organizers and activists having her back, Newsome offered healing to those heartbroken after the murder while simultaneously rejecting the sickening nature of a lone gunman pretending to be well-intended, pretending to come to worship, violently betraying the love, compassion and generosity of those who he murdered and all who had ever worshiped there, all who had hoped we had arrived at a different moment in our national story. A healing that, coexisting with Obama's stirring eulogy, also offered us a sense of hope, a sense of confidence, a sense of victory, a symbol of courage and a radiant light that might drive out fear and some of the grief we were experiencing. Removing the flag that day put Newsome in "a kind of new modern civil rights movement going on" that was responding unapologetically to an "attack on a Black leader in" what has consistently been the most sacred (and safest) of Black spaces, "a church." Doing so was healing for all of us because we could be proud that we, through Bree, did not sit and take it, that we, through Bree, had spoken up and pushed back against the massacre, against racism, against white supremacy, against the state-sanctioned murder of Black people. Newsome's resistance was healing; it altered the circumstances, as she forced the state and the nation to continue examining how we might begin dismantling the vestiges of white supremacy, both its symbols and the pernicious and ingrained institutional policies and practices.

In an interview with NC–based scholar-activist Ajamu Amiri Dillahunt, Newsome explains that we seem to misunderstand what it means to act, to be an activist, to engage in resistance. In fact, she explains that "she went from tweeting to protesting and marching after the acquittal of George Zimmerman for murdering Florida teenager Trayvon Martin and the 2013 ruling on voting rights by the Supreme Court." It is worth considering Newsome's wisdom as we all continue to explore and reconsider how we will contribute to the liberation, the well-being and quality of life for Black people. Newsome explains that our long-term, sustained resistance might look like "everyone ... do[ing] what they're already doing but applying a new consciousness to their actions."

This means that "we need teachers who love our students in the classrooms who understand the need to dismantle the school-to-prison pipeline." We need physicians and other medical professionals, like Philadelphia-based physician Dr. Ala Stanford and her colleagues, who are aware of how racism and implicit bias operates in medicine who can commit to dismantling racism in health care systems. Stanford created the Black Doctors COVID-19 Consortium and sent mobile test units into neighborhoods in Philadelphia to serve people living in communities that were experiencing disturbingly disproportionate rates of coronavirus infections without access to affordable testing and much needed medical care. We need legal minds, like those involved with recent cases of George Floyd and Breonna Taylor, who can help us mount challenges in the court systems and craft new revolutionary policy ideas, like those considered across the nation this summer, in some cases under the clarion calls of "no justice; no peace" and "defund the police." We need conscious social workers and urban planners, like my cousin Kristen Jeffers, who can imagine, design and build institutions that allow communities to flourish with funds redirected from the police and prison abolishment. And, of course, yes, "we need folks who are ready to protest, take to the streets and shut it down when needed. We need all hands on deck and we need everyone to recognize what is at stake in this moment."

Having all hands on deck includes using our social capital and connections to leverage work opportunities for our peers the way a member of the 2019 Xavier University racial healing experience cohort has done. In the midst of budget cuts and wavering and inconsistent institutional support of Xavier University's Stained Glass Initiative (SGI) racial healing, restoration and justice mission, Ishan was able to secure youth employment positions to hire additional staff as a result of his long-standing relationship and work history with the Cincinnati Recreation Commission. So, now, not only does Ishan have the chance to directly contribute to the SGI's racial healing efforts, he also extended himself for the well-being of others by making similar opportunities available to others who, during this challenging period, may not have found employment otherwise, much less the chance to work in a role that contributes in some way to the healing and restoration of Black people.

Resistance might also look like the sisters and brothers who I referenced previously building institutions and creating spaces for Black folks to experience healing and restoration, including programs and classes that are discounted or free during the economic challenges. For example, there are the ongoing daily BIPOC–only classes being offered by Sanctuary in the City, or the Stopping the Clock Remembrance (Grief) Ritual that Eddy and I offered in collaboration with the Bryant Educational Leadership Group (BELG), Chez Alpha Books (Dakar) and Xavier University's Stained Glass Initiative (SGI) to hold space for Black folks experiencing grief and loss due to Covid-19 and (what was at the time) the inhumane murder of George Floyd. Resistance, altering our circumstances, contributing to our collective well-being, looks like folks like our friend and Newark-based educator Christina and Columbus-based social worker and therapist Megan Torres using their networks and social media to consistently and repeatedly organize mutual aid efforts for their communities as folks continue to struggle with hunger and unemployment.[5]

Clearly, there are many ways we can directly be engaged in improving the well-being of Black people. With humility and with our egos in check. With a commitment to the collective, a willingness to engage others "already doing similar work and ... joining up with them so as not to replicate work that's already being done."

At this moment, we need all hands on deck as we grapple with the fact that in the years since Newsome removed the flag, "we [continue to be confronted] with public images of Black death and the flagrant violence of oppressive systems that obstruct justice and our current systems [still] promise complex, compounded and nearly constant trauma for Black people and ensure that we have little resources, space, time or energy to heal and little agency to protect ourselves and our loved ones from facing the same."[6] At this moment, our resistance must also include a commitment to healing justice, which is "an active intervention in which we transform the lived experience of Blackness in our world," according to Prentis Hemphill, former Healing Justice Director at Black Lives Matter Global Network and movement facilitator, Somatics teacher and practitioner, and writer who lives and works at the convergence of healing, individual and collective transformation, and political organizing, who spent many years working with powerful movements and organizations.[7] Healing justice includes identifying ways we can use a range of modalities to "holistically respond to and intervene on generational trauma and violence, and to bring collective practices that can impact and transform the consequences of oppression on our bodies, hearts, minds and spirits." This also means that we recognize that care, self and collective, communal care, conscious emotional labor and resilience are critical to our capacity to sustain ourselves and our well-being. We need space to tap into our bodies as healing resources rather than only as weapons in the fight for justice. We need space to feed and connect with spirit and all we understand to be divine energies. They are key aspects to our resistance, to our efforts to alter our circumstances and fight to change the concrete material conditions and truly transform the lived experiences of Black people. As Hemphill states, "we heal so that we can act and organize."

Resistance also looks like making hard choices that allow us to transform the experience of Black lives, starting with our own. Choices that allow for our own healing and restoration. Choices that allow for our own well-being. Choices we make when we realize that we can no longer contribute to institutions that continue to injure us and do us harm. We resist so we can heal; we heal so we can resist, which means being courageous even when we are scared:

Shout out to all the sistahs (and brothas) who said enough is enough.[8]
The ones who vehemently declared fuck that shit.
The ones who walked away from all of it.
All the bullshit, the conditioning, the perceived notions, the expectations,
the projections that were blocking their light
All the bullshit that was stealing their joy and killing them softly
Shout out to all the sistahs (and brothas)
The ones who can tell you the exact day and time
when their mumble grumble became something else.
When their throat chakra opened
with the fire of courage and conviction from their belly.
When they let out a bellow, a shout, a yell and loud lament for all the world to
    hear—
Yo! Yo! Yo! "Fuck this shit!;

I ain't doing it no more!"
"Nah, I ain't don't this no more!
Fuck this shit!"

Shout out to all the sistahs (and brothas)
The ones who can tell you with the precision of a seasoned
Senegalese tailor cutting fabric for Tabaski
The exact date, the exact day, the exact time,
the exact moment when the shift happened and
Shout out to all the sistahs (and brothas) who can tell you the exact moment
when their Spirit pushed its way out to full expression
like a crumbling levee giving way to hurricane-force winds
and waist-high torrents of rising water.

Yeah! Yeah! Yeah!
Shout out to all the sistahs (and brothas)
standing on the ledge, on the precipice, albeit tentatively,
with a date circled, not in pencil
but in ink,
sharpie-permanent, red,
bleeding through the page marking the day,
And the days that follow
Shout out to the sistahs (and brothas)
the ones with earned leave time payouts calculated
and verified with pay stubs
and and and the most important sistah in HR.

Shout out to the sistahs (and brothas)
The ones with their hopes and dreams pasted, yeah, you know with a glue stick,
on poster boards
or tacked on the cork boards.
Affirming, manifesting, declaring, asserting, breathing life
into their prayers.

Shout out to the sistahs (and brothas)
Pouring milk into the ocean,
lighting white candles that burn all night,
giving away six red kola nuts or
a white cloth slept with the previous night,
smoking out the sticky stuff that no longer serves,
releasing, letting go, making room, clearing space.

Shout out to the sistahs (and brothas)
Prostrating, in child's pose or legs up the wall or savasana
Orrrr, on their prayer mats five times a day.

Shout out to the sistahs (and brothas)
Opening to expansion, to spirit

Listening to their gut, intuition, wisdom, promptings, nudgings, premonitions
Visions....

Shout out to the sistahs (and brothas)
Who are sooooo aware of "coincidences."
Air quote. Air quote. Air quote.
Serendipity and synchronicity
"coincidences."
Lined up numbers, prompting, images in the clouds
Unexpected rain showers and motherfuckin' rainbows!!!
Shout out to all the sistahs (and brothas) who can see the motherfuckin'
    rainbows!!!
And get wet in the unexpected rain showers.

Shout out to the sistahs (and brothas)
Who can see the Red birds. The Red birds. The Red birds.
Or Kite birds flying over you on your first visit to Goree Island.
Or Dragonflies and Butterflies. Or Dragonflies and Butterflies. Or Dragonflies
    and Butterflies.
And the whispy swirling seeds,
and the whispy swirling seeds
and the whispy swirling seeds
dancing down the hallway or
hovering above the ancestral altar
when you ask your grandma,
a question.

Shout out to all the sistahs (and brothas)
Who are calling on their ancestors, calling on divine energy, calling on spirit
to support them and to help them
to guide them and to protect them
As they realize, accept, embrace, and stand fully,
like they in tadasana, yo
Or warrior one
Or warrior two
Or warrior three
Or goddess pose.

Shout out, Shout out to my people, my sistahs (and brothas)
Who are returning to their essence, to purpose, to a calling,
To an expression of of their SOUL,
To an expression of of their true and authentic selves

Yooooo!
Shout out to the sistahs (and brothas) who said enough is enough.
The ones who vehemently declared fuck that shit.

Shout out to the sistahs (and brothas)
whose mumble grumble has become something else.
Shout out to the sistahs (and brothas)
Who began to bellow and shout and yell
And scream for all the world to hear.

Yo! Yo! For real tho, for real tho, for real tho, for real tho!
Fuck this shit.

I'm not doing it no more!
I'm not doing it no more!
I'm not doing it no more!
Naw!
I don't this no more.
Fuck this shit.

For all my sisters and brothers who made this declaration
Jump baby, jump.
You will fly, soar and land
and fly and land and soar again.
Shout out to my sisters and my brothers who finally said,
yo, fuck this shit,
I ain't doing it no more
We ain't doing this shit no more.

Of course, we are all at different places and stations in our lives. However, we all have the capacity to contribute to the well-being, healing and restoration of Black people. So, perhaps you don't quite feel ready to jump, soar and land and jump, soar and land again. Or in Newsome's case, climb. But, we can all contribute as she did to the dismantling of white supremacy and challenge the way that anti–Blackness adversely affects us. As Newsome gracefully and humbly suggests, there is an "entry point to the modern movement" for all of us, if we simply start by "identify[ing] what issue [we are] most passionate about and what talents and skills [we] want to bring to the fold." Ideally, we will "do the work where [we] are, in the and around the institutions and communities [we] are already in." There will always be, as Newsome states, at least for the foreseeable future, a need for us to engage in and protest in order to force our nation to see what it must see. There will always be moments when we are forced to be our authentic selves and accept the call of our SOUL. There will always be moments when we are called to do what feeds it most, when we decide that we can no longer tolerate playing small or playing along, when we must venture out on our own, with the support of our community, of the collective, to imagine, create and build another existence. And, yes—that, too, is our resistance. That, too, is part of our liberation. That, too, is part of our healing, individually and collectively.

And, as you decide where to lend your passion, energy, talents, and love, remember the question that my mentor, well-regarded political advisor and scientist Dr. Ron Walters, often asked: "what does this have do with the liberation of Black people?" When we speak of resistance, we mean the fight for, the insistence upon Black liberation. The demand for our well-being. The refusal to be denied our humanity. As you get involved, as you choose healing and restoration, as you choose resistance, consider what Black Lives Matter and Black Futures Fund Co-Founder Alicia Garza offers us, which is that Black liberation does not look like "replac[ing] one form of power with another form in which Black people or people of color are implementing and enacting the same toxic dynamics that the people who are in power now are enacting." This is why representation, diversity in ranks, cannot and should not be confused with equity, much less liberation, freedom and justice. Putting Black people in a position to perpetuate the same atrocities is not progress, and there ain't nothing resistant about it. Instead, we are at the point where "we fundamentally have to be oriented and organized around transforming the ways that we can be together, the ways [that] resources are distributed in our communities and the ways that we get to make decisions over our own well-being and the well-being of others. And that means that we have to be radical in our caring for each other, caring for communities and caring for the future that is right at our fingertips."

Or as Kelley offers us, our fight is to

remake the world. We must be ruthless in their criticism and fearless in the face of the powers that be. We must be able to model what it means to think through crisis, to fight for the eradication of oppression in all its forms, whether it directly affects us or not. [We must] work to understand and advance the movements in the streets, seeking to eliminate racism and state violence, preserve Black life, defend the rights of the marginalized (from undocumented immigrants to transfolk), and challenge the current order that has brought us so much misery. And, [we cannot] do this work, not without criticism and self-criticism, not by pandering to popular trends or powerful people, a cult of celebrity or Twitter, [IG or TikTok] and not by telling lies, claiming easy answers, or avoiding the ideas that challenge us all.

Yeah, leadership, this work, creating change, ain't about likes or followers. It ain't about being a celebrity or the material things you amass. It's about the people. This work—resistance, liberation—is about the people and their well-being. To do this work, to be this kind of leader, one with SOUL who can collaborate with others to heal our world, you must operate from a place of love, with courage, with a willingness to extend yourself for the well-being of others who are just as committed to your care as you are to theirs. It is this way that our world will change. It is this way with the help of spirit that we will stop the harm, injury and violence of white supremacy, anti–Black racism and other forms of oppression that wound.

So, then, how will you engage in resistance and be part of imagining and creating a culture, a society, a world where Black lives do matter, one that is life-affirming, driven by love and rooted in justice? What Black futures are you imagining and committed to investing your time and energy into creating? What Black futures are you prepared to advocate for, to fight for? When and where and how will you resist so that we can be well? And, at the same time, how will you continue to be well and care for yourself and your communities, those you love, so you can continue to resist? How will you continue to heal and be resilient so you can do the work that must be done? How will you fight for yourself, your capacity to be and express your true and authentic self, for your SOUL, while making sure the world allows others to do the same without fear of harm, injury or violence?

Chapter Notes

Preface

1. Ginwright, Shawn. "Radically Healing Black Lives; A Love Note to Justice." *New Directions in Student Leadership* 148 (Winter 2015): 33–44.
2. Palmer, Parker. "The Vitality of Diversity." *On Being.* https://onbeing.org/blog/parker-palmer-the-vitality-of-diversity/. 30 May 2017.
3. Hemphill, Prentis. "What Is Healing Justice?" https://prentishemphill.com/healing-justice.
4. Gay, Roxane. "Remember, No One Is Coming to Save Us." *New York Times.* 30 May 2020. https://www.nytimes.com/2020/05/30/opinion/sunday/trump-george-floyd-coronavirus.html.
5. Kelley, Robin D. "Black Study, Black Struggle." *Boston Review.* 7 March 2016. http://bostonreview.net/forum/robin-d-g-kelley-black-study-black-struggle.
6. Menakem, Resmaa. *My Grandmother's Hands: Racialized Trauma and the Pathway to Mending Our Hearts and Bodies.* Las Vegas: Central Recovery Press, 2017.
7. Hemphill, Prentis. "Healing Justice Is How We Can Sustain Black Lives." *Huffington Post.* 7 February 2017. https://www.huffpost.com/entry/healing-justice-b5899e8ade4b0c1284f282ffe?4s1vjiol7fxjn61or=.
8. Harrell, S. "Soulfulness as an Orientation to Contemplative Practice: Culture, Liberation, and Mindful Awareness." *The Journal of Contemplative Inquiry* 5, no. 1 (2018).
9. Somé, Malidoma Patrice. *The Healing Wisdom of Africa: Finding Life Purpose Through Nature, Ritual, and Commun-*

ity. New York: Jeremy P. Tarcher, 1998; Some, Malidoma Patrice. *Ritual: Power, Healing and Community.* New York: Penguin, 1997.
10. Diasporic Soul Healing-Centered Leadership Development Experience.
11. Van der Kolk, Bessel. *The Body Keeps the Score: Brain, Mind, and Body in the Healing of Trauma.* New York: Penguin, 2014.
12. Parker, Gail. "Spiritual Activism." Amplify and Activate Summit. 4 December 2020.

Chapter I

1. Harrell, S. "Soulfulness as an Orientation to Contemplative Practice: Culture, Liberation, and Mindful Awareness." *The Journal of Contemplative Inquiry* 5, no. 1 (2018).
2. Ginwright, Shawn. "Radically Healing Black Lives; a Love Note to Justice." *New Directions in Student Leadership* 148 (Winter 2015): 33–44.
3. Wortham, Jenna. "Black Health Matters." *New York Times.* 27 August 2016.
4. Harrell, S. "Soulfulness as an Orientation to Contemplative Practice: Culture, Liberation, and Mindful Awareness." *The Journal of Contemplative Inquiry* 5, no. 1 (2018).
5. Somé, Malidoma Patrice. *The Healing Wisdom of Africa: Finding Life Purpose Through Nature, Ritual, and Community* (1998) and *Ritual: Power, Healing and Community* (1997).
6. Harrell, S. "Soulfulness as an Orientation to Contemplative Practice: Culture,

Liberation, and Mindful Awareness." *The Journal of Contemplative Inquiry* 5, no. 1 (2018)," 9–40.

7. Sey, Seinabo. "Breathe." *I'm a Dream.* Universal Music. 7 September 2018. https://www.okayafrica.com/seinabo-sey-breathe-video-gambia/. Seinabo Sey, who is a Swedish-Gambian singer, wrote "Breathe," which is an orchestral string-backed song about self-love and self-acceptance, while on her first visit to Dakar, Senegal. Sey explains that "she felt at ease in Senegal, but couldn't quite pinpoint why until she realized that she loved it in Senegal because she didn't have to explain herself to people. She realized that as Black women, so much of our time is spent explaining obvious things about our culture or ourselves, when we would rather just be."

8. Cantwell, David. "The Unlikely Story of 'A Change Is Gonna Come.'" *New Yorker.* 17 March 2015. Accessed 19 August 2017. https://www.newyorker.com/culture/culture-desk/the-unlikely-story-of-a-change-is-gonna-come.

9. Harrell, "Soulfulness as an Orientation to Contemplative Practice: Culture, Liberation, and Mindful Awareness." *The Journal of Contemplative Inquiry* 5, no. 1 (2018).

10. As Walker notes in "The Sound of Our Own Culture," "culture is something in which one should thrive—the body and spirit simultaneously. But in the United States, for many [Black] people that is not happening, in part because the dominant culture is typically injurious and disadvantages individuals are not white males" (53).

11. King, Joyce E., and Ellen Swartz. *The Afro-Centric Praxis of Teaching for Freedom: Connecting Culture to Learning.* New York: Routledge, 2016. 2–3.

12. Kelley, Robin D. "Black Study. Black Struggle." *Boston Review.* 7 March 2016. http://bostonreview.net/forum/robin-d-g-kelley-black-study-black-struggle.

Chapter II

1. Nwigwe, Tobe. "Shine." (feat. Madeline Edwards). *Three Originals.* 2019.

2. Salaam Remi & Black on Purpose. "Is It Because I'm Black" (feat. Black Thought, Syleena Johnson, CeeLo Green, Anthony Hamilton & Stephen Marley). 2020.

3. Gay, Roxane. "Remember, No One Is Coming to Save Us." *New York Times.* 30 May 2020. https://www.nytimes.com/2020/05/30/opinion/sunday/trump-george-floyd-coronavirus.html.

4. Hill, Jemele. "NBA Players Put America on Notice." *The Atlantic.* 27 August 2020. https://www.theatlantic.com/ideas/archive/2020/08/nba-players-needed-do/615769/.

5. Hauser, Christine. "Ohio Man Is Shot Dead by a Deputy Searching for Someone Else." *New York Times.* 10 December 2020. https://www.nytimes.com/2020/12/08/us/columbus-police-shooting.html.

6. Parker, Gail. "Restorative Yoga and Racial Trauma Workshop." I Am Yoga. Charlotte, North Carolina. October 2017.

7. Lusk, Julie. *Yoga Nidra for Complete Relaxation and Stress Relief.* Oakland: New Harbinger Publications, 2015. 19–21.

8. Menakem, Resmaa. *My Grandmother's Hands: Racialized Trauma and the Pathway to Mending Our Hearts and Bodies.* Las Vegas: Central Recovery Press, 2017.

9. Menakem, *My Grandmother's Hands.* 15, 44.

10. Leary, Joy DeGruy. *Post Traumatic Slave Syndrome: America's Legacy of Enduring Injury and Healing.* Milwaukie, OR: Uptone Press, 2005.

11. Hughes, Langston. "Harlem." *Norton Anthology of African American Literature.* New York: W.W. Norton, 1997. 1267.

12. In *Restorative Yoga for Ethnic and Race-Based Stress and Trauma* (2020), Parker writes that Leith Mullings coined the term Sojourner Syndrome to refer to gender-specific, high effort coping by women after the extraordinary efforts of Sojourner Truth to resist and overcome racial and gender oppression (68).

13. Hamblin, James. "Why Succeeding Against the Odds Can Make You Sick." *New York Times.* 27 January 2017. https://

www.nytimes.com/2017/01/27/opin-ion/sunday/why-succeeding-against-the-odds-can-make-you-sick.html.

14. Outkast. "Git Up, Git Out." *Southernplayalisticadillacmusik.* LaFace Records, 1994.

15. Neal, Amber. "The Physical and Spiritual Consequences of Racial Battle Fatigue." Sojo.net. 13 May 2020. https://sojo.net/articles/physical-and-spiritual-consequences-racial-battle-fatigue.

16. Foor, Daniel. *Ancestral Medicine: Rituals for Personal and Family Healing.* Rochester, VT: Bear & Company, July 2017.

17. *Foor, Ancestral Medicine.*

18. EFT is a mind-body-spirit self-care approach which involves tapping on acupuncture points while repeating emotionally-charged statements that relate to specific health issues, often referred to as acupressure for the emotions. It is an evidence-based method that has been shown in several dozen randomized controlled trials to be effective for a variety of conditions including anxiety, weight loss and food cravings, depression, PTSD, phobias, pain and other physical symptoms. As a form of energy psychology, EFT addresses the root energetic imbalances that result from trauma and other emotional stressors.

19. Shahid, Kyra T. *Anti-Black Racism and Epistemic Violence.* Austin: Sentia Publishing, 2018.

20. McGee, Ebony, and David Stovall. "Reimagining Critical Race Theory in Education: Mental Health, Healing, and the Pathway to Liberatory Praxis." *Educational Theory* 65, no. 5 (October 2015): 491–511.

21. Inside Higher Ed Staff. "The Black Experience in Higher Education." *Inside Higher Ed.* https://www.insidehighered.com/the-black-experience-in-higher-education. 20 October 2020.

22. Wortham, Jenna. "Black Health Matters." *New York Times.* 27 August 2016. https://www.nytimes.com/2016/08/28/fashion/black-lives-matter-wellness-health-self-care.html.

23. Holmes, Barbara. *Joy Unspeakable: Contemplative Practices of the Black Church.* 2nd Edition. Minneapolis: Fortress Press, 2017.

24. Gates, Rolf. "Day 183: Genograms." *Meditations on Intention and on Being: Daily Reflections on the Path of Yoga, Mindfulness and Compassion.* New York: Anchor Books, 2015. 173.

25. McGee, Ebony, and David Stovall. "Reimagining Critical Race Theory in Education: Mental Health, Healing, and the Pathway to Liberatory Praxis." Reprinted by *Harvard Journal of African American Public Policy* (2016): 44–59.

Chapter III

1. Fish meatballs that are found mixed with tomato sauce and onions on top of the red rice.

2. Accokeek Foundation. "Soul Food: The Food of Love; Panel Featuring Williams, Psyche and Ju Ju Harris, Moderator." 5 March 2015. https://www.accokeek.org/post/soul-food-the-food-of-love.

3. As I prepared to leave Cincinnati in 2016, I learned that the city actually ranked at that time as one of top ten worst places for Black people to live.

4. Brown, Brene. *Braving the Wilderness: The Quest for True Belonging and the Courage to Stand Alone.* New York: Random House, 2017.

5. King, Joyce E., and Ellen Swartz. *The Afro-Centric Praxis of Teaching for Freedom: Connecting Culture to Learning.* New York: Routledge, 2016.

6. Gates, Rolf. *Meditations from the Mat.* New York: Anchor Books, 2002.

7. Palmer, Parker. *Let Your Life Speak: Listening to the Voice of Vocation.* Kindle Edition. San Francisco: Jossey Bass, 2000.

8. King and Swartz. *The Afrocentric Praxis of Teaching for Freedom.* 12.

Chapter IV

1. Sey, Seinabo. "Breathe." *I'm a Dream.* Universal Music. 7 September 2018. https://www.okayafrica.com/seinabo-sey-breathe-video-gambia/. Seinabo Sey, who is a Swedish-Gambian singer, wrote "Breathe," which is an orchestral

string-backed song about self-love and self-acceptance, while on her first visit to Dakar, Senegal. Sey explains that "she felt at ease in Senegal, but couldn't quite pinpoint why until she realized that she loved it in Senegal because she didn't have to explain herself to people. She realized that as Black women, so much of our time is spent explaining obvious things about our culture or ourselves, when we would rather just be." In other words, in "Breathe" Seinabo Sey speaks of Senegal being a place where she can do just that, breathe; a place where she can express herself authentically as a Black woman.

2. Parker, Gail. "Spiritual Awakening: When Spirit and Activism Merge." Amplify and Activate Summit. 4 December 2020. https://www.amplifyandactivate.com/summit.

3. The Serere Sine and Saafi are two of seven sub-ethnic groups that make up the larger Serere ethnic group, which is the third largest ethnic group in Senegal.

Chapter V

1. Diamond, Anna. "The Deadly 1991 Hamlet Fire Exposed the High Cost of 'Cheap.'" *Smithsonian Magazine.* September 8, 2017. https://www.smithsonianmag.com/history/deadly-1991-hamlet-fire-exposed-high-cost-cheap-180964816/.

2. Some, Malidoma. *The Healing Wisdom of Africa: Finding Life Purpose Through Nature, Ritual and Community.* New York: Penguin, 1998.

3. Beattie, Melody. *Journey to the Heart: Daily Meditations on the Path to Freeing Your Soul.* San Francisco: HarperCollins, 1996.

Chapter VI

1. Yusef Kirriem Hawkins was 16 years old when, in August 1989, he was murdered by a mob of white teenagers after going with friends to the insular white neighborhood of Bensonhurst, Brooklyn, to inspect a used car. Horton, Adrian. "Storm Over Brooklyn: Retelling the Devastating Murder of Yusuf Hawkins." *The*

Guardian. 11 August 2020. https://www.theguardian.com/tv-and-radio/2020/aug/11/storm-over-brooklyn-yusuf-hawkins-hbo.

2. Foor, Daniel. *Ancestral Medicine: Rituals for Personal and Family Healing.* Rochester, VT: Bear & Company, 2017.

3. Parker, Gail. *Restorative Yoga for Ethnic and Race-Based Stress and Trauma.* London: Singing Dragon, 2020.

4. *History of Haiti.* https://library.brown.edu/haitihistory/5.html.

5. Somé, Malidoma. *The Healing Wisdom of Africa: Finding Life Purpose Through Nature, Ritual and Community.* New York: Jeremy P. Tarcher, 1998.

6. Arewa, Caroline Shola. *Opening to Spirit: Contacting the Healing Power of the Chakras and Honoring African Spirituality.* Baltimore: Afrikan World Books, 1998.

7. Holmes, Barbara. *Joy Unspeakable: Contemplative Practices of the Black Church.* 2nd Edition. Minneapolis: Fortress Press, 2017.

8. Eden, Donna. *Energy Medicine for Women: Aligning Your Body's Energies to Boost Your Health and Vitality.* New York: Penguin, 2008; Eden, Donna. *Energy Medicine: Balancing Your Body's Energies for Optimal Health, Joy and Vitality.* New York: Penguin, 2008.

9. White, Renee. *African Concepts of Energy and Their Manifestations Through Art.* Master's Thesis, College of the Arts, Kent State University. 2016.

10. Mokgobi, M.G. "Understanding Traditional African Healing." *African Journal for Physical Health Education, Recreation, and Dance* 20, supplement 2 (2014): 24–34. https://www.ncbi.nlm.nih.gov/pmc/articles/PMC4651463/.

11. Parker, Gail. "Spiritual Activism." Amplify and Activate Summit 2020. 4 December 2020. https://www.amplifyandactivate.com/summit.

12. *A Little Juju Podcast* celebrates the rapidly growing number of Black folk reclaiming their indigenous spiritual practices, while creating a space for us to laugh, question, and recommit ourselves to liberation through the ancestral tools given to us. Because the ancestors always call us back. Bae, Juju. *A Little Juju*

Podcast. https://www.itsjujubae.com/podcast.

13. *Ifa* is a faith and divination system with its roots in Olori's family's ancestral homeland, Yorubaland. The region now encompasses the nations of Benin, Togo and Ghana and parts of Nigeria. Like some other religions, *Ifa* includes magic, the use of *traditional* medicines and veneration of the dead. Pitts, Jonathon. "West African Religions Like Ifa and Vodou Are on the Rise in Maryland, as Practitioners Connect with Roots." *Baltimore Sun.* 28 March 2019. https://www.baltimoresun.com/maryland/bs-md-african-faiths-20190315-story.html.

14. Santería, also known as Regla de Ocha, Regla Lucumí, or Lucumí, is an African diasporic religion that developed in Cuba between the 16th and 19th centuries. It arose through a process of syncretism between the traditional Yoruba religion of West Africa and the Roman Catholic form of Christianity.

Chapter VII

1. Somé, Malidoma. *The Healing Wisdom of Africa: Finding Life Purpose Through Nature, Ritual and Community.* New York: Jeremy P. Tarcher, 1998.

2. Cotter, Holland. "From the Deep, a Diva with Many Faces." *New York Times.* 2 April 2009. https://www.nytimes.com/2009/04/03/arts/design/03wata.html.

3. Snider, Amber. "The History of Yemaya, Santeria's Queenly Ocean Goddess Mermaid." *Teen Vogue.* 9 July 2020. https://www.teenvogue.com/story/the-history-of-yemaya-goddess-mermaid.

4. Broner, E.M. "Bringing Home the Light." *Ms.* (October/November 1999): 55–63.

5. Sharpe, Christina. *In the Wake: On Blackness and Being.* Durham: Duke University Press, 2016.

6. Van Sertima, Ivan. *They Came Before Columbus: The African Presence in Ancient America.* New York: Random House, 2003.

7. Kendrick, Lamar. "Bloody Waters."

Black Panther: The Album. Interscope Records. 9 February 2018.

8. Sharpe, Christina. *In the Wake: On Blackness and Being.* 40–41.

Chapter VIII

1. Wamsley, Laurel. "Parks in Nonwhite Areas Are Half the Size of Ones in Majority-White Areas, Study Says." *All Things Considered.* NPR. 5 August 2020. https://www.npr.org/2020/08/05/899356445/parks-in-nonwhite-areas-are-half-the-size-of-ones-in-majority-white-areas-study.

2. Daniel, Pete. *Dispossession: Discrimination Against African American Farmers in the Age of Civil Rights.* Chapel Hill: University of North Carolina Press, 2013.

3. The Black Farmers Market. "Local Black Farmers." https://blackfarmersmkt.com/.

4. The Black Farmers Market. "Food Apartheid." https://blackfarmersmkt.com/.

5. hooks, bell. *Sisters of the Yam: Black Women and Self-Recovery.* London: South End Press, 2005.

6. Lee, Michele E. *Working the Roots: Over 400 Years of Traditional African American Healing.* Oakland: Wadstack Publishers, 2014.

Chapter IX

1. Assata Shakur was a member of the Black Liberation Army who was charged with the murder of a state trooper on the New Jersey turnpike. Ultimately, she managed to escape prison and go to Cuba, where she has been in exile ever since.

2. At the time there was no access to American banks in Cuba.

3. Hodge, Ray. "I Am King." *Braveheart.* 2016.

4. Singleton, Micah. "'To Pimp a Butterfly': Kendrick Lamar's New Album Is Perfect." *The Verge.* 19 March 2015. https://www.theverge.com/2015/3/19/8257319/kendrick-lamar-album-review-to-pimp-a-butterfly.

5. A form of glass-painting with

origins that stretches back to pre-colonial Senegal.

6. Walker, Alice. "Epilogue." *The Way Forward Is with a Broken Heart*. New York: Random House, 2000. 200.

7. Hodge, Ray. "I Am King."

8. Brand, Dionne. *A Map to the Door of No Return: Notes to Belonging*. Toronto: Vintage, 2001. 19–20.

9. Danticat, Edwidge. "We Are Ugly, but We Are Here." *The Caribbean Writer* 10 (1996).

Chapter X

1. King, Noel. "'I See These Conversations as Protective': Talking with Kids About Race." America Reckons with Racial Injustice. Conversation with Ibram X. Kendi. *NPR*. 16 June 2020. https://www.npr.org/2020/06/16/877545848/i-see-these-conversations-as-protective-talking-with-kids-about-race.

2. Dak'art is a bi-annual international art exposition that attracts artists from throughout the Diaspora.

3. The *kora* is a string instrument used extensively in West Africa. A *kora* typically has 21 strings, which are played by plucking with the fingers. It combines features of the lute and harp.

4. Toliver-Diallo, W. "The Woman Who Was More Than a Man: Making Aline Sitoe Diatta into a National Heroine in Senegal." *Canadian Journal of African Studies/Revue Canadienne Des Études Africaines* 39 no. 2 (2005): 338–360. Retrieved August 2020 from http://www.jstor.org/stable/25067487.

Chapter XI

1. hooks, bell. *All About Love: New Visions*. New York: William Morrow, 2000.

2. hooks, bell. *Sisters of the Yam*. New York: South End Press, 1993. 146–47.

3. hooks, bell. *Sisters of the Yam*. 146–147.

4. Jordan, June. "Where Is the Love." *Some of Us Did Not Die: New and Selected Essays of June Jordan*. New York: Basic/Civitas Books, 2002. 272.

5. Jordan, June. "Where Is the Love." 269.

6. Jordan, June. "Where Is the Love." 271.

7. Wilentz, Gay. *Women Writers Curing Cultural Disease*. New Brunswick: Rutgers University Press, 2000.

8. Bondy, Dianne. *Yoga for Everyone: Poses for Every Type of Body*. New York: Penguin, 2019.

9. Palmer, Parker. *Letting Your Life Speak: Listening for the Voice of Vocation*. San Francisco: Jossey-Bass, 1999.

10. Gates, Rolf. *Meditations from the Mat: Daily Reflections on the Path of Yoga*. New York: Anchor Books, 2002.

11. "Ta-Nehisi Coates on HBO Adaptation Of 'Between The World And Me.'" *All Things Considered. NPR.* 23 November 2020. https://www.npr.org/2020/11/23/938131210/ta-nehisi-coates-on-hbo-adaptation-of-between-the-world-and-me.

12. Coates, Ta-Nehisi. *Between the World and Me*. New York: Spiegel & Grau. 2015.

13. Dillahunt, Ajamu Amiri. "Social Justice Work in North Carolina: An Interview with Activist Nhawndie Smith." *Black Organizing Today. Black Perspectives.* 30 January 2019. https://www.aaihs.org/social-justice-work-in-north-carolina-an-interview-with-activist-nhawndie-smith/.

Chapter XII

1. Wittes Schlack, Julie. "Self Care Isn't a Privilege. It's an Act of 'Self Preservation.'" WBUR Radio. 12 May 2020. https://www.wbur.org/cognoscenti/2020/05/12/self-care-commercialization-goop-coronavirus-julie-wittes-schlack.

2. Garza, Alicia. "Radical Self-Care." *Afro-Punk Festival*. Interview. 18 December 2018. https://www.youtube.com/watch?v=NQ7FGkfPwyE.

3. *2020 Amplify and Activate Summit*. Self-Care Panel. 4 December 2020.

4. Parris, Anana H. *Self Care Matters: A Revolutionary's Approach*. YBF Publishing, 2015.

5. Davis, Angela. "Radical Self-Care." *Afro-Punk Festival.* Interview. 18 December 2018. https://www.youtube.com/watch?v=Q1cHoL4vaBs.

6. Wortham, Jenna. "Black Health Matters." *New York Times.* 27 August 2016. https://www.nytimes.com/2016/08/28/fashion/black-lives-matter-wellness-health-self-care.html.

7. *Amplify and Activate Summit.* Self-Care Panel. 4 December 2020.

8. Jeffers-Coly, Phyllis. "Resilience Playlist." iTunes.

Chapter XIII

1. Van der Kolk, Bessel. *The Body Keeps the Score: Brain, Mind, and Body in the Healing of Trauma.* New York: Penguin, 2014.

2. Harrell, S. "Soulfulness as an Orientation to Contemplative Practice: Culture, Liberation, and Mindful Awareness." *Journal of Contemplative Inquiry* 5, no. 1 (2018).

3. The five yama are ahimsa (without harm), satya (truthfulness), asteya (non-stealing), brahmacharya (moderation), and aparigraha (non-possessiveness). The five niyama are saucha (purity), santosha (contentment), tapas (persistence), svadhyaya (self-study), and Ishvarapranidhana (devotion to the Numinous).

4. Walker, Alice. *The Way Forward Is with a Broken Heart.* New York: Random House, 2000. 200.

5. Walker, Alice. "The Sound of Our Own Culture." *Anything We Love Can Be Saved: A Writer's Activism.* New York: Random House, 1997.

6. Sey, Seinabo. "Breathe." *I'm a Dream.* Universal Music. 7 September 2018. https://www.okayafrica.com/seinabo-sey-breathe-video-gambia/.

7. Hathaway, Lalah. "Breathe." *Self-Portrait.* Concord Music Group, 2008.

8. Desikachar, T.K.V. *The Heart of Yoga: Developing a Personal Practice.* Rochester, VT: Inner Traditions International, 1995.

9. Burke, Amber. "A Restorative Practice Inspired by Vinyasa." *Yoga International.* 30 November 2015.

10. "A key component in the relationship between exposure to stress and development of mental illness is coping. High-effort coping, defined as 'sustained cognitive and emotional engagement,' is described as a problem-focused coping strategy when Black individuals appraise stressful situations that are sometimes related to racial discrimination, such as job loss or being passed over for promotion, as situations that can be altered by hard work. However, high-effort coping may be a 'mental health cost' paid by African Americans who maintain greater levels of sustained effort and energy expenditures in order to cope with stress. Additionally, working class and poor Black resilient strivers face a greater potential for illness as from stress, such as diabetes and hypertension; notably, working-class white Americans seemed unaffected by this phenomenon."

11. I start most of my practices in mountain after reading *The Heart of Yoga* in part because I primarily teach beginners and I want to focus on breath awareness.

12. In a retreat setting when I have students for multiple days, I focus on setting a sankalpa that is informed in many respects by why they came to us for the experience. We typically set the sankalpa in the context of our opening session and integrate it into reflective journal keeping. Of course, students may set a class-specific intention if they desire.

Chapter XIV

1. Kelley, Robin D.G. "Black Study, Black Struggle." *Boston Review.* 7 March 2016. http://bostonreview.net/forum/robin-d-g-kelley-black-study-black-struggle.

2. Diop, Arimeta. "We Have to Keep Repeating Ourselves Just to Be Able to Breathe: Black Activists on the Movement for Justice." *Vanity Fair.* 5 June 2020.

3. Newsome collaborated with other

organizers, including Greenpeace environmental activists who taught her how to climb a flagpole.

4. Joiner, Lottie. "Bree Newsome Reflects on Taking Down South Carolina's Confederate Flag 2 Years Ago." *Vox.* 27 June 2017. https://www.vox.com/identities/2017/6/27/15880052/bree-newsome-south-carolinas-confederate-flag.

5. As of 21 December 2020, 12 noon GMT, Megan raised over $12,000 in mutual aid funds for rent relief with the understanding that, as Somara Machel offers, "solidarity is not an act of charity, but aid between forces fighting for the same objective." https://www.instagram.com/p/CJBXWhOjGcx/.

6. Hemphill, Prentis. "What Is Healing Justice?" https://prentishemphill.com/healing-justice.

7. Hemphill, Prentis. "Healing Justice Is How We Can Sustain Black Lives." *Huffington Post.* 7 February 2017. https://www.huffpost.com/entry/healing-justice_b_5899e8ade4b0c1284f282ffe?4s1vjiol7fxjn61or=.

8. Jeffers-Coly, Phyllis. "Fuck This Shit, I Ain't Doing It No More: A Manifesta." I wrote this on Monday 7 December 2020 after being inspired not only by the women I heard from at the Amplify and Activate Summit over the weekend, but as the result of a year of deep self-study and growing acceptance and love of who I have become, how being in Senegal is an expression of my courage, an act of resistance and will continue to be a place where I can learn and grow and deepen my capacity to hold space for others who are tapping into their courage, deepening their self-awareness and deciding to push back and follow their own path, be their authentic self. Our work is to make sure there are loving, affirmative spaces where all of our authentic selves can actually flourish and thrive and not be subjected to injury, harm or violence.

Bibliography

Acosta, Angel, and Zishan Jiwani. "Breathwork for Healing Racial Trauma: A Contemplative-Based Research Journey." *ACHME Webinar.* The Association for Contemplative Mind in Higher Education. 16 December 2020. http://www.contemplativemind.org/archives/6439.

Adrienne, Carol. *Find Your Purpose, Change Your Life.* New York: HarperCollins, 1999.

Amplify and Activate Summit 2020. Let Spirit Lead. 2–6 December 2020. https://www.amplifyandactivate.com/program.

Arewa, Caroline Shola. *Opening to Spirit: Contacting the Healing Power of the Chakras and Honoring African Spirituality.* Baltimore: Afrikan World Books, 1998.

_____. "Opening to Spirit: Contacting the Healing Power of the Chakras and Honoring African Spirituality." The Sanctuary in the City. 9 October 2020. https://www.thesanctuaryinthecity.org/shola/.

_____. "Opening to Spirit: Stepping in Before Stepping Out." *Amplify and Activate Summit 2020.* 3 December 2020. https://www.amplifyandactivate.com/program.

A2MEND. *Diasporic Soul Healing-Centered Leadership Development Experience|June 2019* Participant Focus Group. Video Recording. California. August 2019.

Bae, Juju. *A Little Juju Podcast.* https://www.itsjujubae.com/podcast.

Beattie, Melody. *Journey to the Heart: Daily Meditations on the Path to Freeing Your Soul.* San Francisco: HarperCollins, 1996.

Bondy, Dianne. "Connecting to the Divinity Within/Yoga, Body Image and Empowerment." *Amplify and Activate Summit 2020.* 3 December 2020. https://www.amplifyandactivate.com/program.

_____. *Yoga for Everyone: Poses for Every Type of Body.* New York: Penguin, 2019.

Brand, Dionne. *A Map to the Door of No Return.* Toronto: Vintage, 2001.

Brown, Brene. *Braving the Wilderness: The Quest for True Belonging and the Courage to Stand Alone.* New York: Random House, 2017.

Burke, Amber. "A Restorative Practice Inspired by Vinyasa." *Yoga International.* 30 November 2015.

Burke, Larry. *Tapping Into Health: EFT for Self-Healing.* September 2020. Duke Integrative Medicine. https://dukeintegrativemedicine.org/programs-training/public/tapping-into-health/.

Cantwell, David. "The Unlikely Story of 'A Change Is Gonna Come.'" *The New Yorker.* 17 March 2015. Accessed 19 August 2017. https://www.newyorker.com/culture/culture-desk/the-unlikely-story-of-a-change-is-gonna-come.

Coates, Ta-Nehisi. *Between the World and Me.* New York: Spiegel & Grau, 2015.

Cotter, Holland. "From the Deep, a Diva with Many Faces." *New York Times.* 2 April 2009. https://www.nytimes.com/2009/04/03/arts/design/03wata.html.

CTZNWELL. *CTZNWELL Summit 2020: Politics of Community Care.* 9–13 September 2020. https://www.ctznwell.org/summit2020.

Daniel, Pete. *Dispossession: Discrimination Against African American Farmers in the Age of Civil Rights.* Chapel Hill: University of North Carolina Press, 2013.

Danticat, Edwidge. "We Are Ugly, but We Are Here." *The Caribbean Writer* 10 (1996).

Davis, Angela. "Radical Self-Care." *AFROPUNK*. 7 December 2018. https://afropunk.com/2018/12/radical-self-care-angela-davis/.

DeGruy, Joy. *Post Traumatic Slave Syndrome: America's Legacy of Enduring Injury and Healing*. Portland: Joy DeGruy Publications, 2005.

Desikachar, T.K.V. *The Heart of Yoga: Developing a Personal Practice*. Rochester, VT: Inner Traditions International, 1995.

Diamond, Anna. "The Deadly 1991 Hamlet Fire Exposed the High Cost of "Cheap." *Smithsonian Magazine*. 8 September 2017. https://www.smithsonianmag.com/history/deadly-1991-hamlet-fire-exposed-high-cost-cheap-180964816/.

Dillahunt, Ajamu. Personal Interview. 3 June 2020.

Dillahunt, Ajamu Amiri. "From Hashtag Activist to Street Protester: An Interview with Bree Newsome Bass." Black Organizing Today Series. *Black Perspectives*. 2 July 2019. https://www.aaihs.org/black-organizing-today-an-interview-with-bree-newsome-bass/.

_____. Personal Interview. Skype. 15 June 2020.

_____. "Social Justice Work in North Carolina: An Interview with Activist Nhawndie Smith." Black Organizing Today Series. *Black Perspectives*. 30 January 2019. https://www.aaihs.org/social-justice-work-in-north-carolina-an-interview-with-activist-nhawndie-smith/.

Dillahunt, Rukiya. Personal Interview. 3 June 2020.

Eden, Donna. *Energy Medicine: Balancing Your Body's Energies for Optimal Health, Joy and Vitality*. New York: Penguin, 2008.

_____. *Energy Medicine for Women: Aligning Your Body's Energies to Boast Your Health and Vitality*. New York: Penguin, 2008.

Foor, Daniel. *Ancestral Medicine: Rituals for Personal and Family Healing*. Rochester, VT: Bear & Company, July 2017.

Franklin, Angela. *Pour First from a Full Cup and a Full Heart: My Soul to Keep Series*. Dakar, Senegal, 2018.

_____. *When Feeling Blue, She Reaches for the Redbird: My Soul to Keep Series*. Dakar, Senegal, 2018.

Garza, Alicia. Radical Self-Care. *AFROPUNK*. 17 December 2018. https://www.youtube.com/watch?v=NQ7FGkfPwyE.

Gates, Rolf. *Meditations from the Mat*. New York: Anchor Books, 2002.

_____. *Meditations on Intention and on Being: Daily Reflections on the Path of Yoga, Mindfulness and Compassion*. New York: Anchor Books, 2015.

Gay, Roxane. "Remember, No One Is Coming to Save Us." *New York Times*. 30 May 2020.

Ginwright, Shawn. "The Future of Healing: Shifting from Trauma Informed Care to Healing Centered Engagement." *Medium*. 31 May 2018. https://medium.com/@ginwright/the-future-of-healing-shifting-from-trauma-informed-care-to-healing-centered-engagement-634f557ce69c.

_____. "Radically Healing Black Lives; a Love Note to Justice," New Directions in Student Leadership, 148 (Winter 2015): 33–44.

Hamblin, James. "Why Succeeding Against the Odds Can Make You Sick." *New York Times*. 27 January 2017. https://www.nytimes.com/2017/01/27/opinion/sunday/why-succeeding-against-the-odds-can-make-you-sick.html.

Harrell, S. *Self-Care Ambassador Training Part 1 & Part 2*. SisterCare Alliance. 27–28 June 2020. Zoom Webinar.

_____. "Soulfulness as an Orientation to Contemplative Practice: Culture, Liberation, and Mindful Awareness." *The Journal of Contemplative Inquiry* 5, no. 1 (2018). Retrieved from https://journal.contemplativeinquiry.org/index.php/joci/article/view/170.

Hathaway, Lalah. "Breathe." *Self-Portrait*. Concord Music Group. 3 June 2008.

Hauser, Christine. "Ohio Man Is Shot Dead by a Deputy Searching for Someone Else."

New York Times. 10 December 2020. https://www.nytimes.com/2020/12/08/us/columbus-police-shooting.html.

Hemphill, Prentis. "Healing Justice Is How We Can Sustain Black Lives." *Huffington Post.* 7 February 2017. https://www.huffpost.com/entry/healing-justice_b_5899e8ade4b0c1284f282ffe?4s1vjiol7fxjn61or=.

_____. "What Is Healing Justice?" https://prentishemphill.com/healing-justice.

Hill, Jemele. "NBA Players Put America on Notice." *The Atlantic.* 27 August 2020. https://www.theatlantic.com/ideas/archive/2020/08/nba-players-needed-do/615769/.

Hodge, Ray. "I Am King." *Braveheart.* 2016.

Holmes, Barbara. *Joy Unspeakable: Contemplative Practices of the Black Church.* 2nd Edition. Minneapolis: Fortress Press, 2017.

hooks, bell. *All About Love: New Visions.* New York: William Morrow, 2000.

_____. *Sisters of the Yam.* New York: South End Press, 1993.

Hotter Than July. Amplify and Activate. July 2020. https://www.hotterthanjuly.info/events/.

Hughes, Langston. "Harlem." *Norton Anthology of African American Literature.* New York: W.W. Norton, 1997. 1267.

Inside Higher Ed staff. "The Black Experience in Higher Education," *Inside Higher Ed.* 20 October 2020. https://www.insidehighered.com/the-black-experience-in-higher-education.

Jeffers-Coly, Phyllis. "Fuck This Shit, I Ain't Doing It No More: A Manifesta." 7 December 2020.

_____. (Panel Facilitator). "We Got Soul: Healing-Centered Black College Student Leadership Development." *Universities Studying Slavery 2019 Fall Symposium.* 9–12 October 2019. Cincinnati, Ohio.

Joiner, Lottie. "Bree Newsome Reflects on Taking Down South Carolina's Confederate Flag 2 Years Ago." *Vox.* 27 June 2017. https://www.vox.com/identities/2017/6/27/15880052/bree-newsome-south-carolinas-confederate-flag.

Jordan, June. "Where Is the Love." *Some of Us Did Not Die: New and Selected Essays of June Jordan.* New York: Basic Books, 2002.

Kelley, Robin D. "Black Study, Black Struggle." *Boston Review.* 7 March 2016. http://bostonreview.net/forum/robin-d-g-kelley-black-study-black-struggle.

King, Joyce E., and Ellen Swartz. *The Afro-Centric Praxis of Teaching for Freedom: Connecting Culture to Learning.* New York: Routledge, 2016.

King, Noel. "'I See These Conversations as Protective': Talking with Kids About Race." *America Reckons with Racial Injustice.* Conversation with Ibram X. Kendi. *NPR.* 16 June 2020. https://www.npr.org/2020/06/16/877545848/i-see-these-conversations-as-protective-talking-with-kids-about-race.

Kozak, Deb. "Self-Care Day." *Globe & Feminist.* Women's Health Clinic. 24 July 2020. https://globeandfeminist.com/2020/07/24/self-care-day/.

Lamar, Kendrick. "Bloody Waters." *Black Panther: The Album.* Interscope Records. 9 February 2018.

_____. "D.N.A." *Damn.* Interscope Records. 14 April 2017.

Lee, Michele E. *Working the Roots: Over 400 Years of Traditional African American Healing.* Oakland: Wadstack Publishers, 2014.

Lusk, Julie. *Yoga Nidra for Complete Relaxation and Stress Relief.* Oakland: New Harbinger Publications, 2015. 19–21.

McGee, Ebony O., and David Stovall. "Reimagining Critical Race Theory in Education: Mental Health, Healing, and the Pathway to Liberatory Praxis," *Educational Theory* 65, no. 5 (October 2015): 491–511.

Menakem, Resmaa. *My Grandmother's Hands: Racialized Trauma and the Pathway to Mending Our Hearts and Bodies.* Las Vegas: Central Recovery Press, 2017.

_____, and Erin Trent Johnson. *Coming Home: Embodied Practices for Healing and*

Bibliography

Resilience for Black Women. 4 Equity Partners. 27–28 June 2020. http://4equityleaders. com/index.php/2020/06/16/coming-home-embodied-practices-for-healing-and-resilience-for-black-women/.

Mokgobi, M.G. "Understanding Traditional African Healing." *African Journal for Physical Health Education, Recreation, and Dance* 20, supplement 2 (2014): 24–34. https://www.ncbi.nlm.nih.gov/pmc/articles/PMC4651463/.

Neal, Amber. "The Physical and Spiritual Consequences of Racial Battle Fatigue." *Sojo.Net.* 13 May 2020. https://sojo.net/articles/physical-and-spiritual-consequences-racial-battle-fatigue.

Nwigwe, Tobe. "Shine." *Three Originals.* Tobe Nwigwe LLC. 10 March 2019.

Outkast. "Git Up, Git Out." *Southernplayalisticadilacmusik.* LaFace Records, 1994.

Palmer, Parker. *Let Your Life Speak: Listening to the Voice of Vocation.* San Francisco: Jossey-Bass, 2000. Kindle Edition.

_____. "The Vitality of Diversity." *On Being.* 30 May 2017. https://onbeing.org/blog/parker-palmer-the-vitality-of-diversity/.

Parker, Adrian. *Diasporic Soul Healing Experience Summer 2019.* Participant Interviews, Senegal. June 2019.

Parker, Gail. *Books & Brunch W/BYTA: Feat. Dr. Gail Parker.* 27 September 2020. https://www.union.fit/orgs/black-yoga-teachers-alliance/videos/3ZufB1URjV4VeKJVLFTmJ GaT.

_____. *Restorative Yoga for Ethnic and Race-Based Stress and Trauma.* London: Singing Dragon, 2020.

_____. *Restorative Yoga for Race-Based Traumatic Stress Injury.* I AM Yoga, Keisha Battles. Charlotte, North Carolina. 20–22 October 2017.

_____. "Self-Care & Self-Determination: Recovering from Race-Based Stress and Trauma." 4-week series. The Sanctuary in the City. October 2020. https://www.thesanctuaryinthecity.org/parker/.

_____. "Spiritual Activism." *Amplify and Activate Summit 2020.* 4 December 2020. https://www.amplifyandactivate.com/summit.

_____. *Yoga from the Inside Out: Shining a Light on Racial Wounding.* Yoga Service Council. 5 February-23 April 2019 (Weekly). https://zoom.us/webinar/563771662/ics?user_id=4lz_dzm2TWaqidIDzBFK3A.

Parris, Anana H. *Self Care Matters: A Revolutionary's Approach.* United States: YBF Publishing, 2016.

"Post-Experience Convening and Debrief." *Diasporic Soul Healing Experience.* Video Recordings. 19–21 September 2019. Cincinnati, Ohio.

Sey, Seinabo. "Breathe." *I'm a Dream.* Universal Music. 7 September 2018. https://www.okayafrica.com/seinabo-sey-breathe-video-gambia/.

Shahid, Kyra T. *Anti-Black Racism and Epistemic Violence.* Austin: Sentia Publishing, 2018.

Sharpe, Christina. *In the Wake: On Blackness and Being.* Durham: Duke, 2016.

Sims, Stacy. *True Body Project Leadership Training.* Cincinnati, Ohio. 24–26 June 2016. www.truebodyproject.org.

Singleton, Micah. "'To Pimp a Butterfly': Kendrick Lamar's New Album Is Perfect." *The Verge.* 19 March 2015. https://www.theverge.com/2015/3/19/8257319/kendrick-lamar-album-review-to-pimp-a-butterfly.

Snider, Amber. "The History of Yemaya, Santeria's Queenly Ocean Goddess Mermaid." *Teen Vogue.* 9 July 2020. https://a/story/the-history-of-yemaya-goddess-mermaid.

Somé, Malidoma Patrice. *The Healing Wisdom of Africa: Finding Life Purpose Through Nature, Ritual, and Community.* New York: Jeremy P. Tarcher, 1998.

_____. *Of Water and the Spirit: Ritual, Magic and Initiation in the Life of an African Shaman.* New York: Penguin, 1994.

_____. *Ritual: Power, Healing and Community.* New York: Penguin, 1997.

The State of Union (Yoga) Address: Six-Part Series. Season I. 30 June 2020–10 November 2020. https://stateofunionyoga.com/.

"Storm Over Brooklyn: Retelling the Devastating Murder of Yusef Hawkins." *The Guardian.* 11 August 2020. https://www.theguardian.com/tv-and-radio/2020/aug/11/storm-over-brooklyn-yusuf-hawkins-hbo.

Toliver-Diallo, W. "The Woman Who Was More Than a Man: Making Aline Sitoe Diatta into a National Heroine in Senegal." *Canadian Journal of African Studies / Revue Canadienne Des Études Africaines* 39, no. 2 (2005): 338–360. Retrieved August 2020 from http://www.jstor.org/stable/25067487.

Van der Kolk, Bessel. *The Body Keeps the Score: Brain, Mind, and Body in the Healing of Trauma.* New York: Penguin, 2014.

Walker, Alice. "Epilogue." *The Way Forward Is With a Broken Heart.* New York: Random House, 2000. 200.

_____. "Turquoise and Coral: The Writing of the Temple of My Familiar." *Anything We Love Can Be Saved: A Writer's Activism.* New York, Random House, 1997.

_____. "The Sound of Our Own Culture." *Anything We Love Can Be Saved: A Writer's Activism.* New York: Random House, 1997.

Wamsley, Laurel. "Parks in Nonwhite Areas Are Half the Size of Ones in Majority-White Areas, Study Says." *All Things Considered.* NPR. August 2020. https://www.npr.org/2020/08/05/899356445/parks-in-nonwhite-areas-are-half-the-size-of-ones-in-majority-white-areas-study-5.

White, Renee. *African Concepts of Energy and Their Manifestations Through Art.* Master's Thesis, College of the Arts, Kent State University. 2016.

Wilentz, Gay. *Women Writers Curing Cultural Dis-ease.* New Brunswick, NJ: Rutgers University Press, 2000.

World Peace Yoga. "300-hour Foundation Teacher Training." Cincinnati, Ohio. Completed and Awarded October 2018.

Wortham, Jenna. "Black Health Matters." *New York Times.* 27 August 2016. https://www.nytimes.com/2016/08/28/fashion/black-lives-matter-wellness-health-self-care.html.

Index

Index